GUARDS VC

Blitzkrieg 1940

A Tribute to the First or Grenadier Regiment of Foot Guards

In Flanders formed by King's Decree
A bond of strength & loyalty.
For good King Charles in exile cast
A legend born to ever last.

The very best the Grenadiers
A name their foes would learn to fear.
Through haze of smoke & battle roar
First Regiment of Foot holds fast and sure.

From Waterloo to Western Front,
With 1st Guards too they bore the brunt.
With weapons held from sword to gun
Fought long & hard till battles won.

Only those who have no fears
Will join the ranks of Grenadiers.
This Regiment, First Foot in name
Has courage war will never tame.

Larry McHale, St Albans, February 1999.

GUARDS VC

Blitzkrieg 1940

Dilip Sarkar

Ramrod Publications

Other books by Dilip Sarkar:-

SPITFIRE SQUADRON: 19 Squadron at War, 1939-41.
THE INVISIBLE THREAD: A Spitfire's Tale.
THROUGH PERIL TO THE STARS: RAF Fighter Pilots who failed to return, 1939-45.
ANGRIFF WESTLAND: Three Battle of Britain air raids 'through the looking glass'.
A FEW OF THE MANY: Air War 1939-45, A Kaleidoscope of Memories.
BADER'S TANGMERE SPITFIRES: The Untold Story, 1941.
BADER'S DUXFORD FIGHTERS: The Big Wing Controversy.
MISSING IN ACTION: Resting in Peace?

Dilip Sarkar's next published works will be a Battle of Britain related photographic collection in September 1999, and *Johnnie's Kenley Spitfires*, in conjunction with the RAF's top scoring fighter pilot of WWII, Air Vice-Marshal JE Johnson, in May 2000.

Dilip is currently undertaking background research concerning Operation MARKET GARDEN, and has developed a particular interest in the part played by the Guards Armoured Division in XXX Corps' unsuccessful but determined attempt to relieve Allied Airborne forces at Arnhem. If you were in any way involved, or have a relative or friend who was involved in this inspiring undertaking, please contact the author via Ramrod Publications.

Concurrently, Dilip maintains his interest in the Fall of France and is always pleased to hear from Veterans with stories to tell. He is currently considering organising a guided battlefield tour of the area, including the Poplar Ridge site where Lance Corporal Nicholls won his VC; anyone interested in receiving more details should contact me, Anita, at Ramrod Publications (Tel: 01905 767735, Fax: 01905 424533).

GUARDS VC: *Blitzkrieg* **1940**

© Dilip Sarkar 1999

First published 1999 by Ramrod Publications, 16 Kingfisher Close, St Peter's, Worcester WR5 3RY

ISBN: 0 9519832 6 1

Designed and typeset by Ramrod Publications
Printed in Great Britain by Aspect Print & Design, 89 Newtown Road, Malvern, Worcestershire WR14 2PD

Dedication

Whilst considering this dedication, I was reminded of these words spoken by Sir Jacob Astley before the Battle of Edgehill in 1642:-

O Lord, though knowest how busy I must be this day. If I forget thee, do not thou forget me.

With those words in mind, this book is respectfully dedicated to all those BEF soldiers who became casualties on the road to Dunkirk (whether fatally, physically or mentally), especially the following members of the 3rd Battalion Grenadier Guards:-

Lance Corporal Harry Nicholls VC:	whose supreme gallantry saved the lives of many comrades, although he would never fully recover from his own wounds.
Guardsman Percy Nash:	whose gallantry also deserved recognition.
Guardsman 'Bert' Smith:	my Grandfather, also wounded and captured.
Guardsman Arthur Rice:	badly wounded defending the River Escaut.
Guardsman Les Drinkwater:	who saved Arthur's life.
Guardsman Sam Hayes:	killed alongside my Grandfather on May 21st, 1940.
Lance Sergeant Arthur Rimell:	who became a Guardsman when aged 16 - only to become the 3rd Grenadiers' youngest casualty, aged 18, on May 21st, 1940.
Lance Sergeant Charles Constantine:	who survived to record his experiences for the benefit of history.
Major WRJ Alston-Roberts-West:	and all those who are officially Missing in Action.

Contents

Foreword: 7
Introduction: Something to be proud of   8

Chapter One: Once a Grenadier *always* a Grenadier!   13
Chapter Two: Shadow of the Past   29
Chapter Three: Maginot Line   50
Chapter Four: Eve of Battle   60
Chapter Five: *Blitzkrieg*!   71
Chapter Six: "..a busy time very shortly"   94
Chapter Seven: Guards VC: May 21st, 1940   108
Chapter Eight: Victory along the Escaut   132
Chapter Nine: Flames & Bayonets   142
Chapter Ten: Dunkirk   163
Chapter Eleven: Aftermath   184

Postscript: The War Pilgrim   204

Index: 231

Appendix One: Roll of Honour   234
Appendix Two: German Casualties   242
Appendix Three: Composition of the German 31 ID,
                     Infantry Weapons & Equipment, 1940   245

Acknowledgements: 250
Bibliography: 254

FOREWORD

In the Grenadier Guards we are justifiably proud of a reputation for discipline, courage and success in battle earned over three-and-a-half centuries of service in campaigns over the globe: from Waterloo to South Africa, from Canada to Malaya. We particularly cherish the memory of the 13 Grenadiers who have won the Victoria Cross, Britain's highest award for gallantry. Every year the Corporals' Mess celebrates 'Harry Nicholls Day' to commemorate one of their number who won the Victoria Cross during the early days of World War Two, even before Dunkirk. This book is his story and that of his comrades in the 1st Guards Brigade.

There is nothing romantic about war and Dilip Sarkar makes no attempt to put a glossy coat on those rough days of May 1940, which saw the BEF pushed out of Belgium and France. The horrors of the battlefield, the boredom of prisoners of war, the sorrows of grieving families and the painful legacy of physical and mental wounds are laid out for all to see. What emerges, however, is a strong feeling of family: the author's quest for knowledge about his own Grandfather, who dressed Harry Nicholls' wounds and was captured with him, was the inspiration for this book. There is also the Nicholls family who received the medal from the King, thinking Harry was dead, but who immediately gave it back when they heard the marvellous news that he was still alive and would one day be able to receive it himself. There is the family aspect of a Regiment like the Grenadiers where many Officers and Guardsmen follow their Father's footsteps, and the family feeling of a Battalion where a Duke's son and a dustman's son stand shoulder to shoulder in battle, and indeed lie shoulder to shoulder in a cemetery. Finally too there is the family spirit of a nation at war with its King at its head. Dilip re-creates this feeling of unity of purpose without a hint of romanticism or sentimentality. There is, however, a strong trace of humour, and anyone familiar with French plumbing will enjoy the anonymous Guardsman's description of his first encounter with it at Cherbourg railway station!

Dilip also manages to set the battle in which Lance Corporal Nicholls' VC was won, and in which the 3rd Battalion Grenadier Guards suffered 47 fatal casualties, in the context of the Battle of France. He moves easily from the strategic view of the Commander-in-Chief of the BEF, Lord Gort (also a Grenadier and also a VC holder) to the view of Guardsmen in the trenches by the River Escaut. He does not pretend that the battle fought on this river line made a great difference to the overall outcome of the Dunkirk Campaign, but the bravery of Harry Nicholls and his comrades showed that the German Army was not invincible and could be driven back. In researching his book, Dilip has read widely from both British and German sources, visited the battlefield and talked to many surviving veterans. This book is a tribute to them and their generation. Those of us serving now must attempt to show the same spirit and the same high standards in the very different circumstances of today's world.

Lieutenant Colonel David Hutchison, Commanding Officer of the 1st Battalion Grenadier Guards, December 1998.

INTRODUCTION

Something to be proud of

My Grandfather, 'Bert' Smith, fascinated me from an early age. I knew that he had been a Grenadier Guardsman and, infant though I was, realised that there was something very special about this particular Regiment; why else were Guardsman seen on sentry duty at Buckingham Palace? My Mother had an old photograph of her Father in uniform, probably taken at Wellington Barracks in 1928. This left a lasting impression: something to be proud of.

Guardsman Herbert Henry Smith, Grenadier Guards: the Author's Grandfather pictured sometime between 1928-31.

'Bert' had that unmistakable military gait evident in most former professional soldiers, Guardsmen in particular. He wore a discreet enamel Royal Cypher in his lapel, but rarely spoke of his wartime experiences or attended functions connected with his military days. He always seemed reserved, a good listener but never a talker. My perception was that here was a man who had once suffered great trauma but was nevertheless at peace with both himself and the world. I never once heard him complain or raise his voice. I have since recognised this almost indefinable quality amongst the many other former prisoners of war - of both sides - whom I have met during the course of my various researches. And that was all I knew: Granddad, a former Grenadier Guardsman, had been captured by the Germans. It was almost impossible to draw him on his wartime experiences; he would listen to others but said little himself.

Sadly Bert Smith died of cancer on September 14th, 1983. Considering his attitude, i.e. 'my soldiering is done, it was a long time ago and all I want now is to be left alone', I was surprised at how well represented the Hereford & Worcester Branch of the Grenadier Guards Association was at the funeral. As we walked from my Grandfather's graveside I thanked an old Grenadier for attending. He reminded me of Bert Smith in fact: tall, quietly spoken and possessed of that unmistakable Guardsman's gait; his name was Arthur Rice. Mr Rice told me that he and Bert had served in the 3rd Battalion in 1940, and that together they had run the 'Battalion Wet Bar' in France during the winter of 1939/40. "Of course", he went on, "Bert was captured with Harry Nicholls on the same day that I was wounded". It was said as though I should know of Harry Nicholls; I did not and asked who he was. "Him that won the VC", he replied before leaving me to my thoughts. My mind was in a whirl. Captivated by the Second World War since childhood, it never really occurred to me that my own Grandfather had much of a story to tell. I realised immediately how wrong I had been, and the tragedy of it all was emphasised by the fact that Bert was no longer alive to be asked for his account.

Later I recounted the conversation with my Mother, Bert's eldest daughter, who told me that on rare occasions he had referred to an old newspaper cutting saying "See that, champion boxer he was, Harry Nicholls; big bloke and the Germans made me carry him on my own!" Having never heard of this I was astonished. Suddenly the souvenirs given to me over the years by Granddad himself, 'Nan' (my mother's mother, Bert's first wife Dorothy), and 'Auntie Mary', his popular second wife, became more significant. Amongst them were letters he had written home whilst a prisoner of war, some old photographs and three medals (which had never even been taken out of the envelope in which they arrived from the Army Medal Office, much less worn!). I had treasured them all but this memorabilia was now an important and tangible link with the past. There was obviously much to learn, but at the time I was just 21-years-old and a recently appointed constable in the West Mercia Constabulary; for the time being I had my own life to lead although I sensed that a certain destiny - yet to be fulfilled - was attached to these precious relics.

In 1988, I was assaulted and badly injured whilst on duty, this leading to an operation on my right hand and a period of convalescence. During this time I contacted Mr Rice and spent many afternoons in his home learning about the BEF. I was given a copy of the 1982 *Grenadier Gazette*, in which appeared an article by former Guardsman Les Drinkwater featuring the engagement concerned: stirring stuff indeed. Les was kind enough to correspond with me and we also became firm friends. The road then led to Bournemouth and (the now late) Percy Nash who had been directly involved with the VC action concerned. It was both inspiring and a privilege to meet such august but modest gentlemen. Much later I determined that this story should be recorded, in as much detail as the march of time would permit, and indeed published before it was too late. The result of my quest now lies before you.

During the course of this research I have found that most existing published accounts tend, understandably perhaps, to concentrate on the Dunkirk evacuation itself. Comparatively little material, however, appears available in respect of events leading up to this dramatic and crucial undertaking. It seems to me that those who perished, were captured or wounded during the various rearguard actions fought to make the evacuation possible are today little more than forgotten heroes. I hope that this book will provide them with some long overdue recognition.

This book mainly seeks to provide a platform for those whose experiences have not previously been published. These are essentially those of junior Officers and Other Ranks. Many of the commanders and other personalities of great import have published their auto-biographies, or their biographies have been written, so as this information is already available I have not duplicated it here. If, like me however, the reader wants to learn more of what it was *really* like to be in the 'Poor Bloody Infantry' during 1940 - *from the survivors themselves* - then this book is a must!

We are fortunate that, despite the huge bonfires of May 1945, a surprising amount of contemporary German records survive, including some from those German Army units which fought in 1940. The majority of German records published herewith have either never been published in English before, or indeed appear in print for the first time. Reference to these German records is essential if a balanced account is to be provided.

Also published for the first time, although available for inspection at the Public Record Office since 1975, are extracts from the War Diaries of certain British

Army battalions. The reader will note that the style of writing, and in some cases abbreviations used, naturally varies from unit to unit. Any attempt to provide a uniform presentation would clearly entail tampering with the 'evidence'. These extracts appear largely unedited, therefore, in an effort to preserve authenticity. Likewise, the many first-hand accounts are just that, i.e. straight from the 'horse's mouth', and little or no attempt has been made to edit them. In places, however, it has been necessary to add explanatory author's notes, these being in parentheses thus: '[-]'. Furthermore, Officers' ranks appear throughout the text as they were at the time; the retired ranks and decorations of contributors, however, can be found in the Acknowledgements section.

It is crucial, I believe, that histories such as this - particularly in respect of the personal experiences of the front line fighting soldier - are recorded and published. It is still vibrant living history. A surprising number of 1940 veterans are still alive, in fact, as are the brothers and sisters of many soldiers who died. Many of these casualties, however, exist now only in the sideboards or attics of a close relative. Upon the death of that custodian, all too frequently such apparently insignificant treasures are thrown out and lost forever. Fortunately that will not happen in respect of certain casualties connected with this story. Our research has often located photographs and biographical information, this publication providing a permanent record of these 'ordinary' people. Sadly, even after not quite 60 years, the faces of many thousands have already been lost forever.

Today, too many people are unaware of the great sacrifices, pain and suffering of the 1940s. Every year hundreds of thousands cross the English Channel to holiday on the Continent, or perhaps take advantage of the cheap beer, wine and spirits offered in French ports. As these travellers drive deeper into France, I wonder whether they have any perception of the tumultuous events which once took place on those very roads? I make no apology, therefore, for plunging the reader back into our darkest hour. I can only hope that readers of the post-war generations will in future spare a thought for those men featured in this account.

Neither must our thoughts neglect the deep sorrow of those families left at home to mourn the sudden and violent passing of a loved one; their grief is summarised in this moving inscription on the grave of a Coldstream Guardsman at Pecq Communal Cemetery, Belgium:-

ONLY THOSE WHO HAVE LOST CAN TELL THE PAIN OF PARTING WITHOUT FAREWELL

Without such Servicemen the freedom and lifestyles we enjoy today - and take so much for granted - would not exist. To my mind the sacrifices of 1940 (with which this book deals) are as valid today as they were then.

Dilip Sarkar, Worcester, February 1999

CHAPTER ONE

Once a Grenadier *always* a Grenadier!

In front of me is a Soldier's Service & Pay Book, a rather worn example relating the military record of one 2611042 Guardsman Herbert Henry Smith, Grenadier Guards. The fragile pages indicate that this particular Grenadier was born at 'Powers, Ombersley Nr Worcester' on November 2nd, 1907. A market gardener, 'Bert' Smith enlisted at Worcester on January 2nd, 1928, signing on for '3 years with the Colours and 9 years in the Reserve'. Between January 12th, 1928, and September 4th, 1930, Guardsman Smith served at 'Home' with the 1st Battalion (Bn). For some reason he was later transferred to the 3rd Bn, in which he served until leaving the Regular Army on New Year's Day, 1931. Unremarkable though the content of this ancient document is, it is extremely precious to me as it once belonged to my late Grandfather.

Calm before the storm, summer 1939: 'Bert' Smith, then a British Army Reservist, pictured in Gheluvelt Park, Worcester, with his first wife, Dorothy, and daughters Joan (left) and Janet (right, the Author's Mother). This happy scene was soon to be shattered forever.

After leaving the Army in 1931, Bert Smith returned to Ombersley and worked on Lord Sandys' estate, marrying Dorothy Eva Pointer at the local church on November 21st, 1931. Sadly the couple's first child, a boy, was to die whilst still a babe in arms, but on May 25th, 1933, their first daughter was born, Janet Mabel (my Mother), followed by Joan Dorothy on November 2nd, 1936. Family responsibilities saw Bert become a storeman at the Metal Box factory, the Smiths moving to a town house at No 7 Lansdowne Road, Worcester. The family lived a simple but happy life, soon to be irrevocably affected by current political events. In 1933, Adolf Hitler, leader of the Nazis, had become Chancellor of Germany;

the genesis of events leading up to the outbreak of war, therefore, coincided with my Mother's birth. Although not fully recognised at the time, a sinister shadow had fallen over Europe.

Hitler was determined that Germany would be restored to its 'rightful' place as the most powerful nation in Europe. On June 28th, 1919, The Treaty of Versailles had been signed between the victors of the First World War and Germany, their defeated enemy. The terms of this flawed settlement, which contained hundreds of articles, concerned the League of Nations, boundaries and self-determination, German rights, disarmament, reparations and guarantees. There were three particular articles which infuriated the Germans from the outset: Article 160 limited Germany's armed forces to an Army of 100,000 volunteers with no tanks, a small Navy and no Air Force; Article 231 made Germany accept all responsibility for the war (the 'War-Guilt Clause'), and Article 232 imposed severe financial reparations. Hitler and the Nazis were determined to repudiate this Treaty which the nation appeared united in believing unjust.

Under General Hans von Seeckt, the German Army was, in fact, organised as a highly trained and professional framework for a much larger force which would one day be raised by conscription. The development of tanks, military aircraft and submarines - also banned by Versailles - went on in secret. Much of this work was actually undertaken in the Soviet Union. By the spring of 1935, Hitler was able to renounce the Treaty of Versailles, openly boasting the fact that Germany now had an Air Force and was preparing to introduce conscription with the intention of increasing the Army to 300,000 men.

Britain and France made no effective protest, however, which convinced Hitler that they had lost the will to act decisively. In March 1936, he openly proved this by successfully reoccupying the Rhineland, also forbidden by Versailles. In March 1938, came the *Anschluss*, when Austria was annexed to the Reich. Again this was despite the prohibition by Versailles of a German union with Austria. Again Britain and France took no action. Understandably their governments were determined to avoid war and preferred instead to appease rather than confront Hitler.

In the Autumn of 1938, Hitler made his first overt move against a truly *independent* state, demanding that Czechoslovakia's western border - the *Sudetenland* which contained 3,000,000 Germans - should also be annexed to the Reich. Although the Czechoslovakian Government prepared to resist, Britain and France mounted increasing pressure to obtain an 'honourable' solution. In simple terms, at Munich on September 29th, 1938, the Prime Ministers of Britain, France and Italy decided that the *Sudetenland* would be conceded to Germany in return for a guarantee of peace. In reality, however, the exercise further convinced Hitler that Nazi Germany had nothing to fear from Britain and France.

In March 1939, the Czech Government was induced to ask Hitler for military protection. German troops rapidly completed the occupation of Czechoslovakia; even the British Prime Minister, Neville Chamberlain (a leading exponent of 'Appeasement') then started to realise the true nature of Hitler's plans. The Western powers continued rearming in earnest (having commenced this process after the Munich Crisis), but German forces were by now superior in strength to most of their probable opponents.

After this success in Czechoslovakia, Hitler turned his attentions to Poland. There the 'Danzig Corridor' severed East Prussia from the Reich (another legacy of Versailles) and presented an inviting excuse for Nazi intervention. Europe stood on the brink of war, and, recognising this fact, Britain and France held Army Staff Talks in March 1939, it having been clear for some time that, in the event of hostilities, Britain and France would fight together. It was decided that Britain's contribution to any fighting on the Continent would comprise a ground Expeditionary Force and an Advance Air Striking Force (AASF). On March 29th, 1939, the British Cabinet ordered that the Territorial Army should be doubled in size. On April 27th, 1939, Parliament passed the Military Training Act (as a result of which some 200,000 men aged between 20 and 21 years registered for military service in June 1939). The strength of the British Army that April (according to figures published by the Secretary of State for War) was as follows:-

Regular Army:	224,000
Territorial Army Field Force:	325,000
Territorial Army Anti-Aircraft Units:	96,000
Total of Men Under Arms:	645,000

In April 1939, Britain pledged to assist Poland in the event of a German attack, although, due to the geography involved, the practical military help she could give was limited. Naturally the Allies gave great consideration to the prospect of a major German attack against the West. Political difficulties existed with both the Netherlands and Belgium, however, due to both having declared neutrality unless their own frontiers were attacked. Although the Allies were not confident of providing effective military aid to the Netherlands (which had remained neutral throughout the First World War) if her neutrality was infringed, the British Chiefs of Staff believed that Belgium's *intended* neutrality, *if* respected by Germany, could be to the Allies' advantage. No Staff liaison or planning in respect of either the integration of the Belgian Army or defence of Belgium therefore took place.

The storm eventually broke on September 1st: Germany invaded Poland in an undeclared act of war.

On that day, 3,000 men of the British Army Reserve were 'recalled to the Colours'. Consequently 32 years old family man Bert Smith left home for a most uncertain future. His daughter Janet, then just six years old, remembers 'lots of crying in the house and neighbours saying that "Bert Smith has gone off to war"'. Of course many of those on the Reserve List were, like Bert, mature men with family responsibilities. The prospect of returning to the Army to fight a war was doubtless an unwelcome prospect. Nevertheless, having already completed a period of military service, reservists had learned self-reliance and discipline, and were therefore already imbued with regimental *esprit de corps*; quite simply, each man knew exactly what was required of him.

Guardsman Arthur Rice,
3rd Bn Grenadier Guards.
Mr A Rice.

So far as was possible, every effort was made for reservists to re-join the battalions in which they had previously served. Bert Smith travelled by train to Aldershot with fellow Worcestershire Grenadier reservist, 2613284 Guardsman Arthur Rice. The pair found the 3rd Bn Grenadier Guards at Barrosa Barracks. Another Grenadier reservist, Guardsman Bert Middleton (formerly of the 2nd Bn) remembers:-

In 1939, I was on the Army Reserve List. We all had our call up papers and received instructions over the wireless and in the newspapers to report back to our units. On September 3rd, I travelled to Wellington Barracks in London where I was issued with kit but soon transferred to the Holding Bn at Windsor. Sam Price, from Cheltenham, and myself were then ordered to Barrosa Barracks, Aldershot, to make an inventory of equipment left behind by the 3rd Bn when it went to France. We were then to hand the barracks over to the next battalion coming in.

Lance Sergeant Charles Constantine had been posted to Victoria Barracks, Windsor, as an instructor:-

Amongst the reservists were men who had served their time as regular soldiers. Some had finished three years, some four and others even seven years service, after which they had returned to civilian life only to be recalled because of the war. I will always remember the first time I had to take them on a drill parade. I called one out as a right marker and then shouted the order "Get On Parade". They all came to attention and stepped off with the left foot, sloped their arms in the three drill movements corresponding with the left foot as it touched the ground, and when they reached the right marker formed up on his left, got their distance right between each man, ordered arms and stood at ease with the precision of trained men who had not forgotten how to drill. As they stood there and I looked at them, an old saying went through my mind: 'Once a Grenadier *always* a Grenadier'. Looking at these men I thought how true that saying was. I also wondered what they thought of me, a young Lance Sergeant with just over 18 months service in, drilling them and telling them what to do. After the hours drilling on parade, I found out that these men were pretty good; some had been out of the Army for a considerable time and were a little rusty, but on the whole, given that there had been a few changes in the drilling, it all came back to them rapidly.

Lieutenant Edward Ford:-

There were no better soldiers than the reservists that came back to us. It is a marvellous thing for a young, relatively inexperienced, Officer to be absolutely confident in his men, and to know the quality of his Platoon.

By September 3rd, 1939, Germany had ignored the ultimatum delivered by Britain and France to withdraw from Poland. At the time, Lieutenant The Master of Forbes (now The Lord Forbes) was a subaltern serving with the 3rd Bn Grenadier Guards and remembers that:-

On the morning of September 3rd, whilst the Battalion was engaged in constructing air-raid trenches, we were told that a special announcement was due to be broadcast on the wireless at 11.15 am. All the Officers foregathered in the Officers' Mess where we heard the Prime Minister, Neville Chamberlain, announce to the nation that we were at war with Germany. There was no alternative. The chips were down.

What would the forthcoming war be like: the Battle of Waterloo or a repeat of the First World War? Did anyone really know what it would be like?

It has been said that there was no 'popular excitement' when war was declared, the attitude in Britain being 'Let's get it over with,' and in France: *'Il faut en finir'*. The 'Great War to end all wars', however, fought between 1914-18, was now to have a terrible sequel. During that 'Great War', a certain little boy called Harry Nicholls, of Nottingham, had paraded around his back yard shouldering a broom handle: "If the Germans shoot my Dad then I'll go and shoot them!" Although the boy's father, Mr Jack Nicholls, survived the war, this was a prophecy which would otherwise be fulfilled as Harry's generation now marched off to do battle against a familiar foe on the battlefields of its forefathers.

By the declaration of war, the British Army numbered 1,065,000 men, of which 160,000 were allocated to the British Expeditionary Force (BEF). It is a little known fact that a significant proportion of the BEF were reservists, and many of its battalions and other units were from the newly expanded Territorial Army, also mobilised for service on the Continent.

The French General Gamelin (left) and The BEF's Commander-in-Chief, General The Viscount Gort VC.
Grenadier Guards.

The BEF comprised three Corps, General Headquarters (GHQ) troops and Lines of Communications personnel. The Commander-in-Chief was General The Viscount Gort (formerly a Grenadier). Lord Gort had been Chief of the Imperial General Staff (CIGS) from 1937-39. He had extensive experience of battle having served in the trenches; he had commanded the 4th Bn Grenadier Guards in 1917, fighting at Passchendaele and Cambrai, and the 1st Bn in 1918. He had, in fact, been awarded the Victoria Cross for his gallantry in capturing a German position close to Cambrai in September 1918.

In September 1939, the 3rd Bn Grenadier Guards, commanded by Lieutenant Colonel Sir John Aird, together with the 2nd Bn Coldstream Guards (Lieutenant Colonel Lionel Bootle-Wilbraham MC) and 2nd Bn The Hampshire Regiment (Lieutenant Colonel Pat Cadoux-Hudson MC) comprised the 1st Guards Brigade under Brigadier Merton Beckwith-Smith MC (a former Welsh Guardsman, originally a Coldstreamer).

With the 2nd and 3rd Brigades, the 1st Guards Brigade formed the 1st Infantry Division. Along with the 2nd Division and 48th (South Midland) Division (commanded by another former Grenadier, Major General Andrew Thorne) the 1st Division served in I Corps under Major General the Hon. Harold Alexander, known generally as 'General Alex', a distinguished Irish Guardsman.

The 'War Establishment' of a British Infantry Division (all ranks) was 13,863 men. Each brigade numbered 120 Officers and 2,824 Other Ranks. Each infantry battalion consisted of some 23 Officers and 760 Other Ranks. These were allocated to Battalion HQ and four rifle companies each of three rifle platoons; platoons were then sub-divided into three rifle sections, each comprising a Non Commissioned Officer (NCO) and seven men.

The infantry battalions were largely armed with the Short Magazine Lee-Enfield (SMLE) .303" rifle, a survivor of the Great War to which the blade bayonet could be fitted. Another Great War survivor, together with the squat steel helmet, was the No.36 (Mills) grenade. Each rifle platoon also had three .303" Bren light machine-guns (each weighing 23 pounds) fed by 30 round magazines. Mobility for the Bren was provided by the Universal or Bren Carrier, an armoured, low, tracked vehicle which could travel across country. Every infantry battalion had a platoon of 10 Carriers, each having a driver in addition to a crew of three armed with a Bren. The concept was to provide the Battalion Commander with a reserve of fire power capable of crossing bullet-swept ground. Having said that, it was stressed that although the Bren could be fired through a frontal slit, the Carrier was not intended for use as a light tank; once the crew had been delivered by Carrier they were then expected to dismount and fire. Every rifle platoon was also equipped with a 2-inch mortar for firing smoke and High Explosive (HE) rounds over a distance of about 100-500 yards, and a Boys .55 inch anti-tank rifle; the manufacturer claimed that this weapon could penetrate light armour up to 500 yards. This weapon's disadvantages were its weight (36 pounds) and significant 'kick' to the shoulder of the firer. Also, ammunition for the Boys was in very short supply.

The Headquarter Company of an infantry battalion comprised six platoons: Signal, 3-inch Mortar, ground and air defence, Carrier, Pioneer and Administrative Platoons. Although it was still intended that the infantryman would march to war, a Company Commander could move a platoon by off-loading his four 15-cwt trucks; furthermore the Quartermaster could empty enough vehicles to lift two companies. Having said that, the BEF had a pool of three Royal Army Service Corps (RASC) troop-carrying companies, each capable of lifting a complete brigade without dumping any stores. It is interesting to note, considering later events, that the British Army clearly anticipated a form of warfare involving manoeuvre when the time came. By the outbreak of war, in fact, the British Army was almost completely mechanised. Contrary to popular belief and in direct contrast, however, the German Army, apart from its *panzer* (armoured) divisions, still used horses for almost all transport tasks.

Coincidentally, given the foregoing paragraph, the outbreak of war found the 2nd Bn Coldstream Guards at Bentley Camp practising 'Truck-Scuttling': the lifting of all marching personnel in the Battalion's Motorised Transport (MT) over a short distance. On September 3rd, 1939, the 2nd Coldstream therefore 'Truck-Scuttled' back to Albuhera Barracks, Aldershot, in the shortest possible time.

During late August and early September 1939, when the reservists arrived at Barossa Barracks, the 3rd Bn Grenadier Guards was already busy preparing for war. The old soldiers joined younger Guardsmen still completing their Colour Service. Both Guardsmen Smith and Rice went to No 4 Company, commanded by Major Alston-Roberts-West. Smith joined a rifle section led by 2614908 Lance Corporal Bryant Everitt, a 22 year old from Leeds who had enlisted in 1936. Arthur Rice recalls that his Section Commander was a Corporal Crossman, and that other members of this section included Guardsmen Hairs, Chapman, Worrall and Roberts.

Amongst the regular soldiers of No 4 Company were men such as 2613546

Guardsman Les Drinkwater, a Cornishman then aged 22:-

As the result of a riding accident suffered during the winter of 1937-8 (whilst exercising a Hunter owned by Captain Hutchins) I had spent several weeks confined to bed in hospital at Combemere Barracks, Windsor. Upon discharge I literally had to learn how to walk again. When war was declared I was still not quite fit, and had visions of No 4 Company going to war with Guardsman Drinkwater bringing up the rear. Then my name appeared on Part I Orders to be trained as a Stretcher Bearer, which was the answer to my problem. The 'SB' Section was led by Sergeant Norton Bullock, and comprised Guardsmen Buckley and Christie in addition to myself. We were trained as a team of four by a Captain Valentine of the Royal Army Medical Corps. We practised with a stretcher collecting the 'wounded' and treating them on the spot for various 'injuries'. We became most proficient and were congratulated by the Captain. Little did I know then how much these new skills would be required in the future.

2614846 Guardsman Percy Nash had enlisted at Bristol on April 20th, 1936:-

It was what I really wanted to do, be a Grenadier Guardsman, and I loved every minute of it. When war was declared I couldn't wait to get some action, that was what I had joined for after all. I think we were all prepared to do whatever was required of us.

Guardsman Percy Nash (left),
3rd Bn Grenadier Guards,
before the outbreak of war; the
identity of the other Guardsman
is not known.

Amongst the 3rd Grenadiers' Ranks was one of the most determined and forthright individuals in the British Armed Forces: 2614910 Lance Corporal Harry Nicholls, whose boyhood broomhandle had become a real rifle upon enlistment at Nottingham on June 6th, 1936.

Extracted from a Company photograph, Guardsman Harry Nicholls, 3rd Bn Grenadier Guards, pictured with his Army boxing trophies before the war.
Christopher A. Collins.

Born on April 22nd, 1915, Harry Nicholls was one of 10 children: five girls and five boys born to parents Jack and Florence in Hope Street, Nottingham, a tough area in industrial Nottingham. After surviving the Great War, Jack Nicholls' ambition became to re-locate his family to a better area. This he achieved through sheer hard graft and the Nicholls family were able to move to Lees Hill Street; the new house even provided a tiny rear garden. As Mrs Nicholls said, "Yes, Jack's a worker. If he found an idle bone in his body he'd break it".

Young Harry attended Bosworth Primary in the Meadows area of Nottingham, but he was not a distinguished scholar. Nevertheless, according to *The Illustrated* magazine of August 17th, 1940, he 'held his own pretty well and grew up, strong and sturdy, into a likeable youngster'. At 14 years-of-age, in 1929, Harry left school and became a storeman in an engineering shop. When he enlisted as a Grenadier, his occupation was given as a labourer. He measured five feet and 11 inches tall and weighed in at 14 stones. After successfully completing his training, Guardsman Nicholls was posted from the Guards Depot to join the 3rd Bn.

Since his early schooldays Harry Nicholls had been a boxer, a sport the Grenadier Guards both encouraged and provided the opportunity to practise. In 1938, he won the Army & Navy Heavyweight Championship and likewise became that of the Imperial Forces. It has been said that 'his boxing was never particularly clever or subtle; he was a fighter. He got into the ring and let go, and didn't stop till he'd beaten his man'. The only man he could not beat was the amateur heavyweight champion of England, Constable Porter:-

You had to stay him or knock him out to get the verdict. The last time I met him I just didn't want to fight. I'd fought him many times before and knew all his moves. But Harry didn't give a damn. He came in with a grin. I beat him again - but what a *fighter* he was!

Guardsman Gil Follett adds:-

Quite simply Harry Nicholls appeared invincible. He had a very positive mind-set, just like Tyson of today.

On April 3rd, 1937, Guardsman Nicholls married the 18 year old Constance Carroll at St Patrick's Church in Nottingham. 'Connie' followed her husband around the various camps to which he was posted, living in married quarters. Shortly before the outbreak of war, however, the young Nicholls couple rented a 'real home' in Lower Eldon Street, Nottingham, 'near the old folk'.

Just before his marriage, Harry Nicholls had become an Acting Lance Corporal, but on January 24th, 1938, he was 'Deprived of Lance Stripe by his CO for the offence of "Absence etc"'. On September 1st, 1939, Harry got his chevrons back, and on November 16th, 'Having held the acting appointment for a consecutive period of 21 days is granted the pay of the appointment'. The Meadows lad was doing well, a respected character not only within his own fine Regiment but, due to his boxing ability, his reputation extended far beyond. As Major LS Starkey of the 3rd Grenadiers later wrote, 'As a Guardsman he was first class'.

For all of these members of the 3rd Bn Grenadiers Guards, September 1939 represented a challenging time. Both the 1st and 7th Guards Brigades (the latter comprising the 1st & 2nd Bn Grenadier Guards together with the 1st Bn Coldstream Guards) had already completed their autumn exercises and so there was little opportunity for further training. According to the 3rd Bn Grenadier Guards War Diary, on September 5th, the Colonel of the Regiment, HRH Field-Marshal The Duke of Connaught, inspected the Battalion: 'He told the Commanding Officer he was very pleased with what he saw and wished all ranks the best possible luck'. On the following day 1st Guards Brigade received a signal to the effect that the 3rd Bn Grenadier Guards was 'fully mobilised'. The next morning reservists were given the opportunity to fire the Bren gun. During the afternoon the Bn was visited by His Majesty King George VI, who 'walked down the ranks of the men who gave him three cheers'.

Despite the overall sensation of waiting, the men suspected that they were probably bound for France in the near future. Telegrams sent home from Stanhope Lines by Guardsman Smith capture an urgency and drama not even hinted at by the matter-of-fact War Diary:-

<u>Saturday, September 9th</u> (on which day all companies carried out Anti-Tank Rifle firing):-

DOROTHY GET GEORGE BARTON TO BRING YOU DOWN HERE TOMORROW SUNDAY NO LEAVE.

<u>Thursday, September 14th</u>:-

CATCH 10.22 TOMORROW FRIDAY MAY GO.

Officers of the 3rd Bn Grenadier Guards, Aldershot, July 1939. From rear, left to right:-

Lt PHA Burke, 2/Lt H Reynell-Pack, 2/Lt RH Heywood-Lonsdale, Lt FJRP Needham, 2/Lt AAAD Ramsay, Lt JE Antony, 2/Lt The Hon NI Forbes, 2/Lt EBM Vaughan, 2/Lt The Hon WNSLH Villiers, 2/Lt GH Dixon, Lt PJC Radford-Norcop, Capt PT Clifton, 2/Lt MW Grazebrook, 2/Lt FJC Bowes-Lyon, 2/Lt DJF Beaumont-Nesbitt, 2/Lt LP Aubrey-Fletcher, Lt The Hon GL Hamilton Russell, 2/Lt EWS Ford, 2/Lt R Crompton-Roberts, 2/Lt JD Buchanan, Capt WRJ Alston-Roberts-West.
Capt GC Gordon-Lennox, Capt JNR Moor, Maj ASP Murray, Maj AHS Adair MC, Lt Col Sir John Aird Bt MVO MC, Capt & Adjut LRC Stucley, Capt LS Starkey, Capt RH Lomer, Capt NDM Johnstone.
Lieutenant Colonel (Retd) GA Alston-Roberts-West

On the previous day in fact, the Battalion's Advance Party:-

.... went to the port of Embarkation with the Advance Party 1st Division. The Advance Party of the Bn consisted of 2nd Lieutenant R Crompton-Roberts, his servant No 2614874 Guardsman R

Bennett and his driver No 2615196 Guardsman A Dove. These will have been the first Grenadiers to have landed in France.

Officers of the 2nd Bn Coldstream Guards, Aldershot, September 1939:-
Back Row: Billy Smith, Bob Windsor-Clive, Geoffrey Britton, Cecil Feilden, Capt. Morrison (MO), Peter Macfarlane, Jimmy Langley, Charles Blackwell, Evelyn Boscawen
Centre Row: Gerry Feilden, Peter Flower, Shamus McGill, Bob Combe, Evan Gibbs, Richard Pilkington, Raoul Robin, Jack Bowman, John Pigott-Brown, Charles Fane
Front Row: Angus McCorquodale, Bill Blackett, Reggie Batt, Col. Guy Edwards, Lionel Bootle-Wilbraham, Paddy Chichester, Pop Wyatt, Bunty Stewart-Brown, H.P. Martin (QM)
Reproduced with kind permission of Regimental Adjutant Coldstream Guards.

Guardsman Smith's suspicions were confirmed on September 15th when:-

All MT was ordered to be loaded and personnel proceeding to the Port of Embarkation with the MT were put at 3 hours notice to move from 2000 hours.

For some, the move to France with the 3rd Bn Grenadier Guards was an unexpected turn of events; Guardsman Middleton:-

Prior to leaving, the 3rd Bn was given 24 hours leave, but several Guardsmen failed to return on time. Consequently Sam Price and I were kitted up, joined the 3rd Bn ourselves and went to France with them.

The Battalion's move proper, however, did not commence until 0645 hours on September 19th:-

The first party comprising Major AHS Adair MC, Captain PJC Radford Norcop, Captain RE Abel-Smith, Captain PH Lort-Phillips and 150 Other Ranks (30 from each Coy) paraded and marched to the Government Railway Siding where they entrained for Southampton. On arrival they embarked on the *Maid of Orleans* with 1st Guards Brigade Headquarters and the 2nd Bn Coldstream Guards.

0915 hours:-

The Bn (less Nos 1 & 2 Coys and the first party) paraded under the Commanding Officer. The whole Bn was reported present.

1015 hours:-

The Bn reached the Government Siding and were joined by Nos 1 & 2 Coys who had marched out from billets. The Bn baggage consisted of 3 days rations, 1 Anti/Tank Rifle per Coy and 4 Bren Guns per Rifle Coy. The train was reserved for the Bn but was very crowded.

1330 hours:-

The train arrived at Southampton and we learnt that our first party was to sail in the *Maid of Orleans*, whilst we were to sail on the *Viking*, 1900 Tons. The Bn embarked immediately and was allotted the first deck. The 2nd Bn Hampshire Regiment arrived later and went to the top deck. Later a Field Ambulance arrived and took the lower deck. General Haking, Colonel of the Hampshire Regiment came on board and visited our Officers. He told us that he Commanded the 5th Infantry Brigade and took them abroad from Stanhope Lines in 1914.

1630 hours:-

The *Viking* sailed and we went off to Spithead where we joined convoy and anchored.

2000 hours:-

All lights out of decks and no smoking. Double sentries posted. Our destination at the time of sailing still unknown.

At half-past-midnight the convoy of five troop ships, escorted by two destroyers, set sail. At the time, Peter Halliday was a young subaltern and the Intelligence Officer of the 2nd Bn Hampshire Regiment; his account regarding that day's events and sailing provides a very personal experience:-

After an early breakfast on September 19th, 1939, the Bn marched to Aldershot station and entrained for Southampton. The train ran alongside the jetty where our troopship was lying and we duly embarked. We sailed during the afternoon and anchored off Ryde Pier on the Isle of Wight. Amongst those who saw us off was the Colonel of the Regiment, old Sir Richard Haking, who was unable to restrain his tears as we pulled away from the quay. We lay at anchor until dark and most of us passed the time gazing shoreward at the familiar coastline of the Island, Portsmouth and Hayling. I have a clear memory of a conversation with John Gratton, the Bn Signals Officer, who was about three years older. Looking at the Hampshire coastline he suddenly

turned to me and said "Of course you realise few of us will see that again?". I still could not really believe in such a gloomy prediction, but I started to pray and settled then on a formula, to which I stuck throughout the war - 'that I should be allowed to survive without dishonour'.

We had an uncomfortable but uneventful crossing in convoy with the other ships carrying 1st Guards Brigade. First light on September 20th, showed that we were in the approaches to Cherbourg. For some reason there was a shortage of water on board and none was available for washing and shaving. It was clearly unthinkable to remain unshaven and I wondered what to do. Senior Officers lost no time in pointing out to me that I was the military equivalent of a foolish virgin for not having filled my water bottle before embarkation. There was, however, an issue all round of a mug of tea and, much as I relish early morning tea, I realised that this was my only hope. After a couple of sips I used the rest to shave in. This, I felt, was war in earnest. A trivial incident perhaps, but the memory of it is still vivid.

Peter Halliday of the 2nd Bn Hampshire Regiment pictured later in the war when a Major.
Lieutenant Colonel (Retd) P Halliday.

The BEF's move to France had, in fact, commenced on September 10th, although advance parties and technical personnel had been arriving since September 4th. The plans for the despatch of the Force differed in two important respects from those of August 1914. The possibility of attack by both sea and air made it necessary to use the Western ports of France instead of the closer Channel ports such as Dunkirk, Calais and Boulogne. The troops were landed at Cherbourg and their stores and vehicles at Nantes, St Nazaire and Brest. The programme of loading, embarkation, landing and unloading in respect of the entire I and II Corps was strictly adhered to; this Lord Gort considered 'a feat deserving of the highest praise'.

The 1st and 2nd Divisions of I Corps were the first fighting troops to land, in fact. These formations were rightly proud of their role as the BEF's spearhead, exercised by right of origin from Aldershot Command; yet again the Guards were *en route* to war in Flanders.

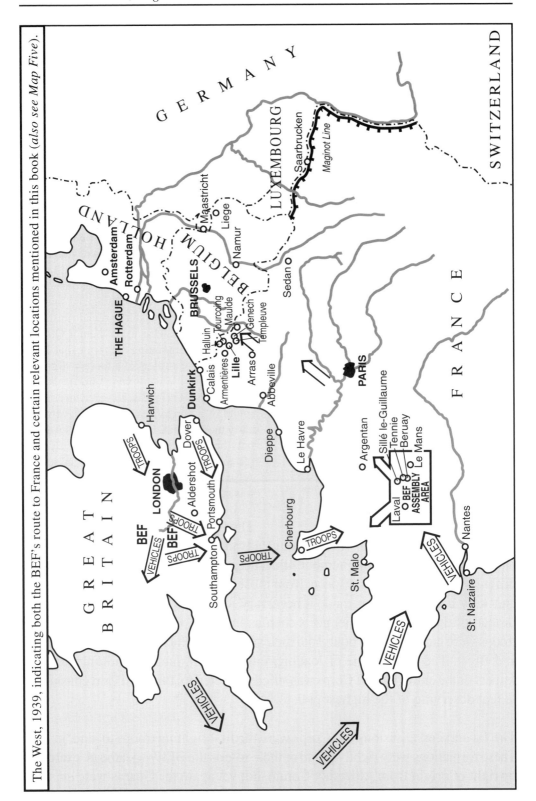

The West, 1939, indicating both the BEF's route to France and certain relevant locations mentioned in this book (*also see Map Five*).

CHAPTER TWO

Shadow of the Past

Although the return to war lacked the popular excitement of 1914, the British remained optimistic; a popular slogan was 'Home by Christmas' whilst the troops enthusiastically sang 'We're going to hang out the washing on the Siegfried Line!' In reality, the autumn and winter of 1939/40 was nicknamed the Phoney War, and later *Sitzkrieg*, by comparison with the events that were to follow. That winter was, in fact, the coldest for 50 years.

The following extracts from the 3rd Bn Grenadier Guards War Diary and first-hand accounts provide an excellent idea of what life was like for a soldier of the BEF throughout this period.

3rd Bn Grenadier Guards War Diary:-

September 20th:-

0730 hours: After a rough two hours which resulted in a good deal of sea sickness we dropped anchor in Cherbourg.

1000 hours: The Bn disembarked and marched to the railway station where we were allotted a huge glass covered waiting room.

Anonymous 3rd Grenadier:-

First Infantry Brigade to France with the BEF. First experience of French railway station lavatories. Crouched down, all money from trouser pockets down the hole. Stood up, pulled chain, floor covered with three inches of sewage.

3rd Bn Grenadier Guards War Diary (September 20th):-

1230 hours: The men were allowed into Cherbourg until 1930 hours. The Officers had lunch at the Casino and spent most of the afternoon at the Field Cashier's changing money. The exchange given was 177 Francs to the £1.

Lieutenant Peter Halliday:-

My first job on landing was to report to the Mairie, which was some distance away in Cherbourg town, to give French officialdom details of our numbers and to confirm the arrangements already made by the staff for a troop train that day. We were the first British Bns to land in France in this war and I suppose French bureaucracy was still functioning on a quasi peace-time basis and regarded us as some sort of tourists. The Orderly Room Colour Sergeant had all the necessary documents and together we set off on bicycles G.S. borrowed from my Intelligence Section. Without thinking, we pedalled off abreast on the left of what was quite a busy street - instantly provoking a furore amongst the local inhabitants! For a moment I wondered whether the natives were hostile. Then I realised how idiotic we were and, with much laughter and cheers, and counter cheers, we crossed the road and pedalled on. Arriving at the Mairie I quickly discovered the inadequacy of my schoolboy French, but somehow managed to complete the necessary formalities to the satisfaction of the French officials.

Our train was not due to depart until the evening and so the Bn was given leave to have a few hours off in Cherbourg. The Bn duly paraded intact at the railway station in the evening but a fair number of men had clearly been surprised by the strength of the local wine. My job was to allocate the train to the various components of the Bn. Officers travelled first class, WOs and Sergeants second class and all other ranks travelled in those French cattle trucks labelled 'Chevaux 8, Hommes 40' and, as I heard one soldier claim, 'Hampshiremen bloody 80!'.

Anonymous 3rd Grenadier:-

Into cattle trucks, '40 men or eight horses' (the latter only recently removed). Crowded in, bale of straw thrown on top of us, sliding door closed. Away, no springs, square wheels, huge cracks in floor boards useful for lavatory. Peeping through tiny windows en route to Belgian frontier. Not encouraged by sight of Great War cemeteries.

3rd Bn Grenadier Guards War Diary (September 20th):-

1900 hours: Began entraining the Bn in darkness. 2nd Bn Coldstream Guards came on the same train. Passenger carriages were provided for all personnel, but were very crowded. A stowaway from a British ship was found in one of the Officers' carriages. He was seized as a spy by Captain PJC Radford-Norcop and the Security Police were sent for. He was removed.

September 21st:-

0830 hours: The train stopped at Alencon where we were met by a Rail Transport Officer (RTO) who officially told us that our destination was Sillé le-Guillaume and our billeting area Tennie.

1030: Arrived at Sillé le-Guillaume where we detrained and formed up as a Bn in the square outside the station.... The men got tea and a ration and the Officers had a meal in the town.

1230 hours: The Bn left Sillé le-Guillaume and went by route march to Tennie (about 7 miles). Nos 3 and 4 Coys went a further 3 miles to Bernay, which was their area.

1500 hours: The Bn reached its billets, which were most welcome. A small village in lovely country. The inhabitants most welcoming and hospitable... The men were billeted chiefly in barns and outhouses.

Lieutenant Halliday:-

It may sound odd but we had no idea where we were going. We assumed it would be eastward, towards the German frontier, even if we were not actually marching towards the sound of the guns. In fact all night the train steamed south and next morning we found ourselves traversing a lovely rolling countryside of streams and apple orchards. We arrived about mid-day at Sillé le-Guillaume, a little town a few miles NW of Le Mans. We were met by the Bn advance party, which had preceded us under the Second in Command, Major John Fowler-Esson. His purple and bewhiskered features were a reassuring sight on the platform as the train drew to a halt.

We marched some 10 miles through a hot and dusty sort of replica of Somerset and, guided by our advance party, went into billets in various large farms in the villages of Neuvillalais and Maison Care. We remained here for 10 days while the rest of the Division assembled in the same general area. The inhabitants could not have been more friendly, and my chief recollection of the area is the astonishing amount of rough cider we consumed. It was impossible to have a conversation with a local without being pressed to down a jug of the stuff!

And so the 1st Guards Brigade reached the BEF assembly area in the vicinity of Le Mans and Laval.

3rd Bn Grenadier Guards War Diary:-

September 21st [continued]:-

The whole atmosphere of the village was most peaceful with no signs of PAD [Panic & Disorder?] and, but for the Bn, no signs of war except the complete absence of any men of military age..... The whole Bn was in great spirits and at the top of its form.

September 22nd:-

1000 hours: The Carrier Platoon with 2nd Lieutenant H Reynell Pack arrived, having come from Sillé le-Guillaume by train from Brest.

1100 hours: The Divisional General (Major General Hon HRL Alexander) visited the Bn accompanied by the Brigadier.

1800 hours: Half the MT accompanied by Captain PT Clifton and Lieutenant JG Rankin arrived having driven from Brest. The MT is sent off to Coys to unload stores and then concentrated in Tennie. Three vehicles had slight collisions during this operation; having motored 200 miles without any accident.

September 23rd:-

The Coys went for route march in the morning. The afternoon was taken up with washing clothes in the rivers and bathing.

September 24th (Sunday):-

1000 hours: The Coys at Tennie attended Church Parade in a field. Captain the Rev Brown took the service, the Commanding Officer read the lesson and the Brigadier took the salute after the service.

In the evening the money was drawn from the Field Cashier at Evron and the Bn was paid out for the first time under active service conditions.

Captain PH Lort Phillips with four other ranks left the Bn to act as Staging Officer for the move forward to the Concentration Area.

On this day, the Commander-in-Chief, Lord Gort, made a personal reconnaissance of the front allotted his BEF: from Maulde (on the River Escaut) to Halluin (just south of Menin), and thence a defensive flank along the River Lys to Armentières. The French 51st Division was placed under Lord Gort's command, and this was employed in the BEF's left sector (along the River Lys), covering the towns of Roubaix and Tourcoing. Within the BEF sector lay the important industrial area of Lille-Roubaix, the ground around which is both flat and low-lying.

It is important to consider the Allied military plans and experience which dictated this deployment. Firstly, the Allied strategy was one of static defence, not offence; there was little or no question of an offensive being launched against Germany. Instead it was a question of patiently awaiting the aggressor's next move. The key to Allied strategy was the Maginot Line, but this was incomplete, extending northwards only as far as the Franco-Belgian border at Longwy. There were actually good reasons why the Maginot Line had not been extended to the coast along this border. First of all due to a perfectly understandable question of cost, and secondly the wish not to isolate the Belgians - Allies in the Great War - on the wrong side of such substantial defences. Aware of the Maginot Line's limitation, however, the Allies were equally haunted by painful memories of the *Schlieffen* Plan of 1914: the massive sweeping thrust through Belgium, aimed at Paris. This is why the possibility of Germany respecting Belgium's neutrality was considered an advantage to the Allies. Naturally Allied plans were based upon the strategy which had provided victory in 1918; conversely the German generals were developing plans arising from *their* experience in 1918. It was to this vulnerable Northern flank, however, that the BEF had been assigned.

The Allied chain of command is also relevant. The Chief of the French Staff and Supreme Commander of all French Land Forces was General Gamelin, his deputy being General Georges (who commanded three Army Groups). Lord Gort's BEF was assigned to General Billotte's 1st Army Group, in what was known as the

'North East Theatre of Operations'. Communication was confusing, however: Lord Gort did not receive his orders, as one might expect, from General Billotte, but from General Gamelin through General Georges! The command structure

Four 3rd Bn Grenadier Guards Officers pictured shortly after arrival in France, September 1939 (from left to right): Captains Lort-Phillips and Gordon-Lennox, Lieutenants Reynell-Pack and Ford. Note the Great War style uniforms.
Grenadier Guards.

could also be considered more impractical given that General Gamelin was not responsible for either the French Air Force or British AASF.
3rd Bn Grenadier Guards War Diary:-

September 25th:-

1200 hours: HRH the Duke of Gloucester [serving as Chief Liaison Officer on Gort's GHQ Staff] visited the Bn.... His Royal Highness walked round the Tennie billeting area and had luncheon with the Officers.

September 27th:-

1300 hours: All Coys began packing their trucks.

1800 hours: The Drums beat Retreat through the streets of Tennie.

September 28th:-

0600 hours: The Bn MT (less Carriers, 5 30-Cwts, 2 Anti-Aircraft (A/A) trucks, 1 water cart and 4 motor cycles) left Tennie under Major AHS Adair MC, to go via two stages to our final destination.

1800 hours: The Bn left Tennie and marched to Sillé le-Guillaume. There they entrained (in cattle trucks - 30 men to a truck) together with half the 2nd Hamps and the Bde Anti-Tank (A/T) Coy. The men had hot tea and then settled down for the night. The MT was put on 'flats'.

September 29th:-

0019 hours: Train left Sillé le-Guillaume for an unknown destination.

1645 hours: The train stopped at Amiens. No arrangements of any sort, and no hot water.

1900 hours: The train arrived at Arras. Here the Bn detrained in the dark, had some tea and was met by Capt RE Abel-Smith and Drill Sergeant Clements, who were the Advanced Party and who led the Bn to our billets in Roeux, about 8 miles from Arras. The Bn arrived there at about 11 pm and found excellent arrangements had been made by Captain RE Abel-Smith. The Bn was quickly settled into billets, had tea and at about 1230 am all the baggage and packs arrived from the station.

Lieutenant Halliday:-

On September 29th, the Division began the 250 mile move by road and rail north-eastward to take over a section of the defences on the Belgian frontier. We understood that we were taking over a sector of the Maginot Line but soon discovered that mighty little work had been done on the Belgian frontier.

Existing field defences in the BEF sector were indeed poor, consisting merely of an anti-tank ditch and some concrete protected emplacements - known as 'pill-boxes' - for the use of small arms. This was hardly comparable, of course, to the impressive fortifications of the Maginot Line proper (in the French sector).

3rd Bn Grenadier Guards War Diary:-

September 30th:-

The Bn settled down into its billets which are good, but no sanitary arrangements of any sort and the village water supply broken down. The village had recently been vacated by two or three thousand French troops.

1200 hours: The Bn is said to have occupied the same billets in the same area during the last war, and a Cypher was found carved in the wall of a dug-out.

1210 hours: An air raid warning. No action taken.

1800 hours: The Bn in fine fettle and setting the highest possible standard.

October 1st:-

1300 hours: The MT arrived under Major AHS Adair MC, having motored about 250 miles.

Leave was granted to the Bn to visit Arras and many men took advantage of this whilst others explored the neighbourhood and came back with many relics of the last war. A very cold, rainy day.

October 2nd:-

1400 hours: Major AHS Adair MC took the Adjutant, Major ASP Murray and Captain MSB Vernon MVO, to the Sunken Road (where the Bn fought in 1918) and to the Vimy Ridge.

1700 hours: HRH the Duke of Gloucester visited the Bn and had tea in the Officers' Mess.

2100 hours: Orders received from Brigade for the move tomorrow.

October 3rd:-

0715 hours: The Bn left Roeux.

The Bn paraded and marched to Bachy station 3 miles away, thence it entrained with the 2nd Bn Coldstream Guards and arrived at Templeuve via Douai and Somain at 11 am. The Commander-in-Chief [Lord Gort] and HRH the Duke of Gloucester were on the platform to meet the Bn, and after detraining the Bn marched past Lord Gort.

1200 hours: The Bn arrived at Genech village [10 miles SE of Lille]....Nos 1, 2 and 3 Coys marched into billets north of Genech, No 4 Coy into billets at Genech and HQ Coy and Bn HQ went into the Château de Genech, a large unfurnished house, built about 40 years ago and left by its owner about a year ago. The Commander-in-Chief and His Royal Highness came to Genech and saw the Bn area.

The Bn is to take over tomorrow a line of Blockhouses (at present garrisoned by the French Army) with the Border Regiment (3rd Inf Bde) on its right and 2nd Bn Hamps on its left. The country is much more pleasant than that round Roeux, and untouched by the last war. The Château was occupied by a German HQ staff during the last war. The Bn area is only about three miles from the Belgian frontier.
The Bn spent the day getting into billets and reconnoitring the position which consists of six blockhouses and a tank obstacle, all constructed by the French in 1937, and very well done.

On this date, I Corps took over from the French the sector Maulde-Gruson on the Belgian frontier. This sector lay between that of the French 1st Army and of the 16th French Corps. General Alexander's 1st Division was on the left, and Major General HC Loyd DSO MC's 2nd Division on the right.

Lieutenant Halliday:-

The 2nd Hampshires were to assume responsibility for a sector about 2000 yards wide in the area of the village of Bachy. A deep anti-tank ditch had been dug parallel to, and generally about half a mile back from the frontier. The ditch went in 1000 yard zig-zags and at each corner there was a concrete blockhouse. The latter's front was solid, but at each side was a gun port to enable the occupants to shoot in enfilade anyone who was trying to cross the anti-tank ditch. Each blockhouse was equipped with a large periscope with which to be able to observe forward. This is all the Maginot Line consisted of in those parts.

The Bn was to be responsible for two of these blockhouses, and I was sent with the advance party, with orders to take over the equipment and orders of their existing French garrisons. I found my way to the first of these blockhouses but was not encouraged to find the French garrison, numbering about a dozen in the charge of a sergeant, fast asleep. They were clearly not expecting me, but finally I managed to establish my credentials. I got the impression that the French were not exactly bursting with information so I only asked whether I could check and take over the periscope.

After a bit of poking about in the inner recesses of the blockhouse, a bearded *poilu* emerged triumphantly lugging behind him a large box about eight feet long and 18 inches wide and deep. "But how does it work?", I said, and insisted that I was not prepared to assume responsibility for it until it had been demonstrated as a periscope rampant, as it were. This caused consternation and, when they raised the lid of the box, I could see why. The whole equipment was in many, heavily greased, pieces. Clearly they had never had it out of the box into which it had been packed at the factory. After about half and hour of furious Gallic altercation, they succeeded in cleaning off and putting together all the bits and pieces. Finally they hoisted the periscope into the cradle, which enabled it to be raised through the roof of the blockhouse. In triumph the Sergeant turned to me: "Voila, mon Lieutenant, regardez la Belgique!" I stepped forward, looked through the eye-piece, and there sure enough was 'la Belgique' - but it was upside down! I started to laugh. This broke the tension and we all ended up having a tremendous laugh about it all. Then the Sergeant and I got down to puzzling out how the thing really should be put together. The little garrison then collected their kit, ran out their anti-tank guns, and withdrew, leaving me the key of the door and the periscope, now suitably rampant. For better or worse I had assumed British responsibility and, with mutual cries of "Bon Chance", we parted. Forewarned, I was able to deal with a similar situation in the second blockhouse more expeditiously!

3rd Bn Grenadier Guards War Diary:-

October 4th:-

0900 hours: The forward companies took over the position from the French, who evacuated the area, leaving behind a working party who are constructing a forward line.
No 4 Coy took over a Guard on the Railway Station and Crossing.

October 5th:-

0900 hours: No 1 Coy took over a further Blockhouse from the Border Regiment.

1400 hours: Baths were arranged at Bn HQ for two platoons of each Coy.

October 6th:-

The Commanding Officer and Major AHS Adair MC carried out a Recce of the front to be allotted to the Bn.

October 7th:-

The CIGS [General Sir Edmund Ironside], the Commander-in-Chief [Lord Gort] and HRH the Duke of Gloucester visited the Bn Front.

The Brigadier accompanied by the Commanding Officer, Major AHS Adair MC and the Adjutant reconnoitred the Bn Front and the Commanding Officer later held a conference of Coy Cdrs.

October 9th:-

Orders were received for occupying the Bn position. Briefly the Brigade area is the area originally occupied by Nos 1 and 2 Coys. No 3 Coy's area is handed over to 3rd Inf. Bde. No 1 Coy's area is handed over to 2nd Bn Coldstream Guards. The Bn occupies No 2 Coy's area, which includes 2 block houses. 2 Hamps occupy the Brigade reserve line.
A pouring wet day which rendered the area round Bn HQ to a lake and flooded the Guard out of the Guard Room.

October 10th:-

1400 hours: Bn HQ moved from Chateau de Genech to Chateau du Fay.
The position is to be held with No 2 Coy on right, No 4 Coy on left, No 1 Coy in reserve on right and No 3 Coy in reserve on left.

October 11th:-

1400 hours: The Royal Engineers [RE, 23rd Field Regiment] instructed Coy representatives in the making of wattle fences for revetting.
Duck boards were constructed and billets in general were improved.

October 12th:-

The forward Coys began the construction of their platoon areas.
Two platoons cut wattles for hurdles.
The Bn took over the duty of providing three double sentries to assist the Customs Officers on the Belgian frontier. These to be provided by 4, 2 & 3 Coys in rotation.

October 13th:-

All Coys began digging and siting Coy positions. Brushwood was cut and wattle hurdles made for revetting. Road ditches were cleared and some of the men helped the local farmer in picking the sugar beet crop.

Lieutenant Halliday:-

The Bn now settled down to constructing an elaborate defensive position based on the anti-tank ditch and the blockhouses. The landscape was mainly flat and open, and the chief difficulty was the water table, which was never far below the surface. We became experts at drainage and, where no amount of drainage ditching would help, we had to build breast-works.

Lord Gort:-

When I Corps arrived in its allotted sector, an almost continuous anti-tank obstacle existed in the form of a ditch covered by concrete blockhouses built to mount anti-tank guns and machine-guns. While defences continued to be developed along the lines of the original plan, based on the close defence of the frontier, it was also necessary to organise the position.... The whole scheme involved the immediate construction of field defences and the duplication of the anti-tank obstacle in the forward zone.

And so the defensive 'Gort Line' on the Franco-Belgian frontier was born.

Lieutenant Halliday:-

The Belgians absolutely forbade any British reconnaissance across the border, and so we relied on our Military Attaché for topographical information of the areas to which we expected to advance. He must have spent a great deal of his time on country picnics with his family in order to cover the areas in which we were particularly interested.

At this stage, however, Belgian neutrality was still considered an advantage by the Allied High Command. On that basis no Staff talks or arrangements for integration of the Belgian Army into the Allied force, or indeed the defence of Belgium, took place.

3rd Bn Grenadier Guards War Diary:-

October 15th:-

Digging was continued in the morning. The afternoon was clear and two voluntary church services were held.
The Drums beat Retreat at Bachy.
Pouring rain.

September 23rd, 1939: a rest during training at Tennie for men of the 3rd Bn Grenadier
Guards.
Grenadier Guards.

September 23rd, 1939: an essential foot inspection, by Captain Lort-Phillips, for men of the
3rd Bn Grenadier Guards during a training exercise at Tennie.
Grenadier Guards.

October 16th:-

A fine day after a very wet night which did a great deal of damage to the trenches. Draining and further digging were carried out all day.

October 17th:-

The Commander-in-Chief visited the Bn in the afternoon and inspected Nos 1 & 3 Coy areas.

October 18th:-

HRH the Duke of Windsor accompanied by the Commander-in-Chief, the Corps and Divisional Commanders inspected the Bn front [HRH had served as a Grenadier Officer in the Great War and had then maintained a close association with the Foot Guards until the Abdication].

October 19th:-

Very heavy rain which resulted in many trenches being abandoned or breastworks substituted.

October 23rd:-

A lovely day. Work was continued on the trenches. Tactical wiring was planned together with proposals for demolition of certain houses and fortifying of others. Fields of fire were cut out in the brushwood and the wattles so produced were turned into revetting material.

October 25th:-

The Divisional Commander inspected the Blockhouses and trials were carried out of their capacity for men, ammunition and stores. Pouring rain.

October 27th:-

HRH the Duke of Gloucester visited the Bn and inspected the trenches which are beginning to near completion as regards digging and revetting. HRH had luncheon at Bn HQ.
Work on our position has been held up owing to heavy rain, water being very close to the surface and continual draining and repairs being required. In some cases trenches have had to be abandoned and breastworks substituted.
Never-the-less the men, with little or no experience of this type of work have got into it extremely quickly and work extraordinarily hard and well in spite of the fact that they work chiefly in pouring rain and thick mud. At the end of a day's work the men are soaking wet and covered in mud and the problem is how to avoid this, as they have nothing to change into. 1lb per man per day for fuel is the present scale for cooking and heating and it chiefly goes in the former. The boots are becoming worn out and at present there is no new issue. The Bn are buying French workmen's' blue canvas trousers and they are invaluable. A small issue of gum boots and thigh boots has been made. At present only 150 second blankets are on charge to the Bn. In spite of all

this the men remain extremely cheerful and the percentage of sickness is not high.

Guardsman Middleton:-

Because I was a country bloke I was persuaded to go out and catch rabbits for the pot whilst we were at Bachy. In this way we supplemented our rations and got a good hot meal. Our spirits were high, we were quite happy to follow the Officers' lead without question.

Lieutenant Halliday:-

The weather was wet and cold and initially a major problem was that, in accordance with War Office instructions, the Bn had gone to war with only one suit of battledress per man and no form of fatigue wear. The theory was that, after a period of operations, each unit would go through a mobile bath establishment to bathe and receive new dry clothing. But we were digging and wiring in filthy, muddy conditions, without foreseeable let up, and inevitably the soldiers' dress suffered.

Colonel Jack Aird, commanding 3rd Bn Grenadier Guards, could stand it no longer and motored into Lille where he bought 1000 French railway-porter outfits. These were blue and caused something of a sensation when his Bn paraded in them. Jack Aird sent the bill to Brigade HQ but, as with many of his other brainwaves, the answer came back from on high: 'Colonel Aird to pay'. Luckily I think he could afford it. Not long afterwards we had an issue of the new denim clothing as fatigue dress.

I remember that Jack Aird, formerly an Equerry to the Prince of Wales (later Edward VIII) was unable to take his soldiering very seriously. I remember one of the first Brigade conferences in France convened to discuss, amongst other things, the desirable scale of issue of maps. On being asked his opinion by the Brigadier, Colonel Aird replied: "I should like to have as few maps as possible. I find they confuse my Officers!"

As Bn IO, I had to organise the construction and camouflage of a number of Observation Posts (OP) to be manned by my intelligence section. I was also detailed, believed it or not, to run a hurdle factory. Each rifle company was detailed to produce two hurdle makers and with these eight worthies we established the factory in the Bois-de-la-Fougere, an area of coppiced woodland (about 1000 by 400 yards) which lay between the anti-tank ditch and the frontier. To begin with we made hurdles to revet the sides of the Bn trenches, and then our remit was extended. Some military genius, sensing that the war might be protracted, had decreed that we must revet the vertical face of the anti-tank ditch. This entailed making an enormous number of 6 by 6 feet hurdles. After a fortnight we were given a yet more improbable task.

Our unknown military genius had decided that the war might last longer than the estimated longevity of our hurdles. The solution was to plant willow cuttings in the bottom of the anti-tank ditch at 18 inch intervals! So my merry hurdle makers and I became foresters. We spent the mornings seeking suitable willow cuttings and the afternoons planting. We planted some 2000 willows and I often wonder how they did!

3rd Bn Grenadier Guards War Diary:-

October 30th:-

An Air Raid Alarm was given at 1145 hours, but the All Clear went five minutes later.

November 1st:-

A bus was hired to run daily between Bachy and Douai, price 11 francs return.

November 8th:-

Work continued on the position.

November 9th:-

The Commanding Officer flew over the Bn position in a reconnaissance plane.

1700 hours: Nos 1, 2 and 4 Coys each manned one platoon post and carried out wiring and digging during the night. They were visited by the Commanding Officer during the night, and he was accompanied by Major AHS Adair MC, and the Adjutant.

November 10th:-

1300 hours: The Platoons of Nos 1, 2 & 4 Coys came out of their trenches.

1530 hours: Twenty-five men of No 4 Coy and 25 men of the 2nd Bn Coldstream Guards together with the massed Drums of the Bn practised for a Guard of Honour at Bachy War Memorial.

November 11th:-

1045 hours: No 4 Coy's Guard of Honour of 25 men under Major WRJ Alston-Roberts-West. This Guard of Honour was made up by 25 men of the 2nd Bn Coldstream Guards and this unique and historic sight of a composite Guard of Honour of Grenadiers and Coldstreamers was at Bachy, where the Guard mounted on one side of the War Memorial with 50 French soldiers on the other. The combined Grenadier and Coldstream Drums grouped in the centre. The Commanding Officer was unable to be present due to illness, but Major AHS Adair MC took his place and Lieutenant Colonel Bootle Wilbraham, Commanding 2nd Coldstream. The Mayor and *Ancien Combatants* marched on with the Tricolor and the names of the dead read out whilst the Guard of Honour Presented Arms. The wreaths were laid and the Drums played the Last Post, then a minute's silence, and the Reveille. Speeches were made by the Curé and Lieutenant Colonel Bootle Wilbraham. The Guard of Honour Presented Arms and Drums played the *Maisel Maire* and God Save the King. The Guard of Honour marched off and the English and French Officers went to the French Officers' Mess where toasts were drunk.

November 13th:-

No 4 Coy moved out of their Billets in Bachy and took over No 3 Coy's Billets in La Posterie. No 3 Coy moved into the Hampshire's Billets in Genech.

1400 hours: Owing to the threat of a German invasion of Holland and Belgium, No 1 Coy and the Carrier Platoon were put at four hours notice to move forward into Belgium under Major AHS Adair MC. The Commanding Officer attended a Brigade Conference and plans were laid for the advance of the Bn.

November 16th:-

Eleven Other Ranks of the Bn attended a concert in Douai given by Miss Gracie Fields. 4 hours notice for certain men of the Bn was lifted.

November 17th:-

The Air Raid Warning was given at 1115 hours and the All Clear at 1200 hours. Gunfire and aeroplane engines were heard close by, but owing to it being overcast nothing was seen.

November 18th:-

The Secretary of State for War [the Rt Hon Leslie Hore-Belisha] accompanied by the Commander in Chief visited the Brigade Front.
The Commanding Officer attended a conference at Brigade HQ and warning was given for a party of 50 Officers and Other Ranks to visit the Saar Front.

November 22nd:-

Work was continued on the position and wiring was done throughout the night. The Carrier Platoon provided the 'enemy' and carried out a skilful 'Tank Attack' at first light at 0530 hours. The attack gave everyone an idea of what to expect and was ruled as not successful.
Work was continued on the position above ground but dinners were eaten in the trenches 'as for the front line'.

November 25th:-

A very wet day, the trenches are getting very wet.

November 27th:-

A party consisting of Major AHS Adair MC, Captain LS Starkey, Lieutenant FJRP Needham, Lieutenant EWS Ford and 12 Other Ranks paraded at 140 hours and went by MT to Templeuve where they entrained for the journey to the Saar Front. They are to be away for three weeks.

Lieutenant Halliday:-

There was a house on the edge of Bachy village with an upstairs window looking towards the Bois and Belgium, which we regarded with great suspicion. In this window there was sometimes displayed a large china cockerel, but not always. We became certain it was a signal, but never proved whether the appearance of the cockerel was a sign of danger or that the coast was clear! However, we thoroughly enjoyed ourselves and hoped at least that we had made life for the local smuggling fraternity more difficult.

3rd Bn Grenadier Guards War Diary:-

December 5th, 1939: HM the King inspects the 2nd Bn Coldstream Guards.
Reproduced by kind permission of Regimental Adjutant Coldstream Guards.

December 5th:-

1200 hours: The King went to Bachy where the Commanding Officers of the Brigades were presented to him.

1230 hours: The King arrived at Bachy Mine Guard where the right of the Bn was drawn up. He got out of his car and walked down the Bn which was drawn up in line and in such a manner that each man could see His Majesty. The men cheered as the King passed. The Bn marched past the Commanding Officer on the way back to billets and worked very well. They appeared appreciably older than when they marched out of Aldershot.

December 9th:-

The week has been spent in maintaining, draining and improving the Bn area.

Lieutenant Halliday:-

One afternoon just before Christmas, I was telephoned by the Bachy village policeman to say that he had taken in for questioning a foreign woman he had found asking questions about the soldiers. I went to his police station and found a not unattractive girl in her early twenties who claimed that, although born in Germany, she had become an American citizen and had that summer in Aldershot married a Guardsman in the 2nd Coldstream. She said that she was only trying to find the 2nd Coldstream in order to be reunited with her husband. It hardly seemed a likely tale and, in any case, the frontier was a no go area for visitors. I gained the impression that, for reasons which seemed suspicious, she had clearly been determined somehow to contact the British Army in Aldershot in the month or so before the outbreak of war. She had first met the Coldstreamer, whom she eventually succeeded in marrying, when he had been in Europe earlier in the year with an Army sports team. I therefore informed the girl that I was arresting her on suspicion of espionage. It was about 4 pm by now. When I telephoned the Brigade IO he informed me that he could not contact a single member of the intelligence staff at Bureau, Corps or GHQ as they were all attending a Christmas concert at GHQ, at which the star was Florence Desmond; a 'Phoney War' it was indeed, it seemed.

The 2nd Coldstream confirmed that they did have the Guardsman to whom the girl claimed to be married, but apparently he wasn't interested as she had left him soon after the wedding. The BIO agreed with me that we had good enough circumstantial evidence to hold the girl. He therefore took it upon himself to make direct contact with the French *Deuxième Bureau* in Lille. I was given an address there where I was to present myself with suspected spy at 10 pm that evening. It was now dark and very cold and my only transport was a 15 cwt truck with a canvas tilt. I took the girl with me to Bn HQ where I called upon the Orderly Room clerks to borrow some blankets, to keep us warm in the back of the truck, as Lille was a good hour's drive away. When they heard what I wanted them for, there was much guffawing and leg-pulling and the Orderly Room clerks never afterwards let me forget this incident!

My problem was that, having reached Lille, I still had nearly two hours to fill before my RV with the *Deuxième Bureau*. I therefore decided that the best thing I could do would be to take this girl to dinner in the restaurant which we usually patronised on our occasional evening forays into Lille. We had a very good dinner. I did my best to entertain her, but I'm not sure I was very successful as she kept returning to the subject of what was going to happen to her. Fortified by wine, she did eventually confide in me to the extent of showing me her address book, in which were the names of more than 20 members of varying ranks in the Army at Aldershot.

In due course we made the RV with the *Deuxième Bureau* where the proceedings were conducted by their local interrogator, who was quite the most dreadful little man I have ever met. He proceeded to question the girl and pretty soon had her in tears and then hysterical. At this point he asked to see inside her little suitcase, upon which she snatched it open and hurled the contents at him. After a while she calmed down and the interrogation continued, mainly I think because she had nothing left to throw. It had, incidentally, been conducted in French and I could not follow all the detail, but clearly our interrogator found grounds for suspicion. He informed me that he would be detaining her and that my role in the affair was at an end. By this time I felt very sorry for my late prisoner, but there was nothing I could do. We were never informed of the outcome. The French had the reputation for shooting alleged spies on little evidence, but she may have got away with deportation on the basis of her claimed US citizenship. I hope she did.

For a long time afterwards I had my leg pulled about taking spies out to dinner. I think one or two senior officers were rather shocked, but no one suggested what else they would have done and certainly the Intelligence Staffs were in no position to criticise my actions!

3rd Bn Grenadier Guards War Diary:-

December 24th:-

The Bn had a cinema show in the evening.

December 25th:-

There was a Service at 1000 hours.
Xmas dinners were seen by the Commanding Officer.
Xmas Day was observed as a holiday.

December 27th:-

The Bn moved by MT to Agny and went into Billets, having handed over 64 and 65 Blockhouses to 2nd Hampshires.

January 4th, 1940:-

The Bn carried out an embussed Adv Gd scheme from Agny to the Canal du Nord.
The Bn formed up on the Sunken Road leading due south from Pronville and marched .... to the position on the Canal du Nord.
The advance across country took 1 hour 10 minutes.

January 9th:-

The Bn moved to Gommecourt and carried out an exercise set by 1 Div to practice a Bn deliberate counter-attack with I tanks. Everything went according to plan. A very cold day.

Lieutenant Halliday:-

In the New Year we were pleased to welcome Lieutenant Colonel Pat Cadoux-Hudson to command the 2nd Hampshires in succession to Stokes-Roberts, who had been posted as GSO of a division in England. I had always got on well with Colonel Stokes-Roberts, but I think we were very lucky to have Cadoux take over the Bn before active operations started. John Fowler-Esson was still 2 ic and the life and soul of what was a very happy mess. His after dinner party piece, if we had guests, was to act as a French General presenting medals to a regiment just come out of the line. For this I used to perform as his ADC and we used to canter into the room astride chairs. About this time I spent a week at Brigade HQ as Brigade IO in the temporary absence of the regular incumbent. This was in accordance with the Brigadier's policy that Brigade and Bn HQ Officers should get better acquainted. The Brigadier was a Welsh Guardsman by name Beckwith-

Smith. He seemed to me to be very old, but I suppose he was no more than in his fifties. He was certainly much older than his Brigade staff and the atmosphere in the Mess was rather like that of a pleasant country house with the Brigadier as our very charming host.

Cadoux very soon assessed that, after our long period of field works, the Bn was badly in need of collective training. To his relief we were ordered to move down to an area NE of Arras for a fortnight's Bn training. The Bn was allotted to a Royal Army Service Corps troop carrying company and moved by road. Normally I should have been on a motor cycle, responsible for navigation and controlling the guides, whom I would post at intervals to direct the flow of the column. On this occasion, however, I was ordered to go forward with the advance party to reconnoitre the training areas allotted to the Bn. Dennis South was ordered to do my usual motor cycle job. The weather was bitterly cold with freezing rain on the roads. Poor Dennis crashed, landed on his head and never regained consciousness.

He was our first casualty. It was particularly tragic as he had only just got married before we left Aldershot. He was older than the rest of the subalterns. We buried him in the British First World War Cemetery on Vimy Ridge. It was another bitterly cold and wet day and I think none of those present failed to be moved by the occasion, especially when the haunting notes of the Last Post sounded across the rows and rows of Great War gravestones. Not for the first or last time I felt lucky to be alive.

With the cemeteries of the Great War all around, and its soldiers based in the same old garrison towns - St Omer, Arras and Hazebrouck to name but three, the BEF was, without a doubt, well and truly in the shadow of the past.

3rd Bn Grenadier Guards War Diary:-

January 12th:-

The Drums of the Bn and the 2nd Bn Coldstream Guards beat Retreat in Arras from 1600 hours to 1630 hours.

January 12th, 1940: the combined Corps of Drums of the Grenadiers & Coldstream at Arras.
Reproduced by kind permission of Regimental Adjutant Coldstream Guards.

January 13th:-

The Bn moved to the forward area by MT.
The Bn went into billets as follows: Nos 1 and 4 Coys - Bachy. 2 Coy La Posterie. Bn HQ and Carrier Platoon - Ch du Fay. HQ Coy and 'B' Ech - Le Riez. 3 Coy - Genech.

January 14th:-

On account of tension on the Dutch and Belgian frontiers with Germany the Bn was placed at 4 hours notice to move and all leave was cancelled.

January 16th:-

Some 2" of snow fell. Orders were received for the Bn to pack and practice a move tomorrow.

January 17th:-

More snow during the night and hard frost. Brilliant sunshine but roads bad.
Leave to the UK re-opens and Bn now at 6 instead of 4 hours notice to move.

January 19th:-

The Bn returns to normal and is no longer at 6 hours notice to move.

Lieutenant The Master of Forbes:-

Life was one of considerable boredom. The long winter evenings were trying and many of the Guardsmen saved up their pay to buy radios in an effort to relieve the monotony. The Belgian frontier was closed to troops and the only relaxation was when a few Officers at a time were allowed to visit the fleshpots of Lille. Lieutenant Tommy Reynell-Pack and I usually managed to go there together. In Lille we discovered an excellent restaurant, which also had a good floor show. Once, at the end of January, when visiting Lille one evening, we each had a most welcome bath in a hotel. This was our first since landing in France, and although we paid through the nose it was well worth it. Then, after a good meal, we struggled back to the Bn, hampered by many stops to free the frozen pedal controls of my vehicle!

And so the 'Phoney War' dragged on. In November 1939, however, Lord Gort had made arrangements with General Georges that a British infantry brigade should take its place in the line on the Saar Front, under the command of a French Division. On December 4th, the first British infantry brigade took over the sector of the French 42nd Division, and since that date further brigades completed short tours of duty. In this section of the Maginot Line, the nearest enemy positions were, on average, just 1,500 yards distant. Clearly this detachment provided an opportunity for some contact with the enemy. In early 1940, therefore, salvation from the monotony of manning the Gort Line was at hand for the 1st Guards Brigade, whose turn to serve in the Maginot Line was fast approaching.

CHAPTER THREE

Maginot Line

3rd Bn Grenadier Guards War Diary:-

<u>February 1st, 1940:-</u>

1st Gds Bde orders were received today for move to the Saar front. Considerable preparation and training has been going on for some time as a result of verbal orders previously issued.

<u>February 3rd:-</u>

The day was spent in packing up and cleaning billets. No 64 & 65 Blockhouses and the Douane Patrols were handed over to the 3rd Infantry Brigade.

<u>February 4th:-</u>

In accordance with Bn Move Orders the Bn entrained for Metz area. The Bn moved by 3 trains ...... The Bn moved from billets by Coys, the Drums playing.
The journey for all three trains was uneventful if long... The Bn marched from the stations into billets at La Maxe.

<u>February 6th:-</u>

The Bn settled down in their new billets and helped to clear the streets of thawing snow and ice that was causing floods in billets.

<u>February 8th:-</u>

The Commanding Officer and Intelligence Officer started at 0745 hours for a recce of the *Ligne de Contact*. Major AHS Adair MC saw Coy Comdrs at 1200 hours and gave out Move Orders for the move to Monneren the next day. The Commanding Officer and Intelligence Officer returned at 1900 hours and saw OC Coys at 2100 hours, explaining the general situation in the *Ligne de Contact*.

Lieutenant Halliday:-

The Maginot Line complex was designed to be a mutually interdependent combination of defensive positions in depth. Nearest the enemy was the *Ligne de Contact*, which was no more than a conventional outpost line. The country consisted of a series of wooded ridges two or three hundred feet high and open valleys about a thousand yards wide. The Bns held a very wide and extended front composed of platoon strong points occupying the forward edges of the woods overlooking the valley of No Man's Land.

Next was the *Ligne de Receuil*, an orthodox Bn field defensive position. Then came the Maginot Line proper. This was a line of mutually supporting forts constructed by tunnelling and excavation of the hills and ridges of the terrain. Finally there was the *Ligne de Arret*. Here the main body of the French field Army was intended to make its final stand by destroying any enemy forces that succeeded in penetrating the line of forts. The theory was perfectly sound. The downfall was that the line was limited in extent. When we asked where it ended, the answer was always 'It extends to the sea', but of course we knew better. In fact it only extended north as far as the Belgian frontier. We were, however, very impressed by the technical achievements of the forts and morale of their garrisons.

In the region of the fortress line the countryside was a bit like downland with the hill features more accentuated and steep. French engineers had driven great galleries into these hills and from the cross-cross pattern of galleries it was possible to ascend to the turrets which held guns of every calibre from long range field guns to medium machine-guns. The turrets themselves could be raised or lowered flush with the ground. The commander of the fort could bring instant fire to bear of whatever calibre he chose on any piece of ground within his area of responsibility. All he had to do was telephone the turrets concerned and quote the appropriate co-ordinates from a lettered grid super-imposed on the map.

3rd Bn Grenadier Guards War Diary:-

February 9th:-

2200 hours: The Commanding Officer saw Coy Cmdrs and gave out instructions for the move up to and the holding of the *Ligne de Contact*.

February 10th:-

0900 hours: Company and Platoon Commanders went forward to recce their positions in the Line, Platoon Commanders going into their positions to stay the night, starting at 1400 hours. Coy MT moved forward well spaced out followed by the Rifle Coys who marched into billets in Bizing and Halstroff. Weather getting cold again.

February 11th:-

10 degrees of frost.
Coys by now familiar with the whole system of defence.
1745 hours: The Bn started to relieve the 1 King's Own Yorkshire Light Infantry (KOYLI).
2000 hours: Relief completed without incident. For the first time in this war the Bn finds itself facing the enemy. Covering patrols 1 KOYLI being withdrawn at that hour.

At this time, the 3rd Grenadiers were starting to receive reinforcements from home. Lance Sergeant Constantine volunteered for service in France and joined

Lance Sergeant Charles Constantine,
3rd Bn Grenadier Guards.
Mr C Constantine.

the Battalion's No 4 Company in the *Ligne de Contact*:-

The Companies, Platoons and Sections we were allocated to were already dug in a mile or so in front of the Maginot Line. We were taken to our trenches by company runners and it was very nearly daybreak when we reached them. Most of the trenches were occupied by a section of men, usually consisting of a Lance Sergeant, Lance Corporal and 10 Guardsman; the one I had to take over did not have a Lance Sergeant, hence me being sent there.

I climbed down into the trench and introduced myself to the Section. I asked the Lance Corporal how things were and to give me a lay out of everything and to put me in the picture regarding what was going on. He explained briefly and said that when it was fully daylight I would be able to see where the enemy were entrenched. This Lance Corporal was, in fact, none other than Harry Nicholls himself.

I think I was just in time for something to eat. Soon it was time for the Section to 'Stand Down' because it was getting light; to explain, when in front line trenches everyone had to 'Stand To' at dawn and dusk, that usually being the time when the enemy attacks.

I was pleased to see that someone had found a tin can and made a few holes in the side of it with a bayonet and from somewhere had managed to get some charcoal and had it glowing nice and red without it throwing out any give-away light to the enemy. It was low down in the trench and very handy for heating water for making tea and gave off a slight warmth. One of the men had filled a receptacle with snow and was beginning to melt it down over the charcoal in preparation for brewing the tea. There had been Compo Rations issued which contained bully beef, cooked sausages, Maconachie's tinned currant pudding and one or two nourishing things that could be eaten. Under the circumstances these had to be eaten cold, also there was a ration of hard Army biscuits which when hungry one would be only too pleased to eat.

After we had had some tea and eaten, Lance Corporal Nicholls explained various things to me, and showed me where, at certain times of day, you could see some movements of the enemy. They must have been dug in as we were. He said that it was rather quiet and neither side were engaging each other in small arms fire because when it did start it would be a big thing; at present neither side wanted to provoke the other. Every now and then there was artillery fire and a shell would screech overhead. Other than that it was a matter of waiting until the real thing started in earnest. Lance Corporal Nicholls told me that sometimes at night patrols would be going out and very often the enemy patrols had dogs with them. These German dogs were extremely viscous and if any of our troops managed to shoot one there was a reward.

The enemy positions were at least a good five hundred yards distant. When I looked, every so often I could see movement. At times, if we were lucky enough to get hold of a pair of binoculars, the Germans could be seen quite clearly. Our trench was fairly long and could hold all the men and provided a reasonable firing position. At the left end of it, facing the front, was a dug-out in which about eight or nine of the section could squeeze in. There always had to be two men on look-out in the trench.

After the first two or three days it began to get very monotonous, but there was nothing that could be done about it. We passed the time telling yarns, but it was mostly quiet until someone thought of a joke or something witty was said to keep us in cheerful mood. At times the rations would come round and there would be a cigarette ration in tins of 50, and a few glucose sweets per man. There was also talk of a rum ration but it had yet to arrive apparently!

The weather was getting colder and there was a few heavy falls of snow. Now and then everyone would start flapping their arms and rubbing hands to keep warm. During the night there would always be two men Standing To and keeping look-out, and I made a duty rota regarding who would relieve who. Through the night Lance Corporal Nicholls and myself would take it in turns to have a spell out there with the two who were on look-out. Sometimes the temperature was so low that the bolts of the rifles and Bren gun would freeze solid. Every 20 minutes we had to work them backwards and forwards to free them.

There were one or two nights when a wiring party had to go out and check on the wire that had already been put down, or sometimes to put new barbed wire in parts that were vulnerable. When doing this orders would be sent from Company HQ with an NCO to supervise the laying. There was also a password which changed every time the men went out. If men were wanted from my Section, either Lance Corporal Nicholls or myself would go with them.

After being in the line for about two weeks the snow was really thick, the weather still bitterly cold. Much to our surprise and delight a rum ration was at last sent round to all the trenches. We took it in our tea and appreciated it very much. The rum ration certainly warmed everyone but I am sure it was the only one we had throughout our time in France.

Lieutenant Halliday:-

The object of taking over a section of the Maginot Line, in contact with the Germans, and 1st Guards Brigade was to hold its sector for 15 days. The plan was for each Bn of the brigade to hold the most forward positions - the *Ligne de Contact* - for five days in turn. Each Bn was required to find a Fighting Patrol 20 strong which would be available for operations throughout the 15 days.

Having conducted some successful patrol operations before the war, I was given the job of training the 2nd Hampshire Fighting Patrol, and Cecil Thomas was put in command. The basic idea was that the patrol was made up of pairs of men, one of whom was responsible for observation and the other for keeping in touch with the next pair ahead. The patrol moved in arrow-head formation of pairs with the commander at his head. The arrowhead was normally well splayed out with pairs at the limit of contact by sight but, if forced to defile, would close in and then open up again as soon as conditions allowed. The last pair of each side of the arrowhead was responsible for observation to the rear. Fire could be brought to bear in every direction on the instant. For these operations each Bn was loaned three Thompson sub-machine-guns (the Chicago gangsters' weapon) from the USA.

The Brigade's three Bn Intelligence Sections and Fighting Patrols assembled in a vacated *Garde Mobile* barracks in the village of Halstroff which was just behind the outpost line. The Grenadier IO was Edward Ford (much later to be knighted as assistant secretary to our present Queen). Brigadier 'Becky' appeared each morning to finalise plans for the fighting patrols that night. There was a curiously pot-hunting atmosphere. The 2nd Bn Royal Norfolk Regiment had been there just before us and their Fighting Patrol, led by Peter Barclay, had surprised a German patrol and captured a prisoner. Peter was given the Military Cross for his exploit and our patrol commanders obviously reckoned they were in the running for another one.

There was a foot of snow everywhere, which made things difficult, but we were issued with white overalls, pillowcases for our heads, bandages for our weapons, and powder for our faces. Due to the conditions, however, the Germans were not venturing out much, the difference being, I suppose, that we were there for a limited time only for the purposes of training and experience.

Lance Sergeant Constantine:-

One day the Company Sergeant Major came round to each trench and said that the Bn was forming a regular Fighting Patrol that was to go out on patrols during the night. One or two volunteers were required in the rank of Lance Corporal and Guardsman to make up the full patrol; was anyone interested in joining it?

Harry Nicholls volunteered and said that he would like to be in it. The Company Sergeant Major wrote down his name and number and said that he would be sent for later in the day. When the Company Sergeant Major had gone I told Harry that I would be sorry to see that he was leaving the Section because all of us seemed to be getting on so well. I accepted that if he craved excitement, however, it was more likely to get it by joining the Fighting Patrol. He said that he preferred to be doing something more active and that the Fighting Patrol appealed to him more than being static, and it would break the monotony. Harry thought that when we came out of the Maginot Line the chances were that he would return to the Section anyway. Later in the day the company runner came for Harry who was to follow him back with all kit. When he was ready to go I shook his hand and we all wished him the very best of luck.

Guardsman Percy Nash:-

I joined the Fighting Patrol from No 2 Company. We became good mates. When in the Maginot Line we went out on patrol across No Man's Land looking for Germans. Harry was that kind of bloke, he was real tough and thirsted for action - so did I. There were 20 men in the unit, led by Lieutenant Ford, and our work was always at night. Harry and me would go on ahead of the others, we worked really well together, but we never clashed with the enemy which was a disappointment - we just wanted to get at 'em.

Lieutenant Edward Ford:-

When we went out at night, I always had Nicholls and Nash in front - they were our spearhead. Very tough, very reliable, they were fine soldiers both of them.

Lance Sergeant Constantine:-

It was either that night or the next that the Fighting Patrol Lance Corporal Nicholls was in passed through near our trench, because there was a special place in the barbed wire that was further out for them to get through. They were all dressed in white, so that they were camouflaged to blend in with the snow; even their rifles and other weapons had white bandages wrapped around them. As they moved along practically everything was invisible. Except for a slight crunch in the snow and the footprints they made, they were very hard to detect. We whispered "Good luck" to them as they went through, and also the password had been given to us for when they returned. We kept sharp look out for them, and after two or three hours could make out a slight movement and crunching noise in the snow. When it got nearer a challenge was given and the right password exchanged. When they came through we could just make out Harry Nicholls and gave him a wave in recognition.

The following day we were talking amongst ourselves trying to pass the time. The routine was much the same which meant that it was very monotonous. The usual artillery fire was in progress and we were discussing the Fighting Patrol to help pass the time. The subject of our conversation was mainly Harry Nicholls. The rest of the Section knew him better than myself, and they were telling me about his Army boxing, and how typical of him it was to join the Fighting Patrol. They said he certainly knew how to look after himself. He was a fine and courageous man, no doubt about it.

3rd Bn Grenadier Guards War Diary:-

February 12th:-

12 degrees of frost.
One of the Brigade Fighting Patrols went out at 0300 hours, returning at 0530 hours. Nothing to report. Stand To 0530 - 0700 hours. A cold night and slow dawn. Between 1105 - 1145 hours some 20 light shells fell in front of 4 Coy right Platoon area 41142884. The French posts immediate to the Bn left was subjected to similar shelling. Both cases were said to be mortar shells. Shelling of this nature was said to prelude enemy infantry activity; all posts were on the *qui vive*. During this first day in the line as far as the iron hard ground and the snow would permit, work out of sight of the enemy was started on the defensive system. The posts were ill sited and badly constructed, being not even bullet proof. The wire was bad. Every effort (was made) to improve the posts, mark out alternative positions, improve the wire entanglements and clear up the Bn sector, collecting wire, duck boards and RE material that was scattered in every direction. This work was continued daily, and when under observation of the enemy - at night throughout the Bn's tour in the line.

3rd Bn Grenadier Guards War Diary:-

February 13th:-

14 degrees of frost.
The Fighting Patrol went out at 0245 hours and returned at 0605 hours. Nothing to report... 15 small shells fell in front of 1 Coy...., otherwise a quiet day.

The Fighting Patrol went out at 1800 hours and returned at 0001 hours 14th Feb. Nothing to report.

February 1940, *Ligne de Contact*, Maginot Line: right-hand sector of the line occupied by the 3rd Bn Grenadier Guards - Section Posts in wood on right.
Grenadier Guards.

Guardsman Middleton:-

One day the Germans sent a shell over. We hadn't 'Stood To' at the time, there was just one Guardsman at each end of the trench. This shell hit some trees near this trench and the shrapnel from it wounded both men. It was a good job that we hadn't 'Stood To' otherwise someone might have been killed, or at least more men injured.

Lieutenant Halliday:-

It was certainly a weird sort of war. There seemed to be a sort of gentleman's agreement that neither side would shell villages or the forward edges of the woods. Movement in the open did however attract shell fire. We were supported by a battery of the famous (i.e. in the 14/18 war) French 75s. We thought they weren't firing enough, so one day I was sent to see them and to try and encourage a little more action. The French Battery Commander wasn't exactly a fire eater, but he did say that, if I let him have my cigarette ration, I could fire a gun myself. Luckily, although a non-smoker, I was carrying the cigarette ration with which I had just been issued and so was able to initiate quite a burst of activity against targets already agreed with the Bn. So much so, in fact, that there was a burst of German counter battery fire. It was inaccurate but unluckily landed near an ammunition limber which was coming up. A French gunner was hit in the knee but his reaction surprised me. Having been knocked off the limber he sat up shouting delightedly: "*Je suis blesse - merci bien - permission - a Paris demain!*"

The Brigade was under French divisional command and one morning the General came to our daily intelligence and patrol planning conference. He came bounding into the room twirling his enormous moustaches saying that he wanted us to mount a '*coup de main*' - a raid on a German forward post. He waved his hand airily about the map and, without actually selecting a target, indicated a triangle crying: "*Ici mitrailleuse - bopbopbop*", and then, lunging into the middle of the triangle of fire with his cane, he shouted: "*Et enfin c'est simple - le coup de main*". There was a moment's awed silence and then splendid old 'Becky' stood up and in slow, deliberately enunciated, schoolboy French said: "*Oui, mon Général - très simple sur papier!*"

3rd Bn Grenadier Guards War Diary:-

February 14th:-

12 degrees of frost.
Movement was heard nearly all day in the direction of Waldwisse and Le Blauenberg. French artillery shelling roads in this area intermittently. Officer Commanding 2nd Bn Coldstream Guards came at 1300 hours to recce the front prior to relieving with his Bn. The Fighting Patrol went out at 2150 hours and returned at 0200 hours 15th Feb. Nothing to report.

February 15th:-

4 degrees of frost.
The Fighting Patrol went out at 0245 hours and returned at 0545 hours. Nothing to report.
Work continued, a quiet day. OC Coys, 2 Coldstream Guards made a recce of Coy areas. Orders for the relief were received.

The following day the 2nd Bn Coldstream Guards relieved the 3rd Bn Grenadier Guards in the *Ligne de Contact*. The Fighting Patrol was disbanded, disappointed to have seen no action; instead of returning to No 4 Company, however, Lance Corporal Nicholls joined No 3 Company: this was later to prove most significant.

The 2nd Coldstream subsequently spent an uneventful five days in the line until they, in turn, were relieved by the 2nd Bn Hampshire Regiment on February 22nd.

3rd Bn Grenadier Guards War Diary:-

February 17th:-

The Commanding Officer had a conference and gave orders for the holding of the *Ligne de Recueil*, the Bn being at 3 hours notice to man this position.
1800 hours: The Commanding Officer had a conference reference the result of the first 5 days in the line.

February 18th:-

Two sentries in the west end of St Francois La Croix village challenged a shadowy figure which did not halt. Three shots were fired, the alarm was blown and the Guard turned out. The house in which the man had disappeared was surrounded and searched but no result. The village was carefully searched next day but nothing was found.

A lovely day, the Coys were employed on wiring according to the French General Plan, and on clearing roads of snow. Shortage of French angle iron pickets limited the amount of wiring that could be done. Work on posts was impossible owing to deep snow and hard ground.

The Bn was ordered to send a Coy to Halstroff on the 19th to be under command OC *Ligne de Contact*, for work on wiring roads etc.

February 19th:-

Thaw and rain made the countryside into a terrible mess. No 3 Coy finished off wiring. The remainder of the Coys were employed draining off what water and slush it could.

The Commander of 1 Corps visited the Bn.

Owing to there being little visibility No 3 Coy was able to move to Halstroff earlier than expected. Wiring and work on signal communication of the Bn position was continued, the ground being too hard to dig.

February 22nd:-

The Duke of Windsor visited the Bn at St Francois La Croix and saw HQ and 4 Coy wiring.

Anonymous 3rd Grenadier:-

February 1940. Maginot Line. A village in the Recoil Line. The Bn still scruffy from two weeks in the muddy trenches of the Contact Line. Guns in the Fortress Line behind us firing shells the size of dustbins and sounding like trains crossing a bridge overhead. A company quickly called out to line the main street. I looked down from the window of a derelict house. A little chap in a greatcoat almost down to his ankles inspected the ranks. The Duke of Windsor. Into his staff car and away.

Lance Sergeant Constantine:-

Upon conclusion of our tour in the Maginot Line were given a souvenir, which I still have: a thin brass medallion which showed a pill box, artillery gun and barbed wire entanglements, a scene representing a fortified position of the Maginot Line. On it are the words *'Ne Passe Pas'*: They Shall Not Pass.

3rd Bn Grenadier Guards War Diary:-

February 24th:-

The Bn marched to Monneren and was lifted from there to La Maxe.

February 25th:-

The Bn bathed in the baths at Metz.

February 26th:-

The Drums practised for the display in Metz with the drums of the 2nd Bn Coldstream Guards. The Bn had a swimming gala in the baths at Metz.

February 27th:-

At 1200 hours the Drums beat retreat through the streets of Metz. Orders were issued for the move of the Bn back to the BEF zone.

February 28th/29th:-

The Bn moved by trains to billets in Nomain. The move was uneventful, the billets at Nomain were very crowded.

And thus the 'Phoney War' continued. Other formations and troops were given time to train, and considerable efforts were made to improve the effectiveness of the Territorial Divisions, while the regular battalions held, and improved, the border defences. Although our story concentrates upon events affecting the 1st Guards Brigade, and in particular the 3rd Bn Grenadier Guards, these experiences were common throughout the BEF; they are therefore fairly representative of the life and times of a British Army infantry battalion in France throughout this long and frustrating period of relative inactivity.

CHAPTER FOUR

Eve of Battle

S ince Germany had defeated Poland in just 18 days during September 1939, the world had waited for Hitler's next move. The Allies rightly anticipated that this would be a major offensive against the West, taking place during the Spring or Summer of 1940. What form this attack would take, however, remained a moot point. Would the Germans strike across the French-Belgian border towards Paris, and therefore assault the Maginot Line, or violate Belgian neutrality in a repeat of 1914? As previously indicated, the *Schlieffen* Plan had seen the Kaiser's Army sweep through Belgium, again towards the French capital. The senior Allied commanders were therefore preoccupied with deciding which defensive strategy to adopt. The Allied Armies in Northern France, however, continued to train and prepare defences.

3rd Bn Grenadier Guards War Diary:-

March 4th, 1940:-

At 2000 hours the Bn had a telephone warning order that it would move to the rear area to guard ammunition and other vital points.

March 8th:-

Bn HQ, HQ Coy and No 1 Coy moved to Fontaine Les Croissilles by MT.
ARH [Ammunition Reserve Holdings] Guard at Ecoust was taken over from 7th Norfolks. The Guard covers 21 miles of small dumps along roadsides. The Bn billets were very good.

March 11th:-

Nos 2, 3 & 4 Coys moved to Cuinchy and Beaumont and took over Douai Aerodrome Guard near Cuincy (2 Coy) and PRH [Petrol Reserve Holdings] Guard at Beaumont.

March 18th:-

Major AHS Adair MC held a TEWT [Tactical Exercise Without Troops] on the ground of the 3rd Bn attack at Moyenneville in 1918, for all Officers clear of duty.

March 22nd:-

Good Friday .... Church service was held in the morning. A tour for all Officers of the Somme area conducted by Major AHS Adair MC.

March 29th:-

A draft of 11 Other Ranks joined the Bn, completing us up to the new War Establishment.

April 7th:-

The Bn paraded for church by Coys. Advance parties left for Nomain. The Commander-in-Chief visited the Bn and walked round the billetting area. He lunched at Bn HQ.
Some pamphlets evidently dropped from the air were found widely distributed.

April 8th:-

The Bn moved to Nomain, more or less into the old billets - but even more crowded up.

On April 9th, 1940, Hitler partially showed his hand when his troops invaded Norway and Denmark. German seaborne troops seized Oslo, Bergen, Trondheim and Narvik. Denmark was totally unprepared for war and consequently surrendered without significant fighting. Norwegian resistance, bolstered by Anglo-French forces (a proportion of whom were partly trained territorial troops not equipped for an opposed landing) was to continue for a further eight weeks (particularly in Narvik which was re-captured by the Allies on April 13th). The campaign was yet another demonstration, however, of German military capability which undoubtedly boded ill for the West. The military operations commencing in Scandinavia on April 9th, therefore, could only have emphasised to Allied forces in France that it was just a matter of time before Hitler attacked them. As the weather improved, the Allies in France continued anxiously to await events. For the ordinary BEF soldier, however, life remained monotonous.

3rd Bn Grenadier Guards War Diary:-

April 10th:-

Nothing outstanding. Working parties have to be found daily on the forward defences, burying signal cable, concreting etc.

April 11th:-

1 Gds Bde orders for Plan 'D' were seen and preparations made, and orders prepared, for Plan 'D'.

What was Plan 'D'? To appreciate later events fully, this requires studying in some detail:-

Lord Gort:-

Very shortly after the arrival of the BEF in their positions on the Belgian frontier I had been invited by General Georges, commanding the French Front of the North East, under whose Command I was, to study the part to be played by the BEF in the event of an advance into Holland and Belgium, or into Belgium alone. *The question of such an advance was one of high policy with a political as well as a military aspect; it was therefore not for me to comment on it. My responsibilities were confined to ensuring that the orders issued by the French for the employment of the BEF were capable of being carried out; indeed events proved that the orders issued were well within the capacity of the Force.*

The subject presented difficulties greatly complicated by the policy of neutrality to which the Belgian Government were wedded. The French authorities were never in a position to obtain reliable and accurate details of the plans of the Belgian General Staff for the defence of their country in the event of an invasion by Germany; staff conversations were out of the question, yet plans had to be framed in such a way that they could be put into instant operation in the event of Belgium asking for military assistance from France or Great Britain when invasion had taken place or was imminent.

Such slender contact as existed between the British and Belgian Military authorities was maintained through the Military Attaché at His Majesty's Embassy at Brussels and General Van Overstaeten, Military Adviser to the King of the Belgians.

Three alternative plans were decided on by the French High Command during October and November 1939, and I had agreed with General Georges on the part to be played in each of them by the BEF.

The first alternative was to occupy the frontier defences, pushing forward mobile troops to the line of the (River) Escaut, while the French 7th Army on my left were to delay the enemy on the line of the Messines Ridge and Yser Canal. This plan was soon discarded in favour of the second alternative, which was to secure and hold the line of the Escaut itself, from the point at which it crosses the frontier at Maulde northwards to the neighbourhood of Ghent where it was intended to effect a junction with Belgian forces.

Later, however, as information became available regarding the defences of the Belgian Army, and its readiness for war, the French High Command formed the opinion it would be safe to count on the Belgian defence holding out for some days on the Eastern frontier and the Albert Canal. It was also ascertained that the Belgians were preparing a *de Cointet* anti-tank obstacle running southwards from Wavre towards Namur.

The line of the River Dyle [which runs roughly North South, some 15 miles East of Brussels] was from the military point of view a better one than that of the Escaut. It was shorter, it afforded greater depth and its northern portion was inundated. In addition, it represented smaller enemy occupation of Belgian territory.

On the other hand it involved the BEF in a forward move of some sixty miles against time, while it also necessitated the holding by the French on our right of the Gembloux gap which contains no natural anti-tank obstacle. This plan was twice discussed by General Georges with me on October 13th at my Headquarters at Le Cauroy and again on November 16th at Folembray Headquarters of the French First Group of Armies; on this occasion there were also present General Billotte, who commanded the Army Group, and Generals Blanchard and Corap, Commanding the French 1st and 9th Armies. At this conference it was agreed that the frontage of the BEF on the Dyle position was to be from Wavre to Louvain, both places inclusive, and a formal instruction to this effect was issued to me by General Georges on the following day. From this time onward, Commanders and Staffs were studying simultaneously two alternative plans for advances to the Dyle or the Escaut; these [respectively] became known as plans 'D' and 'E'.

Both these plans were worked out in the greatest detail, and orders and instructions kept up to date as new divisions arrived and the role of divisions changed.

The Escaut plan was by far the simpler of the two; it involved sending armoured car reconnaissances to the River Dendre to be relieved by divisional cavalry who were later, if necessary, to fight a delaying action backwards to the Escaut; demolitions were provided on both rivers; for the remainder of the force, however, the advance appeared likely to be an easy one, well within a day's march on foot. The Dyle plan, on the other hand, involved an advance of some sixty miles, carried out at a time when every moment was of value over roads not previously reconnoitred, perhaps crowded with refugees moving counter to the Allied armies. Much, too, depended on the resistance with which the Belgians, and perhaps the Dutch, were able to offer the enemy, who at such a time would certainly be making every effort to pierce the line of the Meuse and Albert Canal.

Lord Gort explained Plan 'D' itself:-

The Allied forces were to advance to the line Namur-Wavre-Louvain-Antwerp, of which the BEF sector extended from Wavre to Louvain, both inclusive. On our right was to be the French 1st Army (Blanchard) under whose command was the French Cavalry Corps, and whose task it was to delay the arrival of the enemy on the Dyle position and to block with its main forces the Gembloux gap, with the Cavalry Corps pushed forward to the line Eghezee (8 miles north of Namur)-Tirlemont. On our left the French 7th Army (Giraud) was to advance to the general area Antwerp-Ghent, with the object of supporting Belgian resistance north of Louvain. The plans of this Army included a possible advance into Holland as far as the line Turnhout-Breda, and this was actually carried out. It had been ascertained that a portion of the Belgian Army, if forced to withdraw from the frontier defences, would come into the line on the left of the BEF on the general line from Louvain exclusive, thence northward to the fortified area of Antwerp, known as the National Redoubt.

The British front was to be occupied initially with 1st Corps (Lieutenant General MGH Barker, who had recently taken over command from General Sir John Dill), on a two-division front, on the right, and 2nd Corps (Lieutenant General AF Brooke) on the left, on a front of initially one division.

The advance was to be made in four periods. In the first, 12th Royal Lancers (Armoured Cars) were to move in a general line some eight miles beyond the Dyle in observation of the approaches from the east; they were to be relieved by cavalry regiments of 1st and 2nd Corps when they arrived.

Behind them were to come, from right to left, 2nd Division (Major General HC Loyd) and 1st Division (Major General Hon. HRLG Alexander) of 1st Corps and 3rd Division (Major General BL Montgomery) of 2nd Corps. The whole of the move of these three divisions was to be made by motor transport, and troop carrying companies were allotted to Corps in such a way to complete the move in 90 hours.

At the same time 44th Division was to march into an area north-west of Oudenaarde, with a view to organising the defence of the Escaut in this area.

Movement in the first phase was to be continuous by day and night. The French had decided to restrict movements of their main bodies to the hours of darkness, but I judged the time factor to be of paramount importance and accepted the risk that our air support might be insufficient to prevent enemy interference with the move. Events were to prove that the risk was justifiable.

In the second period, to be completed by the end of the sixth day, 48th Division (Major General AFAN Thorne) and 4th Division (Major General DG Johnson VC) were to move by route march and motor transport into 1st and 2nd Corps reserve respectively, while 1st Army Tank Brigade, consisting of two Bns, was to move chiefly by rail into 1st Corps area.

The third period was to be completed by the tenth day, and included the movement of 50th Division to 2nd Corps reserve, while 4th Division moved into the line on the right of 3rd Division.

The fourth period included the forward movement of 3rd Corps, 5th Division (Major General HE Franklyn) was to move to positions in GHQ reserve, along the River Dendre, north and south of Grammont; 42nd and 44th Divisions to the line of the River Escaut around Tournai and to the south of Audenarde respectively, to organise bridgehead positions pending orders for a further advance.

Detailed instructions had also been issued for the preparation of defences on the three river lines of Dyle, Dendre and Escaut, as also for the necessary demolitions and inundations. Special arrangements had been made for the control of traffic, including refugees for whom routes had been allotted; definite bodies of troops were detailed for these tasks.

There were certain advantages to Plan 'D': the defensive line was shorter than that of Plan 'E'; if successful then Brussels might be saved; behind the River Dyle lay a series of rivers and waterways, each of which would also provide a natural anti-tank obstacle and might therefore be held; and holding the Germans on the Dyle would deny them the Channel Ports. Furthermore there was every liklihood that in the event of the Germans attacking Belgium, the Belgian Army would join the Allies. Also, a defensive line along the Dyle was closer to Germany (and the industrial Ruhr) than that proposed along the Escaut. This reflected, in fact, the French intention to fight the coming battle as far away from its own borders as possible.

Plan 'D' had been approved by both the French Government and the British War Cabinet. BEF Corps Commanders, however, doubted the tactical and administrative feasibility of this plan, involving as it did an advance of over 60 miles across unfamiliar ground. Lord Gort himself preferred to fight along the Dyle than rely upon Belgian 'prepared' anti-tank defences to hold the Germans for a protracted period:-

In April .... I received reports regarding the siting of the Belgian anti-tank obstacle; it appeared that, without informing either the French High Command or myself, that they had sited the obstacle much further to the east than had originally been planned, namely on the line Namur-Perwez-Louvain: furthermore the obstacle was not as yet by any means completed. The matter was discussed with General Georges.

On the British front, the River Dyle was so far superior as an anti-tank obstacle to any artificial work further east which the Belgians might be preparing that I had no hesitation in urging adherence to the existing plan for the defence of the Dyle position.

Information, albeit weak, received from French Military Intelligence suggested that the Germans were likely to attack in the North. Even more significantly, on January 9th, 1940, an enemy aircraft had landed in bad weather at Mechelen: the two German Officers on board were captured together with certain plans providing details of the proposed invasion. These indicated a *Schlieffen* like thrust from the North, but this time through both neutral Holland and Belgium. The execution of Plan 'D', therefore, was a very real prospect for the Allies.

The daily routine of ordinary BEF soldiers, however, still continued much the same as it had since their arrival on the 'Gort Line'.

3rd Bn Grenadier Guards War Diary:-

April 14th:-

Major AHS Adair MC left the Bn for the Royal Military College, Sandhurst.

April 17th:-

Lieutenant The Duke of Northumberland joined the Bn.

Born on July 15th, 1912, Henry George Alan Percy was eldest son of the 8th Duke of Northumberland by his marriage to Lady Helen Gordon Lennox, daughter of the 7th Duke of Richmond. At just 18 years old, upon the death of his father, Henry became the 9th Duke (a title dating from 1766), his distinguished family's home being at Alnwick Castle. At Eton he joined the Officer Training Corps, and was commissioned in the Grenadier Guards (Supplementary Reserve) in 1932 (for call in any emergency). In joining the First Foot Guards, His Grace had followed in his father's footsteps: the 8th Duke, a regular Grenadier Officer, had been the 'official Eye Witness', reporting jointly with General Swinton on the 1914-15 fighting for the War Office.

The 9th Duke of Northumberland was reputedly the largest landowner in the North of England. He was certainly the largest single owner of coal royalties in the North, his income from this source, as one of the 'big five' royalty owners, having been estimated at £69,000 per year. At the coming of age celebrations at Alnwick Castle in 1933, he said:-

I do value the traditions that have been handed down to me, and pray that I may be given wisdom and strength to uphold the name I so proudly bear.

On the same occasion the Duke announced to his tenants that he was about to start a long tour in many parts of the Empire overseas and in foreign countries:-

I hope that by this means I shall the better equip myself to play my part in life and in the management of my estates. In particular I shall try to see something of the agricultural systems of other countries. I should much like to understand better than I do the great industry upon which the prosperity of this country so largely depends.

Interested in politics, the young Duke made his maiden speech in the House of Lords in 1938, when the Coal Bill was debated. Previously he had acted as Parliamentary Private Secretary to Lord Londonderry, when Lord Privy Seal and Leader of the House of Lords, and subsequently to Lord Swinton when he was Air Minister. In his home county, by 1940, the bachelor Duke was assuming responsibilities in public life as a county councillor and president of various charitable, philanthropic, and other organisations. Together with his mother, he was Joint Master of the Percy Foxhounds, and could occasionally be seen in the saddle at North-Country steeplechase meetings - he won his first race at Sedgefield in 1933.

The great interruption to everyday life caused by the Second World War clearly cut across the class and social barriers: both the humble Smiths and aristocratic Percys were in the same boat.

3rd Bn Grenadier Guards War Diary:-

Reminiscent of the trench warfare between 1914-18, these two photographs are from a series of morale boosting publicity shots featuring a rifle section of the 3rd Bn Grenadier Guards in France during the 'Phoney War'.

Grenadier Guards.

April 26th:-

2nd Lieutenant AN Boyd, 2nd Lieutenant P Baring, 2nd Lieutenant LP Aubrey-Fletcher, and 2nd Lieutenant JH Lane-Fox joined the Bn for one month's attachment.

Before the following month was up, however, two of these young subalterns would be buried in the 'Fatal Avenue', and the other two wounded (one of them captured). The War Diary continues:-

April 30th:-

The Bn carried out training exercise.

May 7th:-

Lieutenant Colonel Sir John Aird, Bt, MVO, MC, gave up Command of the Bn on being ordered to the United Kingdom.

On this and the following day a debate on the ill-fated Norwegian campaign was held in the House of Commons. Leo Amery, addressing the government, echoed Cromwell's words when he said "In the name of God, go!" The Phoney War, however, had allowed Britain to mobilise and train more troops. By the end of April there were 394,000 British Servicemen in France, 237,000 of whom were under GHQ command. Lord Gort's BEF had been reinforced to Three Corps comprising 10 Divisions (five Regular and five Territorial), and there were an additional three partly-trained Territorial Divisions in France acting as a labour force.

Whilst the Allies contemplated German strategy, and their reaction to it, Hitler's generals were perfecting a new method of mobile warfare: *Blitzkrieg* (Lightning War). The main principals of this doctrine were surprise, speed and terror. Armoured forces, supported by both motorised infantry and bombers, were to be used to break through the enemy's defences then drive deep into his rear, surrounding large pockets of troops, ignoring and by-passing stubborn defences, and disrupting communications. Some indication of the likely ferocity of any German attack had already been demonstrated in both Poland and Scandinavia. Not surprisingly as the Spring of 1940, wore on, tension continued to mount in the West.

After defeating Poland, the German generals had carefully considered the downfall of France. The first idea was an updated version of the *Schlieffen* Plan, known as *Fall Gelb* (Plan Yellow). This dictated an attack from the North, through the neutral Netherlands and Belgium into Northern France. Its main objective was to capture central Belgium, from where Army Group 'B' (comprising three Armies) was to advance on Ghent and Bruges. It was intended to concentrate the *Panzer* Divisions towards Ghent, but Hitler proposed using them south of Liège, his idea being to breakthrough in the direction of Reims and Amiens. On October 28th, 1939, Hitler decided to attack north and south of Liège, *Panzer* Divisions on each side. Two days later Hitler changed his mind and proposed that an armoured and a motorised division should attack 'Sedan via Arlon'. The Commander of Army Group 'A', *Generaloberst* Gerd von Runstedt, contended that the *Schwehrpunkt* - the point of main effort - must be on the Southern wing. Hitler was unmoved, however, and, on November 5th, ordered the offensive to be launched on November 12th. Two days later these arrangements were cancelled, the first of 30 such postponements due mainly to bad weather.

A third version of *Fall Gelb* was soon issued, taking into account Hitler's intention of attacking through Sedan. Nevertheless, Flanders remained the *Schwehrpunkt*. Von Runstedt, and his Chief-of-Staff, General Erich von Manstein, remained convinced that the *Schwehrpunkt* should be further South, but were unable to gain the support of their Commander-in-Chief, *Generaloberst* Walther von Brauchitsch. Although *Fall Gelb* was suspected to have been comprised to some extent by the capture of Major Reinburger and his plans at Mechelen (on January 9th, 1940) no immediate action was taken to amend them. Indeed, the date for launching the offensive had been set for January 17th, although yet again this was postponed. On February 17th, however, Von Manstein (recently appointed to command the XXXVIII *Armeekorps* in Poland) used a lunch appointment with Hitler as an opportunity to discuss the views of Army Group 'A'. Hitler was impressed, and consequently a new plan was drawn up in which the *Schwehrpunkt* became Sedan, the whole weight of the attack being shifted to the centre. The rest of the offensive - even the attack in the North - became subsidiary to this punch through the Ardennes.

The final plan was therefore *Sichelschnitt*: the 'cut of the sickle':-

Army Group 'B', commanded by *Generaloberst* Fedor von Bock, faced the neutral Netherlands and Belgium. It had been reduced in strength to two *Armees* comprising 29 divisions, including three armoured. The XIIX *Armee* was to seize the Netherlands whilst the VI *Armee* attacked through Belgium; this was, of course, where the Allies expected the *Schwehrpunkt*, but now the German intention was to lure the Allied Armies into Belgium while von Rundstedt made a decisive attack in the south. The deeper the BEF advanced into Belgium, the more difficult it would be to withdraw. Plan 'D' was therefore outdated before the offensive started.

Located South of Liège, opposite the Ardennes and Luxembourg, Army Group 'A' comprised, in contrast, three Armies with a total strength of 45 divisions, seven of them armoured. The spearhead of the all-important *Schwehrpunkt* was the five *panzer* divisions of XII *Armee*: *Panzer Gruppe* (Pz Grp) von Kleist. This concentration of armour was to strike towards the River Meuse, between Sedan and Monthermé, then onwards into France. The *Sichelschnitt* would thus outflank the Maginot Line.

Army Group 'C', with 19 divisions but no *panzers*, was to cover the Maginot Line from Longwy to the Swiss border. Sensibly the intention was not to assault this major fortification but maintain uncertainty within the Allied camp regarding the possibility of another attack developing from this area. In so doing, a number of French divisions would therefore remain committed within this sector.

On the map tables of the *Oberkommando der Wehrmacht* (OKW: the German High Command), *Sichelschnitt* had already defeated the Allied defensive strategy. Providing it could be kept secret, there appeared no reason to expect that it should not achieve victory in practice.

In total, the Allies had 149 Divisions in France which now faced 136 German divisions. The Allies had 3,000 armoured vehicles against 2,700. But, as we have seen, the Allies were still wedded to positional warfare, their armour being assigned to support infantry divisions and spread out along the entire front (with only small reserves maintained). In the air, however, the Germans enjoyed massive superiority with more than 2,000 bombers against the Allies' 800, and 4,000 fighters against 2,500.

The *Blitzkrieg* was about to be unleashed!

CHAPTER FIVE

Blitzkrieg!

From noon on Thursday, May 9th, 1940, frontier posts down the entire length of the Netherlands, Belgian and Luxembourg borders reported the noise of troop movements: Hitler's *Wehrmacht* was on the move at last. At home, the British Prime Minister, Neville Chamberlain, resigned his office on the grounds of ill-health.

Just before midnight a six-man strong German *Brandenburg* (specially trained commando) unit, led by *Oberleutnant* Wilhelm Walther, reached the River Meuse near Gennep. Their orders were to seize the bridge there; other *Brandenburger* units were tasked with capturing river bridges, road junctions and canal crossings elsewhere to ensure the *Wehrmacht's* unhindered advance.

At 0300 hours on Friday, May 10th, the German Government sent a communiqué to the neutral Dutch and Belgians informing them of the *Wehrmacht's* imminent arrival 'to forestall a projected Anglo-French invasion'. This allegation that Allied forces were poised to invade Germany was completely without foundation and therefore a flimsy attempt to justify the act of aggression which followed.

At 0435 hours the *Wehrmacht* crossed the Netherlands, Belgian and Luxembourg borders. The sky was filled with the ominous drone of *Luftwaffe* aircraft heading for many Belgian and Dutch airfields. The Dutch and Belgians - who had naively trusted Hitler's promises to respect their neutrality - were shattered.

Simultaneously almost the entire strength of the German airborne forces - *Fallschirmjaeger* - were dropped over Holland. These well armed and determined paratroopers completely surprised their enemies and seized the crucially important bridges at Rotterdam, Dordrecht and Moerdijk.

One *Fallschirmjaeger* unit landed by gliders in the Maastricht area, seizing several bridges across the Meuse without firing a shot before crossing the (parallel) Albert Canal. The Belgian defences in this sector hinged upon the huge fortress of Eben-Emael - at the time considered the strongest defensive position in existence. A special detachment of *Fallschirmjaeger* from *VIII Fliegerkorps*, *Sturmabteilung Koch*, was assigned to seize the relevant bridges and Fort Eben-Emael. *Hauptmann* Koch's force (which had trained for six months with this mission in mind) was sub-divided into four assault groups. The two Officers and 84 men of *Sturmgruppe*

The opening stage of Germany's invasion of the West, May 1940. As the Allies execute Plan 'D', and advance to the River Dyle in anticipation of the main German attack coming through Belgium from the North, as in the Great War, the actual *Schwerpunkt*, involving the majority of German armour, came through the Ardennes, outflanking the Maginot Line and Plan 'D' in the process. Almost immediately, therefore, the BEF was in great danger.

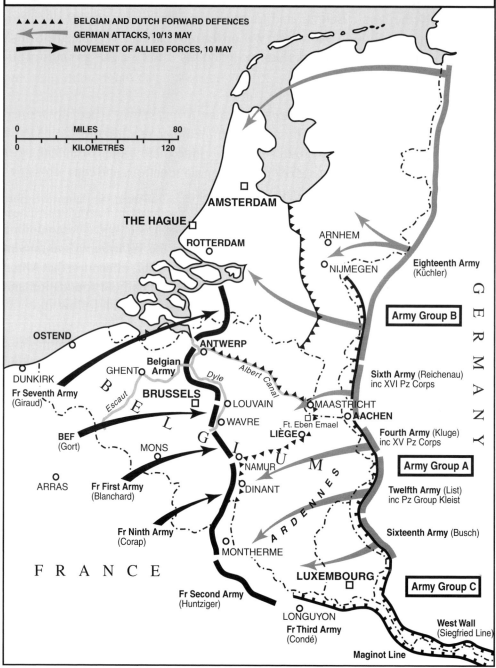

Granit were to attack Eben-Emael; this force was towed in gliders by Ju 52 transport aircraft. At 0405 hours the Fort's anti-aircraft gunners sighted the gliders approaching but took no action until 0420 hours, by which time the troop-laden DFS 230 gliders were actually landing on Eben-Emael's roof! Just 22-minutes later, *Oberfeldwebel* Helmut Wenzel, the leader of Glider 4, reported objective reached. These extremely determined German commandos rapidly placed the newly developed 'shaped charges' on the fortress, killing a number of Belgian soldiers and plunging the fortress into complete darkness. Stick grenades were then lobbed down the lift shaft. Stunned by the speed and ferocity of *Sturmgruppe Granit's* attack, the defenders barricaded themselves in. Throughout this day and into the next the battle raged, the Belgians responding with several resolute counter-attacks, but at noon on May 11th, the defenders surrendered. The Allies' confidence that Belgian forces on the frontier would 'hold out for some days', reflected by Lord Gort's Despatch, was therefore completely unfounded; the consequences of Belgium's intended neutrality were already proving catastrophic.

Whilst the Allies' attention was diverted by events occurring on the Belgian-German border, Army Group 'A' was meanwhile executing the *Schwehrpunkt* some 40 miles further south. The Germans had achieved the necessary and complete surprise in respect of both timing and the placing of the *Schwehrpunkt*, the latter not yet being apparent.

May 10th, also saw German airborne forces mount Operation *NIWI*, the objective of which was to keep roads open east of Neufchateau (25 miles NE of Sedan), to impede Allied troop movements and destroy lines of communication. These operations were highly successful and opened the way for General Heinz Guderian's XIX *Panzer Korps* to cross the 'impassable Ardennes'. The process of completely dislocating and unhinging the Allied defence was well underway.

An hour after the first attacks of May 10th, the Belgians requested Allied military assistance: the long months of waiting were over.

Lieutenant Halliday:-

At the beginning of May, Dick Humphery departed for leave in England, leaving me, with less than three years service, as acting Adjutant. As he walked out of the Orderly Room, leaving me his chair, he said "Oh, by the way, don't forget, if you get the code-word, you have to go to the safe and open the sealed envelope marked Plan 'D' and initiate action accordingly". I laughed, but I was not laughing as I hurried to the Orderly Room soon after dawn on May 10th. I had been woken by the sound of enemy bombing not far away and soon after this received a message by Brigade Despatch Rider giving the code-word for the implementation of Plan 'D'. We were not required to move until the next day, but we spent the 10th of May 1940 in a frantic rush of planning, issuing orders and preparing to meet the enemy.

Lance Sergeant Constantine:-

As from the second week in May, I was to start nine days leave. On May 10th, therefore, I went into town to buy a bottle of something worth drinking to take on leave with me. I never managed to buy that bottle. No sooner had we got to the outlying buildings of the town than we started to hear very large explosions in the distance that seemed to be coming louder and nearer every moment. Very soon we could hear the sound of aircraft, and civilians were running for cover and shouting to each other; so far as we could understand it was the Germans who had started bombing. Seconds afterwards we looked up at the sky and saw a *Stuka* dive-bomber diving and releasing its bombs. I remember throwing myself to the ground beside a low brick wall as the bombs started exploding, one just 25 yards from us. To say that I was not frightened would be a lie. I had not experienced such fear since being knocked down by a tram at the age of 12 and watching the metal wheels grinding into the rails inches from my head. Soon I could see the others I was with getting up off the ground from where they had taken cover. The planes had made their run, and had evidently released all of their bombs. Except for clouds of smoke almost everywhere the sky seemed to be clear. There was a great deal of shouting going on and orders came that all military personnel were to report to their Company immediately.

We made our way back and were all relieved that there were no casualties amongst us, other than shock at the suddenness of what had happened and frustration at not having been able to fight back. We were already beginning to develop a hatred of the pilots who flew those gull-winged planes.

Guardsman Middleton:-

I remember vividly that on the day Germany invaded, Major West lined us of 4 Company up in front of a barn. "We're going to give 'em hell", he said. We were all quite confident that we would.

3rd Bn Grenadier Guards War Diary:-

May 10th, 1940:-

Early in the morning Germany invaded Holland and Belgium. Owing to leave, courses etc., the following Officers were present with the Bn:-

Major OWD Smith. Comd. Offr.
Lieutenant C Earle. Adjutant.
Lieutenant EWS Ford. Intl Offr (vice Lt PF Thorne sick).
Major ASP Murray. Coy Cmder HQ Coy.
Lieutenant FJRP Needham. Sig Offr.
Lieutenant H Reynell-Pack. Carrier Pl Cmdr.
Lieutenant The Master of Forbes. MTO (vice Capt. MGD Clive leave).
Lieutenant & Quarter Master GF Turner MBE DCM.

Captain PT Clifton.Coy Comdr No 1 Coy.
Lieutenant R Crompton-Roberts. Pl Comdr No 1 Coy.
2nd Lieutenant LP Aubrey-Fletcher. Pl Comdr No 1 Coy.
Captain RN Brinckman. Coy Comdr No 2 Coy.
Captain PJC Radford-Norcop. 2nd-in-Comd No 2 Coy.
Lieutenant CG Ford. Pl Comdr No 2 Coy.
Captain LS Starkey. Coy Cmdr No 3 Coy.
Lieutenant The Duke of Northumberland. Pl Comdr No 3 Coy.
2nd Lieutenant P Baring. Pl Cmdr No 3 Coy.
Major WRJ Alston-Roberts-West. Coy Comdr No 4 Coy.
2nd Lieutenant JH Lane-Fox. Pl Comdr No 4 Coy.
2nd Lieutenant AN Boyd. Pl Comdr No 4 Coy.

0800 hours: Three enemy bombers came low down over No 2 Coy Area and dropped bombs that did no damage.

The 2nd Bn Coldstream Guards recorded the following Officers serving on May 10th:-

Commanding Officer:	Lieutenant Colonel L Bootle-Wilbraham MC.
Second in Command:	Major WS Stewart-Brown.
Adjutant:	Captain Hon. APS Chichester.
Signal Officer:	2nd Lieutenant CA Blackwell.
Intelligence Officer:	Captain RC Robin.
Carrier Officer:	Captain CN Fane.
MT Officer:	Captain JH Bowman.
Asst. MT Officer:	2nd Lieutenant The Earl of Devon.
Quartermaster:	Lieutenant (QM) M Jones.
Padre:	Captain Rev. GH Price RAChD.
Agent de Liaison:	Louis de St Genys & Regimental Sergeant Major A Tombs.
OC HQ Coy:	Captain ER Hill.

No 1 Coy: Capt CH Fielden, Lieutenant The Hon EFV Boscawen, 2nd Lieutenant RDE Speed.
No 2 Coy: Major FT Wyatt, Lieutenant RT Combe, 2nd Lieutenants BG Britton and JF Blackwell.
No 3 Coy: Major A McCorquodale, 2nd Lieutenant JH Piggott-Brown, Lieutenant J Langley, 2nd Lieutenant The Hon. MV Broderick.
No 4 Coy: Capt RA Pilkington MP, Lieutenant EL Gibbs, 2nd Lieutenants RC Windsor-Clive and DJ Warde-Adam.

The Commander-in-Chief of the BEF ordered that 1300 hours, May 10th, would be 'Zero Hour'; at 2230 hours that night the armoured cars of the 12th Royal Lancers reached the River Dyle unopposed. Lord Gort later wrote that:-

The Belgian population received the Allied armies in the most cordial manner, and in particular the leading troops were loudly cheered.

The 3rd Bn Grenadier Guards was scheduled to cross the Belgian frontier at 'Z + 28 hours', but due to the 2nd Infantry Brigade having been training in the rear areas at the time of Hitler's invasion, all 1st Division moves were postponed by a further six hours. The 3rd Grenadiers were re-scheduled, therefore, to cross the frontier at 2300 hours on May 11th.

Lance Sergeant Constantine:-

We were issued with hand grenades and three bandoliers of .303 ammunition per man, each containing 50 rounds.

Lance Corporal Ken Hawkins, 1/7th Bn Royal Warwickshire Regiment (48th South Midland Division):-

During the morning of May 10th, we received the news that Belgium and Holland was under attack and we were put under orders to move. All equipment was got ready and personnel were dressed in Battle Order. The whole Bn 'Stood To', anti-aircraft guards were mounted throughout the day. At 1800 hours we embussed in troop carrying lorries and awaited the order to move off. We had been told that we were headed for the Belgian frontier, but little else. Whilst we waited, large quantities of mobile equipment hurried past towards the frontier: tanks, armoured cars, bridging units, artillery, anti-aircraft guns, anti-tank guns, ammunition, supply carriers, other infantry and various other units all trying to move in the same direction.

Whilst embussed, several groups of bombers were seen overhead, but they ignored us as they headed to objectives such as airfields and railways etc. After about one hour's wait, at about 1800 hours our column moved off in the direction of Orchies and Tournai.

As we rolled towards the Belgian frontier with France our spirits rose, the long wait at an end. At last we would see action and be able justify ourselves after the long months of inactivity - now we would be able to settle things one way or another. The general mood was optimistic although I for one felt most uneasy at the prospect of leaving our reasonably well prepared positions on the Franco-Belgian border and moving forward into unfamiliar territory, amongst strangers, and not knowing what conditions would be like at our destination.

As we went through village after village, town after town, many of the inhabitants lined the road, clapping, cheering and waving to us, wishing us well. Our spirits expressed themselves in songs such as "Run rabbit run, rabbit run, rabbit run, run, run", and "We're going to hang out the washing on the Siegfried Line" - in our minds we had already won the war!

The war dead of 22 years before must have been weeping.

During the afternoon of May 10th, Winston Churchill became the British Prime Minister. The scene was now well and truly set for the dramatic events which were to engulf the world in flames over the next five years.

Enemy air activity was intense throughout the first day of the German offensive. The 3rd Grenadiers' No 1 Coy area, which was crowded with troops and civilians, had a lucky escape at 1715 hours when a number of bombs fell but failed to explode. Air attacks were becoming frequent but not intensive.

At 2200 hours on May 11th, the 3rd Grenadiers marched off for Velaines; Guardsman Middleton remembers quite simply that:-

We had to walk it.

Lance Sergeant Constantine:-

We marched all through the night with a 10 minute break in every hour when it was possible, and averaged three miles an hour. During the breaks every man would get down and if possible get their feet up higher than the body to help circulation. Transport was scarce I suppose because of the change in events, and what there was of it was being used in other areas. When it was getting near daylight we stopped for a longer period to eat some of our pack rations and drink from our water bottles which seemed to put life back into everyone. After such a period of rest we would be on the move again. To us the roads seemed endless. As soon as we marched through one stretch and went round a bend or over a hill there was another long stretch that went on for miles, and when we reached that the process was repeated. But morale was high. Sometimes as we marched along one of the men would break into a song and most would join in. There was always a witty remark from someone that would bring a good laugh or smile which helped everyone on their way.

At 2359 hours on May 10th, Major AHS Adair MC arrived at Velaines to take command of the 3rd Bn Grenadier Guards. Allan Adair was from a long-serving Grenadier family. He had been commissioned into the Grenadier Guards (in which Regiment an ancestor of his had been killed at Waterloo) straight from Harrow, in 1916; he was 17 years old. The following year Adair joined the 3rd Bn in France. By the Great War's end he had been awarded the MC and laid the foundations of a distinguished military career. On April 11th, 1940, Major Adair had left the Battalion to command 161 Officer Cadet Training Unit at Sandhurst. When the German invasion was reported, Adair was immediately ordered back to France and appointed to command the 3rd Grenadiers. The problem he faced, however, was how to get there.

In the event he managed to get a place on the last official ferry to leave Dover for five years. Landing at Boulogne he managed to catch a train to Douai. There he found that the only taxi driver prepared to travel onwards and over the Belgian frontier was a former all-in wrestling champion of France! Twelve hours after leaving Victoria Station, Major Adair was in Velaines awaiting the arrival of his Battalion which marched on through the night.

3rd Bn Grenadier Guards War Diary:-

<u>May 12th:-</u>

0630 hours: Marching personnel arrived Velaines after a very tiring march, the roads being blocked with MT columns on the move, the night hot and dusty.

The Bn marched past the Comd Officer in fine style and did not look as though they had done 21 miles.

The Bn rested and cleaned up during the day.

At 1900 hours, troop carrying lorries lifted the 3rd Grenadiers to Huldenberg, near Brussels. By midnight the 'Bn marching personnel reached the de-bussing area having come without incident along the long straight road Renaix-Nederbrakel-Ninove-Guide Kasteel'.

Lieutenant Halliday:-

During this move the main impediment to our progress was the constant stream of civilian refugees moving westward, apparently aimlessly. Most were on foot, pushing barrows, prams and heavily laden bicycles. Trying to thread their way through the pedestrian throng were horse drawn carts, lorries, and cars, all grossly overloaded and the cause of much confusion. It was a pathetic sight, but not yet so dreadful as it became when, later on, the Germans started bombing these columns. A curious thing that struck us was that most of the young women were clearly in their best Sunday clothes, even down to high heeled shoes. They were beginners in this terrible business.

Private Donald 'Elly' Ellingworth was a Despatch Rider of 'J' Section, 1st Division Signals attached to the 1st Guards Brigade; he too remembers the move into Belgium:-

After a quick dash to our forward positions, time came to find where the Bn HQs were, also the Royal Artillery, Royal Engineers and the Medics.

On a ride to the 2nd Bn Hampshire Regiment on the second night I was riding with an old soldier - we rode in pairs for safety. There in the distance was a swinging light and we came to it after a while. 'Darky' was in front. He stopped suddenly then shot off at speed. I caught him up and asked what was the trouble. "That was a Jerry", was his reply.

"Why didn't you shoot him?", I asked, but he only said:-

"The light was on my hands and my side-arm is on the left".

He would not, for some reason, put his pistol on the right side like the rest of us. Anyway we found the 2nd Hampshires and told the IO of what had happened. There was a 'Stand To' and a patrol went out. The light was still shining but after a few shots it was no more, 'Stand Down' order came and we 'DRs' went on our way.

By May 13th, the 3rd Bn Grenadier Guards was at Huldenberg, digging in during

May 10th, 1940: snapped by a local civilian photographer, optimistic BEF soldiers advance into Belgium (Doernik) during the execution of Plan 'D'.
Via Peter Taghon.

the night, resting and hiding in houses during daylight. The 1st Guards Brigade was in divisional reserve holding ground in the rear of 2nd and 3rd Infantry Brigades, which were to hold the line of the River Dyle. The 3rd Grenadiers were disposed across a ridge of higher ground which separated the two rivers, Dyle and Lasne. The Companies dug positions on the reverse slopes from which they could block any German penetration of the river line. The 2nd Hampshires held the centre of the 1st Guards Brigade front; Lieutenant Halliday:-

We began to settle down to the routine of a defensive position in which we expected to remain for some time. We even had to find time for censoring letters home. The German advance soon reached the River Dyle, however, and there was sharp fighting in Louvain which was held by Major General Montgomery's 3rd Division on our left. There was little pressure on our Divisional front, however, but we started to get reports of intense German activity against the French line away to our right. We had a warning that we might have to withdraw. There was a medium RA battery just behind the village. They had dumped a lot of ammunition forward with the guns in the expectation of a defensive battle. That night we realised that withdrawal was more than probable when they began firing off all the ammunition which was surplus to what they could carry away. The noise was tremendous.

Guardsman Middleton:-

At one point we were in a match factory, and I thought 'Blimey, what would happen if a bomb drops on this lot?'

The 2nd Coldstream frontage was 3,000 yards, from the southern corner of Weeberg Bosche wood to the main Louvain-Brussels road. Battalion HQ was established in the village of Schreiberg. Later the Coldstream were supported by a platoon of the 2nd Bn Cheshire Regiment and a troop of anti-tank guns.

On this day the Germans crossed the River Meuse at Sedan and Dinant. The 3rd Bn Grenadier Guards War Diary noted that:-

The presence of the local population and of a stream of refugees made movement difficult and filled the roads.
Low flying bomb and MG [machine-gun] attacks took their toll of this crowd and filled the Bn with a bitter determination. One (Guards) man only was wounded by a bomb splinter.

Lance Sergeant Constantine:-

Everyone on the road started to throw themselves into ditches or whatever cover that was available when a low-flying Messerschmitt riddled the road with bullets; a second later another followed its leader's example. This time we managed to get off a single shot with our rifles and our Bren gunner fired a short burst of automatic fire, but they came in so fast that nobody had time to get their sights on properly. Several of the refugees had been hit, some very severely, and there was no hope for a few of them - and that ranged from young children to old men and women who had no chance of taking cover in time. I think we did all we could under the circumstances but then had to go on our way. As we marched along I am sure all of us were rather shocked and feeling very bitter towards the enemy aircrews concerned. These attacks and casualties made us resolve not to show much sympathy towards the enemy once we made contact.

Back at home, in the House of Commons, the new British Prime Minister, Winston Churchill, delivered his famous speech:-

I have nothing to offer but blood, toil, tears and sweat. .... You ask, what is our policy? I will say: It is to wage war, by sea, land, and air, with all our might and with all the strength that God can give us... You ask, what is our aim? I can answer in one word: Victory - victory at all costs, victory in spite of all terror; victory, however long and hard the road may be.

And a long hard road it certainly would be. Strangely enough the Germans also believed that God was with them; indeed, German Army belt buckles bore the legend '*Gott mit uns*'; given such horrific scenes on the congested Belgian roads, however, Lance Sergeant Constantine and his comrades already found such a claim incomprehensible.

Private Ernie Leggett of the 2nd Bn Royal Norfolk Regiment remembers:-

The roads were choked with civilian refugees, blocking the road as far as the eye could see so we had to take to the fields on either side. German bombers and fighter planes bombed and strafed the columns relentlessly. Carts, wagons, horses, people, children in prams were blown high into the air - coming down mutilated. We could dispatch the animals humanely but there was nothing we could do regarding the humans, some torn to pieces, some with missing limbs but still alive. None of us could understand why these defenceless people were targeted in such horrific manner. We could not stop to help them so were ordered to keep on our way.

We spent early evening in the Foret de Marchienne and our Company Commander, Captain Peter Barclay MC, called us together to give us final instructions. His parting shot was "Now, more than ever before, your previous training will stand us in good stead. From now on when you raise your rifle to shoot, you shoot to kill".

By late evening on May 13th, the 2nd Bn Coldstream Guards were bivouacked in Weeberg Bosche wood, but then orders to start digging were received. The Commanding Officer protested that his men would dig far better after a night's rest so a compromise was reached: one platoon of each company was to dig by night, the remainder relieving them by 0500 hours next morning.

3rd Bn Grenadier Guards War Diary:-

May 14th:-

The day was spent resting and working in houses and cellars putting them in a state of defence, storing up and making second entrances.

More low flying bomb and MG attacks. Each Coy had one or two AA LMGs [Anti-Aircraft Light Machine-Guns] and the men got used to crouching while actually under fire, but firing strongly when not actually being bombed.

Lance Sergeant Constantine:-

We wasted no time digging in, because in that respect when your life is in danger it is amazing the strength that comes into your body when you have to do anything for protection. Each man carried entrenching tools which consisted of a small pick and shovel roughly 16 inches long. Although not the most modern tools for the job I cannot imagine where we would have been without them. Once we were down to the right depth we camouflaged, with whatever was available, the earth we had removed. We were then in a position to study in more detail the area of ground about us.

Guardsman Middleton:-

I was manning a Lewis gun on one occasion when German bombers came over, escorted by fighters, and I let a round off at them but they just kept going on. I said to my second "We'll have to move. They'll radio back and we'll have someone down here very shortly". We hadn't moved about 20 minutes before one came over and dropped a bomb on our previous position.

The 2nd Bn Coldstream Guards were also subjected to air attack. Unfortunately No 3 Company HQ and the Company Cookhouse was hit at Leefdaal, some 11 miles east of Brussels: Company Quarter Master Sergeant (CQMS) Fenwick was killed and Guardsman Seymour was wounded.

On this day the *Luftwaffe* heavily bombed Rotterdam in a demonstration of air power which shocked the world. Despite attacks by the RAF, however, the German bridgehead over the Meuse increased. In anticipation of contact with the advancing Germans, on this date civilians were 'ordered to leave the Military Area'.

On May 15th, the Netherlands surrendered, the Government's will to fight shattered by the previous day's terrifying air attack. While Major General Erwin Rommel - later to find fame in North Africa as the 'Desert Fox' - and his 7 *Panzer* Division (Pz Div) broke through at Philippeville, about 15 miles south of Charleroi, Army Group 'B', north of Namur, began to put increasing pressure on the Dyle Line. In the historic Belgian city of Louvain, the battle started and involved the 7th Guards Brigade from General Bernard Montgomery's 3rd Division. At Huldenberg, however, the 3rd Bn Grenadier Guards still awaited action; War Diary:-

There was fairly heavy shelling during the day, directed by an observation balloon, particularly at the Carrier Section on the right.

During the evening rumours of a general withdrawal were treated as quite improbable, but were confirmed later in the evening.
The A/A Brens at 'B' Echelon brought down one enemy aeroplane this day.

On the 1st Division's front that day, only one attempt was made by the enemy to cross the River Dyle but this was dealt with by artillery fire. The 2nd Division, however, had a tougher time of it and the Germans gained a bridgehead on the western bank. Further south the French line suffered a serious breach which resulted in the BEF's 2nd Division being withdrawn to the River Lasne. The 3rd Grenadiers were put under the temporary command of the 3rd Brigade to fill any gaps which might open between the right of the 1st Division and left of the 2nd. It must have been a depressing sight for the Grenadiers to see the 2nd Division withdrawing over a ridge to their right, and, without having engaged the enemy, it is quite understandable why the rumours of another withdrawal were considered 'improbable'.

The Germans had achieved, however, a complete break-through between Sedan and Mezières. General Corap's French 9th Army was scattered, and the armour of Pz Grp von Kliest began to pour through the 20 mile gap. As these seven *Panzer* Divisions advanced westwards towards the English Channel, the *Panzer Truppen* met only minor and uncoordinated resistance. Soon, therefore, the whole Dyle Line was being outflanked. Unless a general withdrawal, or a major counter move to the South, could be executed quickly, the BEF was in danger of envelopment down the line of its Southern flank, or even encirclement.

Despite the raging *Blitzkrieg*, however, the 2nd Bn Coldstream Guards encountered practical problems of a rural nature: without their masters to care for them, unmilked cows were lowing in increasing distress. Guardsman Potter (Captain Fane's Bren Carrier driver) milked 80 cows that afternoon!

Other units, though, were in direct contact with the enemy. It was the period of May 15th - 16th that saw an 'act of signal valour' for which the first Army Victoria Cross of the Second World War was awarded. The recipient was a Supplementary Reserve Officer serving with the Durham Light Infantry: Second Lieutenant Richard Wallace Annand; his citation reads:-

For most conspicuous gallantry.... when a platoon under his command was on the south side of the River Dyle, astride a blown bridge.

During the night a strong attack was beaten off, but about 11 am the enemy again launched a violent attack and pushed forward a bridging party into the sunken bottom of the river. Second Lieutenant Annand attacked this party, but when ammunition ran out he went forward himself over open ground, with total disregard for enemy mortar and machine-gun fire. Reaching the top of the bridge, he drove out the party below, inflicting over 20 casualties with hand grenades. Having been wounded he rejoined his platoon, had his wound dressed, and then carried on in command. During the evening another attack was launched and again Second Lieutenant Annand went forward with hand grenades and inflicted heavy casualties on the enemy.

When the order to withdraw was received, he withdrew his platoon, but learning on the way back that his batman was wounded and had been left behind, he returned at once to the former position and brought him back in a wheelbarrow, before losing consciousness as the result of his wounds.

Second Lieutenant Annand was to be awarded the first of five BEF VCs.

Despite such courage and tenacity, the overall situation was deteriorating. Lord Gort:-

By May 16th it became clear that a prolonged defence of the Dyle position was impractical. The French 1st Army on my right were unlikely to make good the ground lost on the previous day, notwithstanding the support I had given them in the air and on the ground, and a further withdrawal seemed likely to be forced on them by events in the south.

At about 10 am I received orders (from General Billotte) for a withdrawal to the (River) Escaut, and for the occupation of the positions along that river originally planned. The operation was to begin on the night of May 16th/17th, one day being spent on the Senne and one day on the Dendre positions; thus the Escaut would be reached on the night of 18th/19th May, though the French orders did not rule out the possibility of staying for longer than one day on each bound.

Private Ellingworth:-

It was not too long before the order came to pull back. A night move which was to become the norm. The DRs did their job in getting the convoy moving, then up to the front to lead the way. I went ahead with the Brigade Major, and when a place was found I parked my bike on the road leading to the required place, front wheel doing the pointing, and promptly went to sleep. The convoy passed me, but my pals did not let me miss breakfast. I was then sent to Ninove to direct the infantry, and while plenty of people were going past there was a van wanting to go east. I stopped this vehicle and found, in the back, guns of all sorts. As a couple of Red Caps were passing I called them over and let them deal with it.

By May 16th, General Guderian's *panzer* spearheads had penetrated 50 miles into France; further North, Rommel's 7 Pz Div was closing on Le Cateau. The unexpected thrust across the Ardennes by Pz Grp von Kleist, and the pressure upon the Allied forces North of Namur by Army Group 'B', had radically changed the circumstances upon which the plans for the defence of France had been based. The violation of Belgian neutrality, which had enabled Pz Grp von Kleist to reach the Meuse via routes regarded by the Allies as impassable to armoured vehicles, had led to the request for the Allies to help Belgium as in 1914.

The subsequent 60 mile advance of the BEF to the Dyle, however, without reconnaissance or preparation of supply dumps and defensive positions, and with command arrangements with the Belgians unclear, had exposed the BEF on the Allies' left flank. The *raison d'être* behind Plan 'D' has previously been explained in detail, but, due to *Sichelschsnitt*, this was now out of date. Although Plan 'D' was always a high risk strategy in *military* terms, it was nevertheless a *political imperative* when the Belgian's requested assistance on May 10th. It was not until three days later, of course, that Pz Grp von Kleist seized the Meuse crossings and the *Schwehrpunkt* became apparent. Allied politics had prevented adoption of the safer Plan 'E', but whether this would have led to a different outcome to the campaign remains a matter for debate; this Churchill later described as a 'haunting question'.

On May 16th, the 3rd Bn Grenadier Guards became a rearguard once more, this time for the 3rd Infantry Brigade. By 2300 hours the Brigade had passed through, and 50 minutes later the Grenadiers started their own withdrawal. By 0040 hours on May 17th, all of the 3rd Grenadier forward Companies had passed Huldenberg; five minutes later the bridge there was blown.

Guardsman Percy Nash:-

We were defending a bridge. A civilian male turned up on the other side of the river shouting "Hello Tommy, Hello Tommy!" It became obvious that as he was shouting he was pointing out our positions. I shot him.

According to the Regimental History of the Grenadier Guards (see Bibliography), 'It was a nervous business as the enemy were close on the heels of the 3rd Brigade and well forward on the Battalion's right flank'. Major Adair later wrote that the Commander of the 3rd Brigade 'almost wept with relief when I told him that the Battalion was safely away'.

The 3rd Bn Grenadier Guards then marched via Itzer - Foret de Capucins - Notre Dame Au Bois to the Foret de Soignies. There an Officer from Headquarters 1st Division, checking troops through, was heard to remark "These must be the Guards", as the Battalion marched through the woods, all in step as on parade. The Grenadiers marched on, in fact, south of Brussels, over the Charleroi Canal and into 1st Guards Brigade reserve at Zobbroek, arriving at 1100 hours: it had been a long night.

As the 3rd Grenadiers rested in an orchard at 1400 hours on May 17th, a concentrated dive-bombing attack was carried out by *Stukas*. Fortunately there were no casualties. On this date the Germans entered Brussels; further south Guderian's *panzers* had advanced so far that they were ordered to stop, partly in response to a temporary loss of confidence by Hitler and the OKW owing to the *panzers* having outrun their supporting infantry and horse drawn supplies! Meanwhile the 2nd Coldstream and 2nd Hampshires held a section of the Brussels-Charleroi Canal but no enemy activity was reported. At 2100 hours, Major Adair's Grenadiers were ordered to withdraw behind the River Dendre.

Private Leggett of the 2nd Royal Norfolks remembers the dreaded, crank-winged, *Stukas*:-

We went up to the River Dyle but gradually moved back, fighting small skirmishes. Despite being constantly machine-gunned, bombed and shelled we suffered few casualties. The *Stuka* dive-bombers were more of a nuisance for splitting our ear drums with the shriek from the sirens fitted to their aircraft and fins of their bombs. Some of them were shot down. The towns and villages through which we passed were flattened to the ground, buildings still smouldering. Water cascaded everywhere from burst mains. The desolation and eerie atmosphere was most distressing. The smells of death were obnoxious.

3rd Bn Grenadier Guards War Diary:-

May 18th:-

0100 hours: The Bn passed the Start Point and found the road full of two columns of troops, one on each side of the road, and a double line of vehicles down the middle. A certain amount of shelling and small arms fire on the canal line encouraged all speed to be made, and the Bn led off down a side road. Owing to the dark night and the existence of a number of roads not marked on the map, the diversion was not an unqualified success, and the main column was rejoined after two miles only. Gradually after a long series of delays, movement started and Ninove was reached without further incident at 0900 hours.
The Bn Sector on the left of the 1st Guards Brigade covered two bridges and 400 yards north of the old bridge. On our left was the 1st Bn and the 2nd Bn on the left of that, so all three Bns of the Regiment found themselves in the line together, although in different Corps.
The Bridgehead was being held by the 7th Queen's Regiment and they were to hold the line until 2100 hours. Therefore the Bn rested in a convent school by the old bridge until 1400 hours at which time the Coys dug in, 2 Coy right covering the new bridge - 4 Coy left. Bn HQ was in the Nunnery Hospital at the main road junction in Ninove.

Lance Sergeant Constantine:-

After we had rested and had been issued with rations, that were getting less now, we also washed our feet if there was water available. I might add that they needed it after all the marching that had been done. Our ammunition was made up again making sure that every man had 150 rounds.

Lord Gort:-

At about midnight on the 18th/19th May, General Billotte came to see me, and gave me an account of the situation as he saw it. He also told me of the measures which were being taken to restore the situation on the front of the French 9th Army, though clearly he had little hope that they would be effective. Reports from the liaison Officers with French formations were likewise not encouraging; in particular I was unable to verify that the French had enough reserves at their disposal south of the gap to enable them to stage strong counter-attacks sufficiently strong to warrant the expectation that the gap would be closed.

Thus in my opinion, there was an imminent danger of forces in the north-eastern area, that is to say the French forces next to the sea, the Belgian Army, the BEF and the bulk of the French 1st Army on our right, being irretrievably cut off from the French forces in the south.

The BEF's Commander-in-Chief and General Billotte considered their options. First, in the event of the gap being closed by successful counter-attacks, it would, in theory at least, be possible to maintain the line of the River Escaut, and thence southwards on one or other of the canal lines. The second option envisaged a withdrawal to the mouth of the Somme. This plan was attractive in that the French Army and BEF would be falling back on existing lines of communication and would not entail the abandonment of large quantities of equipment. It would obviously be unwelcome to the Belgians, however, who would be faced with the alternatives of also withdrawing and therefore abandoning Belgian soil, fighting on their own, or seeking an armistice.

Lord Gort's information was not good regarding the state of French defences to the South. He was, however, sufficiently concerned to create the first of a series of *ad hoc* forces to bolster the BEF's Southern flank and protect his lines of communications. On May 17th, Lord Gort ordered that MACFORCE should cover the right flank between Raches (South of Maulde, on the River Scarpe) to St Amand. This move had significant implications for GHQ: the detachment of the BEF's Director of Military Intelligence, Major General FN Mason-Macfarlane, fragmented the work of GHQ's Intelligence Branch which consequently denied Lord Gort key information at critical stages of the battle. A second force was set up on May 18th to defend Arras: PETREFORCE, commanded by Major General RL Petre.

The final option for Gort and Billotte was the possibility of a withdrawal north-westwards or northwards towards the Channel ports, making use of the successive river and canal lines. Lord Gort appreciated from the outset that this course of action was a last resort given that it involved the BEF's departure from the theatre of war at a time when the French might need all the support which Britain could give them; Lord Gort:-

It involved the virtual certainty that even if the excellent port facilities at Dunkirk continued to be available, it would be necessary to abandon all the heavier guns and much of the vehicles and equipment. Nevertheless I felt that in the circumstances there might be no other course open to me. It was therefore only prudent to consider what the adoption of such a plan might entail. On this day therefore at about 1.30 pm I telephoned to the Director of Military Operations and Plans at the War Office and discussed this situation with him.

So just eight days after the German offensive started against the West, the evacuation of Allied troops via Dunkirk was being mooted. Given the relatively static trench warfare of the 1914-18 conflict, the significance of such a prospect cannot be over emphasised. It was indeed *Blitzkrieg*.

Survivors remember the long road back through Belgium:-

Lieutenant Halliday:-

The men were tired, having done little but dig and march for the last four days and nights. They were oblivious as to the time (many of them slept as they marched) and reacted like automatons to the whistle orders. On the second whistle they collapsed where they were on the road.

Shortly after dawn we were surprised to see an MT column coming from the direction in which we were marching. When they reached us we saw that it was Brigade HQ! The Brigadier was more than pleased to see us, but shaken by what might have happened had they not done so. Later on we caught up with a halted convoy of trucks. We found that the driver of the leading vehicle had fallen asleep over the wheel, the whole convoy had halted and everyone was fast asleep. They were quite surprised to be woken and set on.

At a little village called Eychem I was walking down the village street when machine-gunned by an Me 110; fortunately I was unscathed but remember being vaguely surprised to see the machine-gunner's face.

Somewhere on our route back across Belgium we were to be met by an RASC troop carrying company, but to get to that road we had to move about 2,000 yards up a forward slope of open farm land. My orders were to be off at first light to reconnoitre covered lines of withdrawal for the forward companies, who were fully committed holding the line against German probes. In fact, soon after dawn, the Germans opened up with heavy mortar and machine-gun fire and gave every sign of being about to launch a major attack. In the event nothing materialised, the Bn successfully broke contact and, without losing a casualty, gained the ridge behind which was our road back. At one stage we were sharing the sunken road up to this ridge with a company of the Coldstream Guards who had not been so lucky. I passed one of them lying, as I thought, asleep under his gas cape. Thinking this was no place for sleeping I raised the cape to rouse him and was startled to find him dead. I remember this particularly as he was the first corpse I had seen at close quarters.

With the Carrier Platoon acting as rearguard, the Bn set off once more marching westwards. We had no idea when we would meet the transport and were vastly relieved to see them after two hours marching. We were beginning to feel that we were not nearly far enough back from the River Dendre, particularly as we had been seen by a German *Storch* reconnaissance plane which flew parallel with us for some time.

After two hours our lift was over and the RASC unit was forced to leave us on the road while they hurried off to another job. The Bn resumed its march, still very weary, but glad to have gained the 30 miles lift. As we set off we were surprised by two hedge-hopping aircraft which flashed past the length of the column. We had got used to assuming that all aircraft were German and would undoubtedly have opened fire if we had time. But, as they disappeared, we realised they were RAF Hurricanes. The troops gave them a rather derisive cheer. We know now that the RAF was engaging the enemy many miles away, but in our area the *Luftwaffe* had complete air superiority.

Private Ellingworth was with the 1st Guards Brigade HQ:-

On our next night move everything was going fine until dawn broke. There was the sun rising in our faces - we were going east! We pulled into a field in a very orderly fashion. One lad, feeling the call of nature, went into some trees at the edge of this field but came out very fast: "Jerries in the next field!" No order was given but every truck got moving, one exception being the cook wagon which got stuck. We had to leave it along with all our food plus the DR's gear, but at least we got away and were heading west again.

Through all these night runs the DRs had to do their DRLS runs, and it was taking its toll. On one move I nearly fell off my bike I was so tired. I was so exhausted that I just had to get rid of the bike, but not before I had fired six .38 bullets into the mag and dynamos and slashed the tyres. I then climbed up onto the roof of a wireless truck and went to sleep, but then I had to find another bike with which to resume my duties.

Once I saw an RAF Lysander being attacked by German fighters. It stood no chance and eventually crashed in flames. The pilot and wireless operator were thrown clear, their uniforms blazing, but unfortunately we found them both to be dead. A Red Cap came and took charge but we had to get out quick because the German planes returned. One of these pursued me as I rode towards some trees. The pilot fired, but fortunately I was not hit.

Guardsman Follett:-

Being in the Carrier Section it was much easier for us. If we fell behind due to the congestion, we could easily catch up the Bn which was marching. We were, by this time, under pretty constant air attack and I will never forget the sight of bodies and debris pushed to the roadsides.

Guardsman Middleton:-

By this time there were a lot of people on the road, clogging it up, pulling handcarts and so on full of their worldly goods. Then German aircraft started strafing the roads, so of course there were the dead bodies of people and animals everywhere. Guns were just ditched at the roadside.

Guardsman Rice:-

There were saboteurs and spies - 5th Columnists - all around. During one march I noticed that a man was walking alongside us who was wearing what appeared to be German Army jackboots. I went on ahead and told our Officer who had him arrested. That night we stayed in a large wood. I heard shots ring out - the next day the man wasn't there anymore.

Lord Gort:-

On the night of May 18th/19th, the 1st, 2nd and 3rd Corps completed their withdrawal to the line of the Escaut without interference, and prepared to defend the line of the river. Soon after arrival the level of water became dangerously low, at places less than three feet deep. It looked, therefore, as if apart from the unusually dry weather, some of the sluices in the neighbourhood of Valenciennes had been closed in order to produce inundations in the low lying ground in that area - even if at the expense of the water on the front of the BEF.

1st Guards Brigade War Diary:-

May 18th:-

A MG raid by five Messerschmitts on orchard (in which the 1st GB HQ was located) was warded off by two Spitfires.

The reference to 'Spitfires' is actually incorrect. The Air Officer Commander-in-Chief of Fighter Command, Air Chief Marshal Sir Hugh Dowding, was wisely preserving this type of fighter aircraft for the defence of Britain itself (see *Bader's Duxford Fighters: The Big Wing Controversy*, also by Dilip Sarkar). He had, however, despatched a number of Hurricane squadrons to France, and indeed these now even operated from England's forward fighter stations on a shuttle basis. Undoubtedly, therefore, it was two Hurricanes responsible for driving off the *Jagdfliegern* in this particular engagement.

1st Guards Brigade War Diary:-

May 19th:-

.... we commenced a further withdrawal. We left the orchard and withdrew to a village two or three kilos to NW where the convoy stopped for breakfast. The village was left just after 0900 hours. Several civilians were still residing in the village. Within 30 minutes of leaving both orchard and village were heavily shelled.

3rd Bn Grenadier Guards War Diary:-

May 19th:-

0130 hours. Orders were received from 1st Guards Brigade for withdrawal at first light.

0145 hours: Comd Officer 7th Queen's Regiment arrived at Bn HQ stating that his Bn had been ordered to relieve the Bn in the line forthwith. This was confirmed by 1st Gds Bde and the details of the relief were proceeded with as rapidly as possible as daylight was approaching, but owing to lack of warning of this move and the absence of the 7th Queen's Coy Cmdrs the relief could not be completed before daylight, at which time activity started on the whole of the Bn front, particularly on the left. Enemy snipers and men with Tommy guns harried the relief, and one of the latter killed 2nd Lieutenant P Baring as he was leading the incoming Pl to their position.

0700 hours: After a most anxious time on the left, when the Carriers and No 3 Coy took up position to cover the relief of 4 Coy, the Bn got away without further casualties and RVd in an orchard at Muijen where they rested until 1000 hours and withdrew to the line of the Escaut. Orders for this withdrawal were issued verbally by the Brigadier at about 0800 hours.

The Bn marched as far as Nederbrakel, being shelled on its way to the main road, and the 'A' Ech Tpt which went ahead under Lieutenant EWS Ford was bombed and machine-gunned from the air, receiving four casualties.

The Bn embussed in troop carrying lorries at Nederbrakel at about 1200 hours, debussed 45 minutes later at Quaremont, then crossed the river at Berthen and marched to lay up in a wood north of Pont-a-Chin.

A very long march owing to the frightfully crowded state of the road, dust and heat, it was a very tiring one.

On May 20th, the breach south of Arras, opened by Pz Grp von Kliest, deepened and widened. Enemy armour bore down on two objectives: the Somme valley towards Abbeville, then swinging round to the North and the Channel Ports via Hesdin and Montreuil. Early that day *panzers* were reported approaching PETREFORCE in Arras from a direction of Cambrai, but these were held off by the 1st Bn Welsh Guards. Later, more *panzers* were reported 10 miles west of Arras. The *panzers*' advance was rapidly reducing the options available to the Allies - the proposed Southwards counter move was now impractical, although Lord Gort had plans in hand to counter-attack at Arras. Unfortunately, gallant and courageous though the action at Arras proved to be, much more than isolated local successes were required now to save the Allied Armies from defeat.

The BEF had withdrawn from the River Dendre to the Escaut line on May 18th and 19th. Three British Corps were now dug in along the new line. Lord Gort understood that he had to maintain the defence of this important anti-tank obstacle with the French 1st Army on his right and the Belgian Army to his left. On May 20th, he would be mainly concerned with the next Theatre-level moves: co-ordinating the important counter-attack with French forces at Arras, and with the options to withdraw to the coast. These vitally important options would depend, in fact, upon the outcome of the major defensive battle the BEF was now poised to fight.

CHAPTER SIX

"... a busy time very shortly."

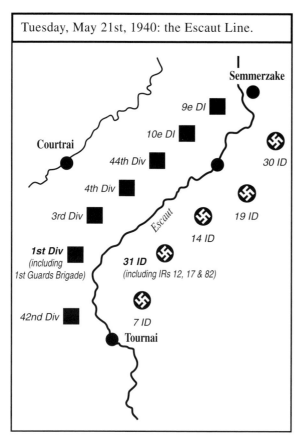

Tuesday, May 21st, 1940: the Escaut Line.

The BEF's previous front on the River Dyle had measured some 22 miles. The allotted sector of the River Escaut, however, was 32. In an effort to close the gap torn through the French further south, Lord Gort sent two Divisions (5th and 50th) and all his tanks to help. This meant that the most weary British Division, the 1st (which included the 1st Guards Brigade), had to take its place in the line. Seven Divisions, in fact, were deployed along the BEF line, running from North of Oudenaarde to Maulde on the French frontier. All brigades were deployed forward, leaving the line's centre with scanty reserves. Defence in Depth was sacrificed in favour of defending the riverline. The River Escaut (or Schelde) itself was just enough to be a significant obstacle, being on average 50 yards wide, but the lowering of the water level made it hard in places to observe the water due to the high banks created. Although demolition attempts were made, grounded barges and bridge piles provided footholds for the launching of boats or assault bridges. Furthermore, in this generally flat landscape, it was unfortunate that significant high ground suitable for observation lay on the east bank.

The Brigades of the Divisions of II Corps were lined up along the Escaut (from the left) in the following order: 9th, 7th Guards and 8th astride the Helchin Sector (3rd Division), and the 1st Guards, 2nd and 3rd Brigades (of the 1st Division) at Pecq. To the right of 1st Division, across the Corps Boundary, was the ancient town of Tournai, guarded by the 42nd East Lancashire Division (less one brigade which was deployed to Arras, fighting with MACFORCE); the 126th Brigade was on the town's northern side with the 1st Bn The Border Regiment forward along some of the many canals which criss-crossed the area. The 125th Brigade defended Tournai itself (5th Bn The Border Regiment left, 1st Bn The East Lancashire Regiment right) deployed along the River Escaut which ran through this historic town. South of Tournai, the 6th Brigade (2nd Division), were deployed beside the 143rd, 144th and 145th Brigades of the 48th (South Midland) Division (although on the night of May 20th/21st, the 6th and 143rd were relieved by the 4th and 5th Brigades of the 2nd Division).

The enemy advance beyond Arras had involved mainly *panzer* and motorised divisions comprising tanks and supporting infantry in both armoured personnel carriers and lorries. The situation regarding the enemy's normal infantry divisions - now about to confront the BEF - remained a largely unknown quantity. Lord Gort's forces, as we have seen, were now lined up Division upon Division to make a determined stand against the anticipated onslaught.

Guardsman Follett:-

At the Escaut we were told that we were 'going to fight to the last man and the last round'.

1st Guards Brigade War Diary:-

May 19th:-

1400 hours: HQ 1 GB established in a chateau south of Estaimbourg.
During the afternoon a woman spy (Mme. Soldenal) arrested. Some suspected parachutists were taken to Division.
Several casualties suffered by 3 GG, 2 CG and A/T Coy.

2nd Bn Coldstream Guards War Diary:-

The line to be held by the Bn was altered on several occasions. It was finally fixed by Brigadier Beckwith Smith in the evening to run from the bend in the River Escaut at 906396 to the big tannery and the river in front of it at 898412. This front was 1,800 yards. The Grenadiers were on our right, the 2nd Hampshires in Brigade Reserve and the 3rd Div on our left. For a few hours the 1st Bn and Capt Fox's Coy of it was on our left but was later relieved.
This evening Brigadier Jack Whitaker [Commanding 7th Guards Brigade] visited the Bn at the Religious Institution, Pecq.

At the tannery, situated in the northern outskirts Pecq, No 4 Company secured an excellent vantage point: overlooking the river, the building's windows provided a superb field of fire.

Throughout the day on May 19th, the nearby town of Tournai had been subjected to heavy air attack in preparation of the enemy's offensive. 2nd Royal Norfolks:-

Tournai was being bombed from the air and was being rapidly demolished as the Bn approached.... In Tournai there was a certain amount of confusion owing to this bombing. There were no guides and a great shortage of maps.

During the evening of May 19th, Captain PJC Radford-Norcop held the 3rd Grenadiers' allotted section of the canalised River Escaut with a composite 'covering party' made up from all 3rd Grenadier Companies; Lieutenant The Master of Forbes:-

We dug in, just South of Pecq. We really were a 'thin red line' along the River Escaut.

To the Grenadiers' right was the 2nd Bn North Staffordshire Regiment, of the 2nd Brigade, the Commanding Officer of which also chose to deploy his rifle sections along the riverbank: 'C' Company on the right, 'D' centre and 'B' left. 'A' Company was held in reserve at Bn HQ which was situated in the cellar of a small house to the east of the Pont-à-Chin - Pecq road. According to the War Diary, during the night 'Digging was commenced and fighting patrols sent out along the river line but no contact was made with the enemy'. To the 2nd Staffordshires' right was the 6th Bn The Gordon Highlanders; the latter's War Diary relates:-

Bn withdrew and embussed along the Ninove Nederbrakel road and proceeded via Renaix, northern outskirts of Tournai to position on west bank of Escaut Canal about Esquelmes. Enemy fairly active along road particularly against refugee camps.

To the right, near Pont-à-Chin, was the 1st Bn The Loyal Regiment:-

During the night 19/20 May enemy forward elements advanced into wooded country along east bank of canal and sniping was then prevalent throughout the day.

2nd Bn Coldstream Guards War Diary:-

May 20th:-

At 0130 hours the main bridge over the River Escaut was blown. This explosion broke most of the glass in the town and Bn HQ was moved to a chateau a few hundred yards away at about 1000 hours. At dawn the Bn started to dig itself in.
The town of Pecq was practically deserted and we were able to get a certain amount of food. Our position here, besides being overlooked by the opposite bank, was also dominated by Mont St Aubert.

To appreciate fully the advantage that Mont St Aubert offered the Germans it is important to understand the topography involved. The West bank, for as far as the eye can see from Pecq, remains a constant 20 metres above sea level; so does most of the east bank. Mont St Aubert, on the other hand, situated directly across the river and about two miles South East of Pecq, and half that from the Grenadier positions at Esquelmes, rises to a most significant 149 metres (490 feet). This wooded hill, crowned by a church, dominates the landscape and its tactical advantage is immediately obvious. From the summit, the Germans were easily able to observe the BEF's preparations throughout this sector and indeed well beyond, and to adjust artillery fire during the coming battle.

Corporal Christie, 2nd Bn Coldstream Guards:-

Our Carrier Platoon was billeted in a large building in Pecq on the first night. We were wakened by a mighty crash as all the windows were blown in when the nearby bridge was blown by the REs.

Pecq itself was a small town of red brick built around a central square off which led several roads running parallel with the River Escaut. A road also came from Lille in the West and ran Eastwards over Pecq bridge (demolished during the night). Lieutenant Colonel Bootle-Wilbraham deployed his Battalion as follows:-

Nos 1 and 3 Companies right and left, with all rifle sections on the riverbank able to bring fire to bear on anyone crossing the water. No 3 Company was also responsible for the bridge approaches.

No 2 Company was held in reserve along the main Pont-à-Chin road, and No 4 Company held the roads leading into the village.

Bn HQ was established in an 'un-named château on the road to Lille'.

1st Guards Brigade War Diary:-

May 20th:-

1050 hours: Two German bombers over HQ 1 GB at height of 700 feet.
1230 hours: Suspect brought in by Coldstream Guards during morning, in the evening further suspects (one dressed as a Belgian soldier and four as priests).
Light forces now in contact on River Escaut. All bridges over river blown.
Own troops digging in, very little enemy artillery activity by day.

Lieutenant Halliday:-

This time we of the 2nd Hampshires were to be in Brigade reserve, holding the village of Estaimbourg, just west of Pecq. We were to link up with a reserve company of Grenadiers in Bailleul. Bn HQ was in a chateau situated in the middle of a large lake. The owners had obviously fled precipitately as the place was full of valuable furniture and pictures. We occupied the cellars, the windows of which were just above the lake's water level. We were heavily shelled fairly continuously. Curiously I felt the apparent safety of the Chateau's cellars not very good for morale because it made one feel all the more vulnerable when one left to go round the Bn area. Shells bursting in the lake did give us one bonus: stunned fish which we collected and cooked!

At one stage two of my Intelligence Section appeared with smoke blackened faces having been shelled out of the farmhouse where they had established an OP. They were in no way shaken and only came for new orders! This was typical of our spirit at that time.

On May 20th, South of Tournai at Froidmont, civilians were found to be a problem; 2nd Royal Norfolks:-

Troops rested and fed during the day. During the morning a recce of the River Escaut between Tournai and Antoing took place and after dark the Bn moved into position. Prior to this move the Bn was just about to have tea when it was suddenly ordered out to arrest or shoot the villagers who had refused to evacuate and were beginning to demonstrate. So far as can be ascertained order was restored. These civilians may have been Germans in disguise.

During the late afternoon shelling increased against the factories on the River Escaut near Calonne. First the brunt was borne by the 1/8th Bn The Royal Warwickshire Regiment, then the 1/7th Bn.

Lance Corporal Hawkins, 1/7th Bn Royal Warwickshire Regiment:-

On May 19th, we took up position amongst some old quarries and spoil heaps from what looked like old limestone workings. We spread out along the tops of these tips and workings which overlooked the River Escaut which was partly canalised and in a small valley. Immediately below us was a large cement producing works with a large brick chimney. We dug in and, during the night, those not rostered for guard duty could sleep. It was impossible to sleep for long, however, due to the noise from the heavy guns' spasmodic shelling. At dawn the next morning there was the usual 'Stand To' and we saw a man and woman emerge from the base of the chimney - the lady had given birth there overnight!

At mid-morning we were astonished to see a small group of soldiers riding bicycles towards our position but on the far side of the canal. They were talking as they rode but then we realised that their uniforms were neither English, French or Belgian - Germans! This was a Jerry cycle patrol on reconnaissance. A Bren gunner quickly scattered them, I don't know who was more surprised - them as they fell or us.

Inside the factory building we occupied was a staircase that led up above roof level, and it made an ideal observation point. From there we kept watch on our front and in particular on the village on the other side of the canal - Calonne. During the late morning we could see enemy troops and equipment moving up, and knew that we would be in for a busy time very shortly. First of all came the sniping as the enemy moved up closer to the canal. Then the shelling of our position commenced, shells landing all around us, in the open, on the factory buildings; some dislodged heaps of masonry from the top of the building, some punched holes in the walls overlooking the canal - some burst inside the main building with an ear splitting crash that made our ears ring continuously.

In the early afternoon we noticed that the water level in the canal had dropped considerably. We did not know at the time whether this had been caused by Allied or enemy forces, but what it meant was that here and there the bottom of the canal was visible, the boats tilting over almost onto their sides. It would now be possible for men to wade through the mud and gain access to our side of the canal.

Later in the afternoon the enemy began to increase his fire at us, shelling, mortar bombing, machine-gunning, sniping; the noise was incredible in our confined space within the factory walls. Nevertheless we felt much safer there, and everyone was fully alert whilst waiting for the enemy infantry to attack, as we knew they would shortly. However, evening came and light of day waned. Soon it was dark and we dared not show a light anywhere, though outside was lit up now and then by flares which turned the darkness into lurid light a few minutes at a time. Our position was almost continuously under fire from the enemy who were just yards away on the other side of the canal. Heavy shelling was constant, causing brickwork and masonry to fall and fly about all over the place. None of us slept that night.

The night banged, clanged and crashed on and by dawn most of us were in a state of mild shell shock. Our ears ached, our heads felt as though our brains had been poured out; fiery painful lances seemed to be being driven right into the very innermost recesses of our minds. When we moved it was as if we were zombies, it taking longer for our reactions to carry out the simplest task. Then at Stand To we were surprised when our relief arrived. Four men of the 1st Bn Royal Scots Regiment took over from my Section at dawn on May 21st. We made our way out of the back of the factory and up the road past where Bn HQ had been. The enemy must have been aware of our movement and began plastering the road and the quarry with all kinds of fire. Then, at last, we were clear of that line on the canal and moved quickly away whilst the sound of gunfire now seemed to come from both front and rear. Half a mile from the front we came across an awful sight: a DR had been hit by a shell and his bike was blown to pieces. He lay in the ditch at the roadside; 10 feet separated both halves of him. It was appalling.

During the evening, activity increased on the BEF sector north of Tournai; 2nd Bn North Staffordshire Regiment War Diary:-

It was not until late evening that the enemy commenced registering on our front - spasmodic rifle and MG fire broke out during the stand to at dusk and slight enemy activity was reported.

It was certainly an indication of what lay ahead. After the apparently constant period of withdrawal, it was clear that the time had come to stand and fight. By

A battle damaged Calonne, May 1940.
Via Peter Taghon.

Enemy soldiers moving through Calonne, May 1940. German infantry often used pedal
cycles for practical transport during this campaign.
Via Peter Taghon.

1700 hours the 2nd Hampshires had started digging in at Estaimbourg: 'X' Company right, 'Z' Company centre, 'W' Company left with 'Y' Company in reserve.

3rd Bn Grenadier Guards War Diary:-

May 20th:-

A quiet day.
Bn HQ moved to Bailleul. The Bn dug in during the night, 1 Coy right, 2 Coy centre, 4 Coy left and 3 Coy reserve, immediately east of Bailleul.

German infantry under fire whilst advancing on Tournai.
Via Peter Taghon.

After dark on May 20th, so as to deny the Germans the advantage of observation, the 3rd Grenadier Guards moved down to the River Escaut. Like the 2nd Coldstream the Grenadier forward companies were deployed along the riverbank, about one mile south of Pecq and in front of the hamlet called Esquelmes. The main Pont-à-Chin road ran parallel with the river about half-a-mile west, and Bn HQ was situated a mile Westwards from the river in the village of Bailleul. Captain Starkey's No 3 Company and the Lieutenant Reynell-Pack's Carrier Platoon were held in reserve there. On the riverbank itself, Major Alston-Roberts-West's No 4 Company covered the Grenadiers' left flank while No 2 Company were in the centre and No 1 Company to the right.

Two No 4 Company men remember these events:-

Guardsman Middleton:-

I reckon it was about midnight when our section was taken along this path, along the side of a wood, and we were shown a slit trench to occupy on the riverbank. Of course you can't really sleep properly standing up so we stayed awake all night waiting for it to get light. There was a lot of heavy gunfire. We were pretty isolated in our position, I could not see anyone to our left or right. We must have been pretty thinly spread.

Guardsman Rice:-

It was dark when we arrived on the riverbank and our lot must have been the Company's extreme left section. We did not need to dig in as such where we were because there was a sloping flood bank which we just lay up against.

The 2nd Bn Coldstream Guards were also digging in but were struck by tragedy during the night:-

Guardsman Joe Nixon, No 1 Company:-

Enemy activity was very evident right up to the opposite bank. A recce patrol was very much needed, especially to make contact with the adjoining Grenadiers. Consequently I accompanied my Officer, Lieutenant Boscawen, in pitch darkness. We set off along our side of the Escaut and carefully counted our steps. It was very tense and eerie. I could hear splashes coming from the other bank and have no doubt that the Germans were undertaking their own recce. After about 500 yards we were challenged by a Grenadier sentry, which would have been on their No 4 Company's extreme left flank. Although we were all very edgy the Lieutenant and I passed safely through the platoon position. We went on to see the Company Commander, Major West, again being challenged strongly by another Grenadier sentry. Lieutenant Boscawen gave his report of the very vulnerable gap existing between our Company and the Grenadiers. It was

Guardsman Joe Nixon, 2nd Bn Coldstream Guards.
Mr J Nixon.

quickly agreed with Major West that we would return immediately to extract the centre platoon of our Company and place it in a position to cover the gap by fire. Lieutenant Boscawen and me then quickly paced back as near as possible to the halfway mark. Lieutenant Boscawen stayed some distance back from the bank to receive the platoon. I hurried back to No 1 Company's front line position on the Escaut bank to request that No 8 Platoon pull out and accompany me back to the Lieutenant's position. Nos 7 and 9 Platoons were warned of the urgent adjustment. I guided No 8 Platoon to Lieutenant Boscawen who arranged with the Platoon Commander how best to place the Platoon to cover the bank with effective defensive fire. He instructed me to return with all speed to No 1 Company HQ, situated on higher ground some distance back from the platoon positions, and advise the Company Commander, Lieutenant Fielden, of the gap and the emergency action taken. I carried out these instructions but although willing the return of Lieutenant Boscawen was then ordered by the Company Commander to man a slit trench as manpower was very low. Sadly about half-an-hour later when still pitch black, a Coldstream sentry challenged a figure looming out of the darkness and - not receiving the correct response - fired and fatally wounded Lieutenant Boscawen.

As his Orderly, and having become his Runner in action, I was told to retrieve the Lieutenant's Coldstream Star cap badge (which I had previously put into his small pack when we exchanged caps for steel helmets). Having collected the Star I wrapped it in a 4 by 2 weapon cleaning cloth and put it in the left-hand pocket of my battledress.

Despite the tragic death of Lord Falmouth's son in this accident, the story of Lieutenant the Hon. Evelyn Boscawen and his Coldstream Capstar was, in fact, far from over.

Lieutenant The Hon. EFV Boscawen, 2nd Bn Coldstream Guards, leading the King's Guard, London, July 1939.
Lieutenant Colonel HGR Boscawen.

Throughout the night, Allied artillery continually fired upon the enemy's East bank positions, the German guns responding in a heavy barrage between 0310 - 0330 hours. According to the official history of the *IV Armee Korps* on May 20th:-

The *Korps* ordered continuation of the pursuit of the BEF. The intention was to create deep bridgeheads on the west bank of the Schelde [German name for the River Escaut or Scheldt]. Attempts during the night at various locations by the Advance Units to force a sudden crossing of the Schelde failed because of heavy enemy defence.

Attacks by the 18 *Infanterie-Division* [contemporary German records record Divisional numbers in Arabic numerals and abbreviate *Infanterie-Division* to 'ID' which is used hereafter] to cross the Schelde before lunch were prevented by our English adversary. The 7 ID established a small bridgehead of just two *Kompanies* on the west bank. The enemy was well supported by artillery, mainly the medium calibre weapons firing from the French fortifications east of Lille.

At about 0930 hours the IV *Armee Korps* was ordered by the 6th *Armee* to cross the Schelde and push in the direction of the French fortifications at Seclin. For this purpose the IV *Armee Korps* received support from the 35 ID and 5th Heavy Artillery Bn.

Divisional reports arriving throughout the afternoon gave the impression that isolated and individual attacks by our divisions would be unsuccessful. Success could only be expected given an attack of the whole IV *Armee Korps* with heavy artillery support. The current attacks were called off, therefore, whilst a plan was made. Should the enemy move off again before this new attack could be launched, an immediate pursuit would commence.

Orders for May 21st involved an attack of the entire IV *Armee Korps*, the centre point being south of Tournai:-

a) Starting point as near as possible to the river.

b) From midnight onwards fighting patrols to put the enemy under fear of imminent heavy attack.

c) At 0310 hours, all available artillery to fire at the farthest line of enemy field.

d) At 0330 hours, sudden stop of artillery fire.

e) 0720 hours, artillery preparation against enemy infantry positions.

f) 0730 hours, infantry commences attack. Target: Belgian-French border. *Schwehrpunkt* of this attack should lay on the inner wings of 7 and 18 IDs.

During the night before the attack, the enemy heavy artillery fired harassing bombardments. Our artillery fire between 0310 and 0330 hours decreased this enemy activity. Later, however, it resumed as before. The adversary had fortified the Schelde. Observation posts identified some 16 enemy batteries, of which six are believed hit. It proved impossible, however, to suppress the

AERIAL PHOTOGRAPH TAKEN BY AMERICAN RECONNAISSANCE AIRCRAFT, MAY 17TH, 1943.

DISPOSITION OF OPPOSING FORCES, MAY 21ST, 1940

KEY

1. **Pecq** 2nd Bn Coldstream Guards
2. To **Estaimbourg** & 1st Guards Brigade HQ 2nd Bn Hampshire Regiment
3. Main Pont-à-Chin - Pecq Road
4. To **Bailleul** & 3rd Bn Grenadier Guards HQ
5. **Esquelmes** 3rd Bn Grenadier Guards
6. **River Escaut**
7. **Ramegnies-à-Chin**
8. **Pont-à-Chin**
9. IR 17 (Divisional Reserve)
10. III/IR 82
11. II/IR 82
12. II/IR 12
13. III/IR 12
14. **Léaucourt** IR 12 *Gefechstand*
15. **Mont-Saint-Aubert**

Air Photographs reproduced by kind permission of the Controller HMSO

enemy artillery.

Facing the 1st Guards Brigade was the 31 ID, commanded by *Generalleutnant* Kaempfe. This Division included three *Infanterie-Regiments* (IR): 82, 17 and 12, respectively commanded by *Obersts* Hozbach, Berthold and Ribstern. According to the 31 ID history:-

During the afternoon of May 20th, the 18 ID failed to occupy the Schelde's west bank. It was therefore decided to mount a concerted attack of the entire IV *Armee Korps*. The entire IV *Armee Korps* artillery fired from 0310 - 0330 hours, intending to entice the English batteries into giving away their positions to our observers. This was important because a successful attack on May 21st would only be possible if the enemy batteries were previously eliminated. The fire attack succeeded in provoking the English but it was not possible to exploit fully the observers' results quickly enough. Owing to the enemy artillery not having been neutralised, the 31 ID requested that the attack be postponed until 1100 hours but this was denied.

IR 82 *Kriegs-Tage-Buch* (KTB or War Diary):-

A two hour reconnaissance revealed that the enemy was strengthening his position behind the Schelde along the road Pecq-Tournai. The 31 ID ordered an attack on the sector in front of the three towns Tourcoing, Roubaix and Lille. The attack orders were essentially:-

1. The enemy has only relatively light defences on the Schelde's west bank. Some entrenchment work has been observed.

2. 31 ID is to force a crossing of the Schelde with IR 82 on the right, IR 12 on the left and IR 17 in reserve.

3. Contact lines to be:-

On the right, 14 ID.
On the left 7 ID.

Contact lines between IR 12 and IR 82: Menhart (12)-Leacourt (82)-Royere (82).

4. The first objective is to create a bridgehead on the lines Soraille-Sonoqier-Croazet. If the enemy takes evasive action he is to be pursued and the bridgehead extended to the line Leers North-Nechin.

The objective of IR 82 is the town of Pecq. To facilitate crossing the Schelde we have the support of a sapper company and a bridge-building column from the IV *Armee Korps*. The emphasis of the 31 ID attack will be IR 12, which will cross the river in relays and safeguard the north flank.

IR 82's reconnaissance during the late afternoon of May 20th, indicates that, contrary to '1' above, that the Schelde Sector is held by strong enemy forces and is well fortified. The recce patrol was strafed by enemy fire. The English have at their disposal on the west bank strong British and French batteries, up to 30 cm, with which they can cover approach roads to the Schelde.

At 2230 hours IR 82 got ready and in relays dug itself in, III/IR 82 to the right, II/IR 82 to the left. By 0100 hours the preparation area has been occupied and we are ready for daylight.

On the west bank, the 2nd Bn Coldstream Guards were also ready - to meet II and III/IR 82 (the 2nd and 3rd Battalions of 82 Regiment) in battle.

Preparing to assault the 3rd Bn Grenadier Guards position was II/IR 12, the Commanding Officer of which was *Hauptmann* Dr Lothar Ambrosius:-

During the afternoon of May 20th, II/IR 12 received orders to cross the Schelde on the morning of May 21st and establish a bridgehead in the direction of Bailleul. Additional support was to be given by two platoons of combat engineers and the Anti-Tank Platoon of I/IR 12. III/IR 12 was to stand by for action in reserve. All of 31 ID's artillery was to be active over II/IR 12's front.

Between 1830 - 1930 hours I held a conference with my Officers. Between 1930 - 2330 hours a detailed reconnaissance took place to establish the enemy positions. It was decided that the crossing was be made with No 5 *Kompanie* (Kp, i.e. 5/IR 12) on the left, 6 Kp (6/IR 12) on the right. The right flank border of 6 Kp would be with IR 82 near Leacourt. 7/IR 12 will attempt to make another crossing to 5 & 6/IR 12's left, just in case difficulties should arise in respect of the major assault. 7/IR 12 will also act as a decoy. 5 & 6/IR 12 will also have the direct support of one platoon of combat engineers and one machine-gun platoon. II/IR 12 *Gefechstand* [Battalion Command Post] will be centrally located between 5 Kp and 6 Kp.

At 0000 hours on May 21st, II/IR 12 set off for the Start Point which was reached at 0100 hours. During the early morning darkness rubber assault boats were advanced along the Tournai-Herinnes Road, but the enemy artillery fire made progress difficult. Our artillery will fire a barrage between 0720 - 0730 hours. At 0715 hours I intend to go forward with my Adjutant, *Leutnant* Engel, to lead the attack at 0730 hours.

And so as the artillery of both sides was noisily in action throughout the night whilst these young infantrymen of Britain and Germany prepared to meet each other in a major confrontation. For many it would be their last night alive. Others would find their lives irrevocably changed; so literally explosive would the next day's events be, in fact, that they can still be found indelibly etched into the memories of survivors well over half-a-century later.

Lance Sergeant Constantine:-

I will *never* forget.

CHAPTER SEVEN

Guards VC: May 21st, 1940

L ieutenant The Master of Forbes:-

After what had seemed a long night, just before first light on May 21st, the whole Battalion 'Stood To'. We were at the ready. There was an air of tension. In front of us we could see nothing, as a heavy early morning mist hung like a blanket all along the Escaut. At times we could hear what sounded like the breaking of the odd twig, or a little rustling noise on the other side of the waterway. We did not know, however, whether those confusing noises we made by animals or humans.

As an attack failed to materialise, the order was given to 'Stand Down'. Consequently the Guardsmen relaxed a little, breakfasting, shaving and cleaning their weapons. The early morning mist rising off the water and enveloping the low-lying landscape perhaps provided a feeling of security.

Lance Sergeant Constantine:-

Our Section (of No 4 Coy) dug in a little distance in front of an old house or cottage which was the same distance behind us as the River Escaut was to our front. We had a good view and could see well over a thousand yards the other side of the river. The fields on the East bank had long grass and a mixture of trees and bushes. The early morning mist was clearing very slowly but suddenly in the distance we could see a mass of movement which looked like ants. Of course these were German soldiers hurriedly dispersing and separating into ones and twos, disappearing into the undergrowth and other cover to mount a frontal attack.

In a scene similar to that in the Pecq sector, German infantrymen of the 30 ID move their rubber assault boats towards a water obstacle.
Via Peter Taghon.

Complying with the German plan, at 0715 hours the enemy artillery and mortars began pounding No 4 Company in advance of II/IR 12's assault. It may not have been coincidence that this determined attack was to be launched against the vulnerable 3rd Grenadier and 2nd Coldstream inter-Battalion boundary: from the top of Mont St Aubert, the enemy were able to observe BEF positions along a significant section of the Escaut line. The early morning mist rising off the water also worked in the enemy's favour given that it shrouded, to some extent, their preparations. The enemy's intention was to approach the River Escaut from the village of Leacourt, mount a river crossing and strike inland (some 200 metres) for an avenue of established poplar trees rising up to the main Pont-à-Chin to Pecq road. From there, II/IR 12 was to press on, over the road and a further half-a-mile due West and seize Bailleul.

Guardsman Rice:-

We were in trees by the canal. We were all eating breakfast when suddenly there were explosions all around us - I remember seeing the Company Runner, Guardsman Brind, showered with earth and thought 'Well that's just ruined his breakfast!' I took cover with Guardsman Chapman on 4 Coy's extreme left flank. We were hit by a bomb and all that was left of Chapman was his pack; I remember thinking 'Funny, he was wearing that a second ago'.

Guardsman Drinkwater:-

Guardsman Les Drinkwater,
3rd Bn Grenadier Guards.
Mr L Drinkwater.

Suddenly all hell broke loose. The enemy opened up on No 4 Coy with artillery, trench mortar and machine-gun fire. Our left flank took an extreme battering and Major West naturally became very worried about this position - we were with him at that time in No 4 Coy HQ, situated a in large barn completely screened from the enemy by a line of trees. The shells consisted of both shrapnel and high explosive - within seconds the call for Stretcher Bearers went up so at Major West's order, Sergeant Bullock and myself made our way forward to the far extremity of 4 Coy's line. Before leaving the Company Sergeant Major gave us each a cotton bandolier containing a further 50 rounds of .303 ammunition. These were hung around our necks, our pouches being already full of bullets. We also carried our rifles and a Red Cross haversack containing shell dressings. We also wore armbands indicating the Red Cross.

Upon leaving the shelter of the trees and bushes we ran into the full force of the enemy's fire - the din was terrible. We ran, doubled up - the ground was flat and devoid of cover. Again and again we dropped to the ground to miss bursting shells. As we went along I treated several casualties with flesh wounds. One poor fellow was caught by machine-gun bullets when returning to his trench (I assumed nature had called). He lay on his back some 20 yards from the canal. As I neared him I flattened myself to the ground. A shell landed alongside him, tearing him apart. This was the first fatality I had seen - I felt sick.

The distance from 4 Coy HQ to the extreme left flank was approximately 800-1000 yards. When we arrived there it was immediately apparent that the Germans were trying to wipe out this position. Sergeant Bullock and I lay down behind a bush, the grass around us was alive with bullets which cracked over our bodies. To our amazement through all this noise we could hear the familiar sound of a Bren gun, firing as if defying the whole German Army. The Bren was positioned on the other side of the bush, on the canal bank. I admired the guts of the two men operating the gun but realised they were the reason for the high concentration of enemy fire.

Suddenly a terrific explosion rent the air. The Bren Gun had received a direct hit which blasted Guardsman Arthur Rice clean through the bush. He looked in a dreadful mess, his knee was smashed, his leg and arm riddled with shrapnel, he also had a head wound and was bleeding profusely. Sergeant Bullock and I immediately set to with shell dressings in an attempt to stop the bleeding. In the meantime Arthur's mate lay somewhere on the canal bank - terrible screams of fear and agony came from him. He had received a nasty head wound and blood and seeped into his eyes, temporarily blinding him. Sergeant Bullock decided to investigate, found this Guardsman and applied a shell dressing. We also noticed that since the Bren had been destroyed, all firing on this position had ceased - this was because the Germans were starting to launch rubber assault boats from the other bank. Sergeant Bullock made an instant decision and came through the bush leading the wounded Guardsman by the hand. He looked at the severity of Guardsman Rice's wounds and decided that if we took him with us our progress would be so slow that all four of us would be killed or at the very least captured. He ordered me to "Leave him, pull back!". I continued to give Arthur what attention I could. On looking up I saw Sergeant Bullock still leading the other wounded Guardsman by the hand - they were running like blazes. He turned once and waved me on, then they both disappeared over a slight rise.

Although firing had ceased on the position Arthur and I still occupied, it had intensified all along the canal bank, especially in the direction of 4 Coy HQ, I also realised that this was our only escape route. On getting Arthur up he said "Leave me, I've had it". This I refused to do.

Lance Sergeant Constantine:-

When the Germans were approaching 500 yards range I told the Section and Bren gunner to fire at their own discretion at each individual target as seen. From then on I seemed oblivious of the others and was finding targets for myself to fire at. Very soon they were within 200 yards or less. Every shot that I fired looked to me that it found its target. I can recall my feelings at the time which was a coolness and concentration when I aimed and fired. At least half of those I fired at got up again and ran for cover; the others did not. As the attack progressed we had to open up the spare box of ammunition, one of which each section had been given when taking up position. Despite our efforts, some of the enemy got across the water and overran some of 4 Coy's trenches by the river (to the left of our section). I told my Section to increase its firepower, otherwise the enemy would cross in front of our trench. Every so often we were helping ourselves to extra rounds from the ammunition box. After making sure that there was plenty for the Bren gunner I knew that the box was getting low. I checked the Section to see how much each man had left - all were getting close to their last bandolier of 50 rounds so I told them not to waste any, and also to be sure of each target before firing. We heard a rumour that our artillery was getting low on shells, but if we had run out of .303 it would have been disastrous.

The river crossing had not, however, been straight forward for II/IR 12. *Hauptmann* Ambrosius:-

The river crossing was very difficult. The English were firing at us with rifle and machine-gun fire from all directions and it became obvious that there were many well constructed and camouflaged fox holes on the west bank which would have to be taken individually. In spite of our heavy losses, strong return fire and steep river banks, we manage to cross on our pontoons. A large pontoon was then paddled across, followed by our remaining *Kompanies* together with heavy weapons and communications. During this crossing under heavy fire *Oberleutnant* Michael distinguished himself.

Even when on the west bank my men faced a most difficult task. There is much marsh land here and we were often wading through deep mud and water up to our waists. Enemy fire increased from all sides and in spite of our own fire and the maximum physical effort, only a few of us reached the small wood some 200 metres inland from the Schelde. Many of my soldiers had already sacrificed their blood: 40 dead and 100 wounded, amongst the latter being *Oberleutnant* Michael, *Leutnant* Ziermann, *Leutnant* Linemann and Dr Stromsky.

By now No 4 Company's position had been completely overrun. Like II/IR 12, the Grenadiers had also suffered many casualties. Amongst them was 28 year old Guardsman Sam Hayes, killed fighting next to Guardsman Bert Smith who was wounded in the head and captured. Also taken by the enemy at this time was their Section Commander, Lance Corporal, Bryant Everitt. No 4 Company's Commander, Major West, was dead, as was one of his Platoon Commanders, Second Lieutenant Boyd (who had joined the 3rd Grenadiers on a month's attachment on April 26th). Owing to the artillery barrage, which involved such scenes of carnage as that witnessed by Guardsman Drinkwater, a number of

Men of *Panzer Jäger Abteilung* 7 pictured in a somewhat less hazardous river crossing than that undertaken by II/IR 12 on May 21st, 1940. This picture shows just how prepared the Germans were, however, for negotiating the many waterways throughout Belgium and Northern France.
Via Peter Taghon.

Officers of II/IR 12 (from left to right): *Hauptmann* Subklew, *Oberleutnant* Dieterichs & *Hauptmann* Ambrosius (*Kommandeur*).
Via Peter Taghon.

Guardsmen would either never be found or not identified.

| Guardsman Sam Hayes, 3rd Bn Grenadier Guards: killed in action May 21st, 1940. *Mr D Clark.* | Corporal Bryant Everitt, 3rd Bn Grenadier Guards (kneeling at left), was amongst the prisoners taken on May 21st, 1940. *Mrs E Hancock.* |

Pioneere (combat engineers) attached to 7/IR 12 pictured sometime during the morning of May 21st, 1940, and during the attack on the 3rd Bn Grenadier Guards at Esquelmes. The foremost man appears to be crouching in a rubber boat.
Peter Taghon.

The land between the River Escaut and the main road consisted of large corn fields. Having taken No 4 Company's position, men of II/IR 12 were also working their way slightly inland and in a southerly direction, intending to cut off Nos 2 and 1 Company of the Battalion.

Lieutenant The Master of Forbes:-

The Master of (now The Lord)
Forbes (pictured whilst a 2nd
Lieutenant), 3rd Bn Grenadier
Guards: wounded, May 21st, 1940.
The Lord Forbes.

Major WRJ Alston-Roberts-West
(pictured whilst a Lieutenant),
3rd Bn Grenadier Guards: missing
in action since May 21st, 1940.
Lieutenant Colonel GA Alston-Roberts-West.

Major Reggie Alston-Roberts-West at once formed a defensive flank in an effort to stop the Germans from cutting off the forward units of No 2 Company - my Company - from its Headquarters. The Germans were attacking all along our front with mortars and small arms fire. At times we could see them on the far side of the Escaut and we would open fire. Since the attack started, I had been lying near the lip of the canal-bank trying to locate any movement on the far bank. Our artillery was replying and so there was considerable noise of battle.

Suddenly I felt a thud on my left leg. My immediate reaction was to get lower down the bank for some extra cover. I tried to move, but my left leg would not respond. When I looked at it, I saw a tear in my battledress trouser by my knee. There was also blood. I looked behind and saw one of my Platoon close to me. He had been hit in the arm and was receiving assistance from another

Guardsman. I guessed that we had both been hit by the same mortar bomb. Then Guardsman Evans of my Platoon saw my plight, and dragged me down from the lip of the canal bank. Mortar bombs were bursting all around by now, and the larger calibre German artillery barrage continued to separate us from Battalion HQ and our reserve Company, a mile to the rear of our front line.

I could hear heavy rifle and machine-gun fire around No 4 Company, to my left, and the next moment their commander, Reggie Alston-Roberts-West, appeared, followed by George, Duke of Northumberland [who must have been sent forward from No 3 Company, in which he was a Platoon Commander, to ascertain the situation]. Reggie told me that he wanted to try and make contact with Battalion HQ, so as to organise a counter-attack and try to push the Germans back across the Escaut. He then asked whether I would prefer to be left where I was and captured, or to risk being pulled back towards the Regimental Aid Post. Without any hesitation I opted for the latter. Next moment Reggie and George, crouching down to avoid being an obvious target, were pulling me along the ground by my shoulder straps, rather like a dead stag being pulled off the hill by its antlers. We had not gone far when I passed out.

Lieutenant The 9th Duke of Northumberland, 3rd Bn Grenadier Guards: killed in action, May 21st,

Guardsman Drinkwater:-

By this time the enemy was almost across the canal - it was obvious to me that it would be foolhardy of the enemy to follow Arthur Rice and me along the canal bank into their own fire. This proved to be correct, as on crossing the canal they proceeded straight out from the bank and were veering slightly to their left in an effort to cut off Nos 4 and 2 Coys. Again Arthur said "Leave me, I've had it" - yet he never complained about his wounds. As we progressed blood was running down my hand - 'Hell, I've been hit', I thought, but I wasn't - the blood came from Arthur's arm. As we moved slowly along the canal bank, a couple of Guardsmen pulled out of a trench, then two more. I thought 'Good, here's some assistance', but these fellows were in no state to help anyone. Then I spotted Major West running along the bank towards us, exposing himself to enemy fire. When I looked again he had disappeared.

We eventually got into Coy HQ and I found a stretcher and blankets for Arthur, and a nice pile of straw for myself where I lay completely exhausted. The shelling had stopped by now but bullets were ricocheting off the roof and walls of the barn. Hearing a voice call my name I moved across to Arthur's stretcher. He gripped my hand and said "Thanks pal". It was my pleasure to shake his hand. I then returned to my pile of straw knowing that we were surrounded. The enemy were closing in.

As the enemy closed in around the barn into which Arthur Rice and I had taken refuge, drastic action was required to enable us to escape. Two company trucks, loaded with equipment, stood in the centre of the barn. It was decided to offload them. Two senior NCOs set up a Bren outside the large double doors - once they started firing we had to start the vehicle motors (the noise of the Bren disguising this sound). The stretcher on which the badly wounded Arthur lay was positioned diagonally across the lorry. Except for the driver's position, and excepting the side and tail boards, there was no cover whatsoever. I crouched alongside the stretcher, rifle at the ready. We were very fortunate as the building's large double doors faced the canal - the enemy were closing in from the rear. The decision was made for the first truck to turn right, the second left, just in case the first got hit.

On clearing the barn we ran straight into the enemy but the essence of surprise was with us! At this stage the enemy dared not fire in case they hit each other; once we were through a hail of bullets hit the truck, wounding our driver, but we continued and we soon over a ridge of higher ground and out of the enemy's sight.

A lucky escape indeed; Lieutenant The Master of Forbes was also lucky enough to be evacuated in a vehicle, driven by Platoon Sergeant Major Cassford, but the adventures of all concerned were far from over.

Lance Sergeant Constantine:-

A Company Runner then got through with a message that we were to withdraw from our position and get behind a building a few yards to the rear of our trench. We managed to crawl there but once behind the building it was confirmed that the enemy had broken through between the left of our own trenches and the 2nd Bn Coldstream Guards. We were also told that the enemy had occupied a large cornfield to the rear of our positions. It was decided to put in an attack with whatever men were available.

My Section joined up with the rest in a long ditch about 100 yards from the corn. We were given the order "Fix bayonets!" A few minutes after we had done so the order was given to advance, crawling forward. We hugged the ground as the enemy raked the area with machine-guns. We charged the last 20 yards leading into the cornfield, small arms fire intensifying. Added to the din were the screams and cries of the badly wounded. We started moving through the corn in a crouching position when I realised that at least six of my Section must have been caught by enemy fire before we reached the corn. Only three of us were left: the Bren gunner, a Guardsman and myself.

The corn was fairly high, at least four to five feet, but it was impossible to stand upright because the enemy's fire power was so great that it would have been fatal. It was not long before I realised that we had lost direction. We moved onwards but suddenly there was a movement in the corn to our right. I was just about to fire when there was a groaning sound and I saw a Guardsman trying to pull himself along in agony. He had been wounded in the leg and was in real pain. A trouser leg had been ripped off and he continued to lose plenty of blood despite a dressing applied over the wound. He was trying to speak but I could not understand what he was saying. I was making up my mind whether to leave him there and try to find out which part of the cornfield we were in, when one of my companions confirmed that we were just a few yards from the edge of the field. I crawled to him and saw that we had crawled over half way, lost our way then ended up at this particular edge.

Lance Sergeant Constantine was now facing west towards the main Pecq - Pont-á-Chin road (which was sparsely lined with poplar trees), 'Poplar Ridge' - occupied by *Hauptmann* Ambrosius and his men - being about 200 metres to the north. Lance Sergeant Constantine continues:-

I had a quick study of the ground and found that we were about 50 yards from a line of poplar trees that looked as though they had a long ditch running parallel with them. We both crawled back to the Bren gunner and the wounded Guardsman, and then I said that we would get him to the edge of the cornfield. When we had managed that I asked the Bren gunner what he thought about running the 50 yards to the ditch; after giving us two minutes we would then run, carrying the wounded man, under the cover of his fire. Also, directly he started off we would give him covering fire. I made it clear that he did not have to do this, and that if he preferred I would run with the Bren instead. He was agreeable to the first plan and was soon running hardest to reach the ditch. We fired as quickly as possible over the corn stalks, and soon saw that he had reached the ditch safely. We slung our rifles over our backs, stood the wounded man up on his good leg (by now he was very near unconscious), crossed our wrists and gripped each other's hands, getting the man in a sitting position between us. We then ran across the open ground as best we could with our Bren gunner firing away until we reached him safely. We found several others from our Company in that ditch.

Hauptmann Ambrosius:-

The soldiers remaining with me continued to move forward up the small wooded ridge where we dug ourselves in. On my left was the Adjutant, *Leutnant* Engel, and on the right the Machine-Gun Company Commander, *Leutnant* Barthels, with a part of 5 Kp. On the left flank was *Leutnant* Hasselmann with 6 Kp. Altogether we had about 70 men dug in here. The position was held despite heavy artillery fire and determined counter-attacks.

Although the dead, dying and wounded lay scattered all around, as indicated by the German Battalion Commander the Grenadiers rallied and mounted several *ad hoc* counter attacks. Given that the main thrust of the German attack had fallen upon No 4 Company, Nos 1 and 2 Companies, situated to the right, were able to hold firm. The open country held by these forward Companies was still being observed from Mont-St-Aubert - any movement provoked a violent reaction from the enemy machine-guns and mortars situated on the East bank. These particular Grenadier companies were also subjected to fire from German snipers who had infiltrated the cornfield behind the River Escaut. Captain Clifton organised an immediate counter-attack with the reserve platoon of No 1 Company and some Guardsmen of Captain Radford-Norcop's No 2 Company. The position formerly occupied by No 4 Company was reached, but the Grenadiers were beaten back with further losses: Captain Clifton and Captain Radford-Norcop were both wounded.

The lethal MG34 mounted on a sustained fire tripod.
Via Peter Taghon.

To the right of these Grenadier companies was the 2nd Bn North Staffordshire Regiment, whose left flank the Germans also attacked, as recounted by that Bn's War Diary:-

Heavy fighting continued for approximately two hours but the Bn stood its ground, 'B' and 'D' Coys both suffering some casualties. All telephone lines with Bde and the Coys were cut by shell fire and it was some time before the situation became clear and could be reported to Bde HQ. The Bde Comdr then told the Colonel that he was to attempt to re-establish the line on our left by putting in a counter-attack. The Colonel then ordered Major FG Matthews, who was in command of 'A' Coy, to counter-attack with 2 Pls in the direction of Esquelmes, supported by our Carrier Pl. This counter-attack was put into force immediately but it was learnt later that co-ordination between 'A' Coy and the Carrier Pl was never properly established. Shortly after the two Pls of 'A' Coy had started to advance a message was received by the Colonel from CO 6 Gordons (in Bde Reserve) offering to support the counter-attack with their Carrier Pl and one Coy. The Colonel accepted this and it was arranged that one Coy and Carrier Pl of the 6 Gordons should come in from the direction of Bailleul and advance due East joining up with the 2 Pls of ours.

After these arrangements had been made the Colonel went forward to co-ordinate the attack but on arrival at the northern edge of wood 894393 he could find no trace of the 6 Gordons. En route up to the corner of the wood the Colonel received two messages from Major Matthews stating that his counter-attack was going according to plan, the last message adding that he had taken under his command and into the counter-attack two pls of the Grenadier Gds. Shortly after this enemy shelling and MG fire became intense and it was obvious that the counter-attack had failed to reach the line of the river but had prevented enemy penetration west of the road Tournai-Courtrai. Seeing the situation the Colonel returned to Bn HQ and reported what had occurred to Bde, stating that he did not consider that it was of any value to put in a counter-attack with any less than a Bn.

At about 0945 hours odd men from the two Pls of 'A' Coy who counter-attacked began to pass through and on being questioned it was learned that Major Matthews had been seen to fall whilst leading his men into action, and that Captain Birch had been seriously wounded. A considerable number of men were missing. As soon as the remnants of the two counter-attack Pls had been reformed, the Colonel made detailed enquiries as to the location of Major Matthews and Capt Birch and posted elements of the Bn including the Carrier Pl and some of the Gren Gds to form a defensive flank on the left of the Bn area, which was at that time entirely open. Corporal Wade stated that the approx position where Major Matthews fell as in a cornfield at 901397. Corporal Wade stated that he had carried Captain Birch back to a small farm building just off the road by the shrine about 897395 and that he could find his way back to the spot.

Although help was at hand for Captain Birch, the 2nd North Staffordshires had lost six men killed and around 40 Officers and Other Ranks wounded. The 3rd Grenadiers fighting alongside these men lost one man: Lance Sergeant Arthur Rimell, of Severn Stoke, Worcestershire, who at just 18 years old became the youngest Guards casualty to date. Although Major Matthews would later be recommended for a posthumous VC, on the basis that his counter-attack had prevented any German penetration beyond the main road, such an award was not forthcoming. The 2nd Bn North Staffordshire Regiment War Diary continues:-

Major FG Matthews, 2nd Bn
North Staffordshire Regiment:
killed in action May 21st, 1940.
Mrs Pat Jordan.

The Colonel sent for Corporal Wade and Company Sergeant Major Foster of 'A' Coy and again investigated the possibilities of sending out a search party for Major Matthews and Captain Birch. Corporal Wade was convinced he knew where they were and volunteered to go out in a Carrier and bring them in, to which the Colonel agreed. A Carrier was procured driven by Lance Corporal Showell and set out, returning at about 1600 hours with Captain Birch and a Corporal of the Gren Gds. No trace could be found of Major Matthews. Captain Birch was seen by the Adjt just prior to being evacuated by Ambulance and he stated that he had not seen Major Matthews, but that he and the Corporal of the Gren Gds had been captured by the enemy whilst lying wounded, but that whilst the enemy had gone back for stretchers our Carrier under Corporal Wade had arrived. Hardly had the two wounded been placed on the Carrier than the enemy returned and opened MG fire, but the whole party and the Carrier managed to return safely to Bn HQ.

The 2nd Bn Hampshire Regiment, in 1st Guards Brigade reserve, was used to bolster the line; War Diary:-

0930 hours: 'Y' Coy moved off under command Coldstream to assist their right in Pecq. Employed Pl of HQ Coy formed up and took up defensive position under Major JM Lee.
1005 hours: Brigadier Beckwith-Smith visits Bn HQ. Orders - enemy apparently trying to push west up stream towards Pas-de-Wasmes 8839. 'Z' Coy ordered to go East down stream from Estaimbourg with one Section Carrier Pl. A Coy of 3rd Grenadiers also pushing up stream from Bailleul.
1215 hours: Grens found nothing in stream so pushed on. 'Z' Coy took over defence of Bailleul.

A German patrol had crossed the main road just north of Poplar Ridge, and was making its way along the same direction as the Wasmes stream towards Bailleul and Estaimbourg; Lieutenant Halliday:-

There was only one block house in our new sector but it was locked. After a good deal of ferreting about the key was discovered in the safe of the local *Mairie*. The block house was occupied literally a minute before the first German patrol appeared. I was with Cadoux visiting 'Y' Company at the time and saw the whole extraordinary performance from a flank.

We could see a German patrol approaching up the road covered by the blockhouse while, from the other direction, one of our bicycle orderlies came waving the key and pedalling furiously towards the block house. We found Major Hugh Phillips, who was commanding 'Y' Company and one of our more elderly Majors, in the last stages of exhaustion. Cadoux immediately sent him back to take over HQ Coy and the latter's commander, James Lee, was summoned to take over 'Y' Company.

We spotted a second German patrol of six men moving across our front. Our Section opened fire at about 300 yards and the patrol dived for cover behind a house. Their problem was to get away along a row of three or four houses with gaps of about five yards between each. The corporal evidently decided to make his men run one at a time across each gap but did nothing about organising any covering fire. We therefore had some jolly snap shooting practice. Cadoux and I each borrowed a soldier's rifle to have a go at the last gap but I have to admit that the lot of us only managed to wing one of the enemy. We were however not much impressed by their field craft or tactics. They obviously withdrew fairly hot and bothered and I doubt that they returned with a very detailed report of our positions.

Hauptmann Ambrosius and his men nevertheless steadfastly maintained their position on Poplar Ridge itself, effectively driving a wedge between the 3rd Grenadiers and 2nd Coldstream. The counter-attack from the south undertaken by the 2nd North Staffordshires with elements of the 3rd Grenadiers had failed to dislodge II/IR 12, weakened though the enemy were. The situation for the 3rd Grenadiers, and indeed the defensive position of the 1st Guards Brigade, was critical as *Leutnant* Barthels' two MG 34 machine-gun teams continued to dominate the battle.

The Commanding Officer of the 3rd Bn Grenadier Guards, Major Allan Adair MC, went forward from Bailleul in a Carrier, taking with him the commander of his reserve Company, No 3, Captain Starkey. Consequently No 3 Company was sent forward with orders not merely to link up with the 2nd Bn Coldstream Guards but also to push the Germans back across the river.

Guardsman Nash:-

We were in our positions beyond Bn HQ, from where we could hear lots of firing coming from the direction of the river. Captain Starkey came and told us that the Germans had crossed the river and had established themselves on a ridge near the main road. As usual I was with Harry Nicholls, who had the Bren gun. We moved up to the main road and formed up in a ditch, but Harry was hit there in the arm by a piece of shrapnel. It didn't bother him too much as he was determined to grab this opportunity for proper action. So was I. The news was bad. These bastards had driven our men back, and we knew the situation was serious with many Guardsmen either killed or trapped in the corn.

At about 1130 hours, supported by a section of three Carriers led by Lieutenant Reynell-Pack, Captain Starkey advanced from the Forming Up Position (FUP), leading his men towards the German position on Poplar Ridge.

Lance Sergeant Constantine:-

Through the line of trees and ditch I saw a number of men, probably the strength of a platoon, who were coming from the rear. Once they were through the line of trees they started towards the cornfield. They were a good 500 yards to my right and I remember waving my rifle in the air, trying to attract their attention, as I thought that if we could make contact I could provide a better idea of the situation. They did not see me, however, and increased their pace until breaking into a run, charging into the corn shouting at the top of their voices. Again cries and screams came from the cornfield but there was little we could do.

These photographs were taken at Louth on October 3rd, 1940, and show men of the 4th Bn Grenadier Guards demonstrating the counter-attack made by Captain Starkey's No 3 Company of the 3rd Bn on May 21st, 1940. Strangely, in the top photograph, the Carrier's supporting infantry are wearing gas masks!

Grenadier Guards.

Amongst No 3 Company's men was Guardsman W Lewcock:-

From the start it was a suicidal attack as we advanced across the cornfield towards the wood in open formation. We were met with a hail of machine-gun bullets and in a short time there were the cries of the wounded and the dying. The Duke of Northumberland, who waved us on with his ash stick, was killed near me.

The advance had started off well supported by mortar fire, but this ceased too early as it was wrongly believed that No 3 Company was too close for safety to the exploding shells. Unfortunately Captain Starkey had no means of communicating with the Mortar Platoon and so his men were suddenly adrift in the corn, unsupported by heavier fire and in range of the German MG 34 machine-guns. Losses increased and Captain Abel-Smith, No 3 Company's Second-in-Command, also fell. According to the 3rd Bn Grenadier Guards War Diary 'the attack went in with great dash .... but the men were mown down by hidden machine-guns'.

Lieutenant Reynell-Pack then attempted to use his Carriers as light tanks, but as the small tracked vehicles dashed forward towards Poplar Ridge his gunners were unable to bring their Brens to bear due to the rough ground. The Carriers charged the Germans head-on; all were destroyed, the gallant Reynell-Pack being killed just 50 yards short of his objective.

Hauptmann Ambrosius:-

A massive counter-attack took place which was preceded by a heavy artillery barrage. Suddenly three enemy tanks put in an appearance, followed by a whole English company. One of these was immediately eliminated, the crew killed. The other two were stopped between our dug outs and forced back together with the rest of the counter-attacking company. The tanks were engaged with rifle fire and anti-tank ammunition. Every man stood upright between the tanks driving here and there. Our men fired and threw stick grenades into the tanks. In this battle *Leutnant* Schlinke and his machine-gun team distinguished themselves.

Guardsman Lewcock:-

Our numbers were dwindling rapidly and as we started to take cover, unable to proceed due to our mounting losses. It was then that Harry Nicholls dashed forward.

Guardsman Nash:-

It was desperate. These German machine-guns were unbelievable. Harry just turned to me and said "Come on Nash, follow me!" So I did. He had the Bren, firing from the hip, and I had my rifle. I fed Harry ammunition, and we attacked by means of short rushes forward. Harry was hit several times and hurt bad, but he wouldn't stop. He just kept on shouting "Come on Nash, they can't get me!" Once the enemy guns in the poplars were out of action we fired on Germans who were crossing the River Escaut. Harry said "Wait till their half way across then we'll sink 'em". I reckon we sank two boats, each containing about 10 men, before Harry turned the Bren on other Germans located both sides of the canal. By then we were drawing a lot of small arms fire ourselves.

Hauptmann Ambrosius described the shattering effect that Lance Corporal Nicholls' gallant attack had on his position:-

This attack caused panic amongst the soldiers of our 5 and 6 Kps [on Poplar Ridge], many of which fled and jumped in the Schelde to escape. *Oberleutnant* Shrumpel and *Leutnant* Schlinke then rallied these men who held their position on the riverbank.

Leutnant Engel, the Adjutant, was killed, shot through the head just a metre from me. It was he, with his fresh and daredevil personality, who had led the *Kompanies* forward. His death created quite a gap in II/IR 12, which he had helped to build up.

After this attack we had no more machine-guns operable and no more anti-tank ammunition. Indeed, by this time nearly all of our ammunition of all types was used up.

The effect of Lance Corporal Nicholls' attack on the advance of II/IR 12 was extremely significant and changed the tactical situation in the locality. Ambrosius' assault force, of near-Company strength, which had been well supported by several MG34s and light anti-tank weapons, had been digging in on Poplar Ridge where it threatened cohesion of the 1st Guards Brigade's defensive position. After the counter-attack, however, the II/IR 12 strength on Poplar Ridge had been reduced to that of a platoon, without machine-guns and with little ammunition. The attack by Lance Corporal Nicholls therefore destroyed the momentum of the assault crossing, and wrested the initiative from the Germans.

The immediate effect was that many Grenadiers were now able to escape from the cornfield in which they had previously been trapped by the MG 34s' withering fire. Grievously wounded and probably unconscious, however, Lance Corporal Nicholls himself sank back into the corn.

Guardsman Lewcock:-

I met up with Harry Nicholls and Percy Nash in the corn. I could see that Harry was badly wounded but appeared just about conscious. At that moment a Lysander flew over and the enemy turned their attentions to it. This enabled the few of us left to drop behind a low bank at the back of the field. The CSM was almost in tears as he counted us: 39 alive out of over 100 men. I was the only one who insisted that Harry Nicholls was still alive, but Percy Nash took the opposite view.

THE PECQ/ESQUELMES BATTLE, MAY 21ST, 1940

KEY

1. **Pecq**
2. Tannery, No 4 Coy 2nd Bn Coldstream Guards.
3. No 1 Coy 2nd Bn Coldstream Guards.
4. No 3 Coy 2nd Bn Coldstream Guards.
5. No 2 Coy 2nd Bn Coldstream Guards.
6. To **Estaimbourg** & 1st Guards Brigade HQ & 2nd Bn Hampshire Regiment (Brigade Reserve).
7. To **Bailleul** & 3rd Bn Grenadier Guards HQ.
8. Main Pont-à-Chin - Pecq Road. The 3rd Bn Grenadier Guards were pushed back to this line after the initial German assault.
9. **Poplar Ridge.**
10. Shrine.
11. No 4 Coy 3rd Bn Grenadier Guards.
12. No 2 Coy 3rd Bn Grenadier Guards.
13. No 1 Coy 3rd Bn Grenadier Guards.
14. 2nd Bn North Staffordshire Regiment & direction of counter-attack led by Major FG Matthews.
15. Assault river crossing by II/IR 12, 5 *Kp* on left, 6 *Kp* on right. These troops took No 4 Coy's position before pressing on and digging in on Poplar Ridge, from where their MG34s were able to dominate the battle.
16. IR 82. Due to lack of artillery support, only 10 *Kp* managed to cross the River Escaut.
17. **Leácourt.**
18. FUP of No 3 Coy, 3rd Bn Grenadier Guards and direction of counter-attack across cornfield towards Poplar Ridge. Having destroyed the two MG34s located there, Lance Corporal Harry Nicholls then attacked German infantry massed behind the poplars (the field sloped downwards towards the River Escuat from that point), creating panic amongst their number. This act of supreme gallantry wrested the upper-hand from the Germans who later withdrew back across the River Escaut.
19. **Esquelmes**

Air Photographs reproduced by kind permission of the Controller HMSO

AERIAL PHOTOGRAPH TAKEN BY AMERICAN RECONNAISSANCE AIRCRAFT, MAY 17TH, 1943.

Lance Corporal Harry Nicholls VC
Grenadier Guards.

Another photograph taken at Louth: Guardsman Jack Nicholls, brother of the VC and also serving in the 3rd Bn Grenadier Guards, stands in for his brother with the Bren, whilst Percy Nash - his Sergeant's chevrons having been won on the field of battle - re-enacts his own part in the famous engagement.
Grenadier Guards.

Lance Corporal J Hudson, 3rd Bn Grenadier Guards: killed in action May 21st, 1940.
Mrs Ruth Grocott.

Guardsman W Lewcock, 3rd Bn Grenadier Guards: a survivor of the 'Poplar Ridge' counter-attack which he describes today as 'suicidal'.
Mr W Lewcock.

Hauptmann Ambrosius:-

After this attack the enemy resistance reduces. Some strong reconnaissance patrols are sent forward to follow up the enemy, in which manner we hope the entire area will eventually be cleared of the enemy. Our strength is now about 40 men. Approximately 60 prisoners have been taken, these men are Grenadier Guards - the *best* professional English soldiers. They are all 1.80 metre tall. The youngest have served six years, the oldest more like 18. In this situation the English have rarely used such elite regiments.

Among the prisoners, in fact, was Lance Corporal Nicholls, discovered in the cornfield just clinging on to life. After the Germans brought the badly wounded Nicholls out of the cornfield, it was Guardsman Smith who carried him and tended his wounds until more appropriate medical attention could be found.

Grenadier Prisoners of War taken by II/IR 12 at the River Escaut. The Guardsman fifth from left is believed to be the Author's Grandfather, Bert Smith. In the original photograph, Mont St Aubert can be seen on the East bank, locating this photograph as being towards the extreme left flank of No 4 Company's position.
Via Peter Taghon.

The local tactical situation was now one of stalemate. About 40 Germans remained on Poplar Ridge but their strength along the West bank itself was unknown. From about 1300 hours, the 1st Guards Brigade decided to maintain the line along the main road; in the ditch there could be found men of the 3rd Grenadiers, 2nd Coldstream, 2nd Hampshire, and 2nd North Staffordshire Regiments.

Lieutenant Edward Ford:-

My brother, Lieutenant CG Ford, had taken part in No 3 Company's counter-attack. Although he was six feet and seven inches tall, he survived, but returned to Major Adair's Battalion Headquarters very shaken indeed. Of course he had seen many of our chaps killed, including the Duke of Northumberland.

Some British soldiers, however, had remained in their riverside trenches throughout the morning:-

Guardsman Middleton:-

Although we were in No 4 Company, we seemed to be in a remote location and saw nothing of this battle which must have gone on inland and some distance to our left. No-one came down to us with any instructions so we remained in our trench. By lunchtime we were all starving, so I set off along the towpath to try and find Coy HQ. As I walked along I found a dead German soldier lying across the path so I realised then that the Germans had got across the river. Obviously I had no way of knowing the enemy strength or even what the situation was on our bank. As I moved inland and into the cornfield I found the body of Major West, our Company Commander. He was wearing his Sam Browne and still had his pipe in his hand. I couldn't find anybody about so I went back to the others. We pulled out, back inland, but just could not find anyone else, the place appeared deserted by this time.

Lance Sergeant Constantine:-

After we had eaten some rations, filled our water bottles and had our ammunition made up we had to get what rest we could as it would soon be dark. The news was received that our Company Commander, Major West, had been killed in the attack on the cornfield, which we were all sorry to hear, and also that No 4 Company had been reduced considerably in strength. My Section was now made up with four or five different men, although another two of the original Section managed to get through which made us up to strength again. The plan was for us to re-take the riverbank after dark, so we just rested up and waited for dusk.

Contrary to previously published accounts, however, the enemy did not withdraw immediately after No 3 Company's counter-attack, although given that certain German soldiers fled and jumped into the River Escaut it is easy to understand this perception. The German records available to us today enable a balanced account to be presented. *Hauptmann* Ambrosius:-

The Ordnance Officer, *Leutnant* Winkler was kept back at the II/IR 12 *Gefechstand* which he moved forward, following the river crossing, to the Schelde. From there he maintained constant telephone contact with the Regiment until enemy artillery fire severed the connections and contact with all *Kompanies* was lost. All radio equipment was also destroyed. The Bn Commanders instead prepared hand-written situation reports but only a few of these reached their destination.

During the course of the day such reports were prepared in triplicate by *Leutnant* Engel and after his death by *Leutnant* Haersler. These were sent by voluntary runners but hardly anyone managed to get back without being wounded.

IR 12 HQ apparently gets the impression that in view of the severity of the English counter-attacks and gravity of our losses, the bridgehead is unlikely to be sustainable. This was later confirmed when news was received that none of the other Bns which had crossed the Schelde could either maintain their bridgeheads on the west bank. 31 ID and IV AK decided, therefore, to re-group and try again after heavier artillery fire.

II/IR 12 received orders to return across the Schelde to the point from where the attack had commenced. I only agreed to go back after being told for a second time and also given *Leutnant* Kuthe's report that, according to our aircraft reports, two strong enemy columns are approaching our direction from SW. The overall picture is different, therefore, from the local one seen around our bridgehead. It requires taking back the survivors of II/IR 12 and so does not permit the other two Bns of IR 12 to follow up our attack as planned. With a heavy heart, considering the heavy losses suffered in crossing the Schelde and maintaining our small bridgehead, I have withdrawn in order to save the lives of my remaining men.

The withdrawal follows quietly and is complete within two hours. All wounded and nearly all equipment is safe. The English have been thrown back so far that they do not even notice our withdrawal.

Hauptmann Ambrosius was quite correct. 1st Guards Brigade's line remained along the main road, and no further attempts were made in daylight to recover the riverbank. Screened by the poplars and no doubt withdrawing via ditches, hedgerows and whatever other cover was available, the remnants of II/IR 12 safely completed their withdrawal. They left behind some 66 dead, however, and 133 German soldiers had been wounded.

Lance Sergeant Constantine:-

With darkness the time came too for us to move off with our hurriedly made up sections. The area was more familiar to us now and we had been told that the enemy had been driven back across the river. Nevertheless, every precaution had to be taken in the event that they may have returned to the west bank.

I led the Section through the ditch from where we had started the attack on the cornfield, trying our hardest to make as little noise as possible we made our way to the end nearest the river. We then slowly climbed out and moved right towards the cottage that was behind the trench that we had vacated that morning. Everything was silent except the noise of artillery. When we reached the cottage I signalled that half of the men were to go round to the right, the other half with me to the left. We moved around the building without a sound. When I drew level with the door I heard a slight creak and fired a shot at where the noise had come from. I must have re-loaded with a second and got the door open but there was nobody there. I felt that I had over-reacted as the shot had made a terrific noise due to the overall surrounding silence. We managed to continue without further mishap, however, and re-occupied the trench.

We got into position immediately because it was not long afterwards that all types of small arms fire was coming in our direction from across the river. We fired back, aiming at the flames their weapons made although it was impossible to see whether we had hit our targets. We were pleased to see that the enemy fire was coming from the other side of the river which meant they had not tried another crossing. As the night went on there was more shelling and mortar bombs being directed at us and these were exploding very near our positions. Our own mortars were kept very busy returning this fire. We had orders to pull out of the trenches before dawn, I remember that when we left there was an infantry unit behind some cover digging themselves in. They had already suffered casualties from the shelling and mortaring. As we passed through the lines I did not envy them and felt that we were just leaving them there.

That night, other Grenadier patrols struck out along Poplar Ridge itself. The Intelligence Officer, Lieutenant Edward Ford, led such a sortie, his men comprising the Battalion Tailor and other men of HQ Company:-

It was very quiet and we found both Poplar Ridge and the riverbank devoid of Germans, living ones anyway. We found a number of dead enemy soldiers; from some of these bodies we took identity discs as it was most important for us to establish against whom we had fought.

According to the 1st Guards Brigade War Diary:-

Positions on the River Escaut retaken during evening. The following articles were brought to Bde HQ: 1 sub-MG, 1 gas mask container, 1 *soldbuch* and 1 identity disc captured from the enemy.

3rd Bn Grenadier Guards War Diary:-

Towards dark enemy MG fire died down, and patrols sent forward found our banks clear of the enemy, and the line was re-established. The remainder of the Bn being organised into one Coy under Captain RN Brinkman who came up from 'B' Echelon during the night. More and more men were collected from weapons pits of the forward area.

A roll call indicated that the 3rd Grenadier casualties were high: 47 Grenadiers had been killed, including five Officers. Three more Officers had been wounded and Other Rank casualties amounted to 180 (this figure including those killed, missing and wounded). It was the Regiment's first major engagement of the Second World War; the action was II/IR 12's first since having re-formed after the Polish campaign. For the Grenadier Guards, however, this battle carved a special place in the Regimental History: Lance Corporal Nicholls would later receive the Victoria Cross for his 'signal act of valour'.

CHAPTER EIGHT

Victory along the Escaut

Although the 2nd Bn Coldstream Guards had expected a major assault on Pecq, in the event the town itself was not bitterly contested. Nevertheless there was a considerable amount of action, as indicated by the following account.

IR 82 KTB:-

All crossing places were covered by continuous enemy artillery fire of all calibres. The *Schwehrpunkt* of our own artillery was at the point of IR 12's crossing point, it only occasionally being directed outside that area. Without appropriate artillery support, our advance was much more hazardous. Because of the lack of artillery support our attack failed and *Oberst* Hozbach stopped the attack. Refusing to continue, he demanded that the 31 ID and IV *Armee Korps* should provide sufficient artillery before IR 82 would attack further.

Elements of IR 82 had, however, managed to cross the River Escaut, as related by the KTB of 10 *Kompanie*:-

One platoon got into the rubber factory of Pecq-Herrinnes, we are in the very front of the line.

Corporal Christie:-

My section of Bren Carriers were sent to support one of the rifle companies which was being attacked. It was my first experience of air burst shells - not nice. We moved forward under constant shell fire to support No 2 Company, commanded by Captain 'Pop' Wyatt. Our three Carriers were spread around the company area. Mine was between two houses and well dug in. We were never in any danger of being shifted!

2nd Bn Coldstream Guards War Diary:-

..... it was reported that the enemy had crossed the river by No 1 Coy's position. Major Stewart Brown was, therefore, sent to restore the situation, taking with him the Carrier Platoon under Captain Fane, who was shortly afterwards killed when making a recce.
The situation on the Coldstream front was soon restored as it was found that only a few Germans had managed to get across despite the intensity of German covering fire.

Guardsman Joe Nixon:-

When the shelling started I was at No 1 Company HQ, but we were forced to withdraw, covering each other as we went. We moved from a high piece of ground along a wooded pathway which led out on to the main road. A ditch there created a natural defensive position and from it we

Captain CN Fane, 2nd Bn Coldstream Guards:
killed in action May 21st, 1940.
*Reproduced with kind permission of Regimental
Adjutant Coldstream Guards.*

could see the Germans on our side of the River. Behind us was a blazing chateau. We did what we could with our .303 rifles, the range concerned being about 500 yards. I am certain that the enemy were using what I would term an 'infantry assault gun', i.e. a *Pak* 35/36, which could easily have been brought across the river. This meant that we were rather outgunned.

Reinforcements soon arrived in the shape of four Bren Carriers which charged along the road towards us. The Germans opened up with this *Pak*, scoring a direct hit of Captain Fane's Carrier. He received a nasty head wound and was killed, the same shell also wounded Guardsman Sanderson and myself. Someone put a field dressing on me and I hobbled off towards the Casualty Clearing Station at Pecq. There I found the Royal Army Medical Corps people to be real experts, extremely professional. I was later evacuated by stretcher before running the gauntlet from Pecq to Calais on a Red Cross train, but that is another story!

No 2 Company of the 2nd Bn Coldstream Guards then formed a defensive flank towards the 3rd Bn Grenadier Guards and attempted to reduce the gap existing between them. As the Grenadiers counter-attacked, the 2nd Coldstream Bn HQ received a direct hit which killed Company Quarter Master Sergeant Burnett and several pioneers. By 1700 hours, Captain Fielden's No 1 Company was able to return to its riverside trenches - there Platoon Sergeant Major Frank 'Pete' Court was found dead, having held his ground regardless. His brother, also a Coldstreamer, was an Intelligence Sergeant at HQ 1st Guards Brigade:-

Sergeant LHT Court:-

I heard the sad news about my brother during the afternoon so went on my motorcycle to the Grenadier HQ at Bailleul - to where my brother's body had for some reason been taken. There I met Drill Sergeant Randall who had been i/c burial party. He showed me where my brother was buried, in the garden of the local padre. He asked me to accept personal articles belonging to my brother which I retained all the way back home.

2nd Bn Coldstream Guards War Diary:-

Our casualties in this encounter were not so heavy as at first appeared, numbering about 30 killed and wounded, which included 2nd Lieutenant Sir John Pigott-Brown who was evacuated with a scalp wound. Lieutenant CH Fielden who was commanding No 1 Coy was also ordered back to rest at 'B' Echelon with a very badly burned hand.

From No 4 Company's vantage point in the tannery, overlooking the River Escaut just north of Pecq church, Guardsman Archie Swaby shot 14 Germans, with Sergeant Eastwood marking, from an upper window. Lieutenant Bob Windsor-Clive recalls that the tannery's windows provided the opportunity for 'an excellent shoot'.

British casualties in Pecq.
Via Peter Taghon.

The 2nd Coldstream left behind some 15 dead at Pecq. For the 2nd Hampshires, being mostly in reserve, casualties were fewer: one killed and 10 wounded. For all of the units involved - British and German - this would become just one of many bloody battles fought across Europe during the next five years.

There was, in fact, another act of conspicuous gallantry recognised on May 21st, 1940, this brave deed taking place just south of Tournai itself. Opposing the BEF

BEF Prisoners of War in Pecq.
Via Peter Taghon

units in that area was the 18 ID; the KTB of which for May 21st states:-

During the nocturnal advance to the starting point, IR 51 was subjected to heavy artillery fire. *Artillerie Regiment* (AR) 81 eliminates the enemy guns.

A feint attack with artillery support indicates that the enemy intends to offer stubborn resistance. The attack begins at 0730 hours but makes slow progress.

At 0900 hours IR 54 reports via radio that there is a concentration of enemy artillery fire near Calonne. So far two *Kompanies* have been moved across the Schelde. A third is in the process of crossing. By 1000 hours IR 54 takes a second Bn across the Schelde.

1150 hours: the English then drive a tank attack against the bridgehead of IR 54. The attackers suffer heavy losses and are repulsed. 40 British *gefangegen* (prisoners) have been taken by IR 54.

1440 hours: on orders of VI *Armee* the attack ceases. The 18 ID prepares to defend the line it has reached on the west bank. III/IR 30 is placed at the disposal of 18 ID to reinforce the area of Warchin; the bridgehead is consequently fortified and maintained.

The 7 and 35 IDs are able to form a weak bridgehead across the Schelde but are unable to maintain them. By winning their battle of the bridgehead at Calonne, the 18 ID is able to move towards the citadel of Lille. Our radio monitoring units warn our troops, however, that the enemy is tapping our wires and is listening.

Supply Company 18 buries 65 British soldiers, all burnt by flame throwers on the Leuze-Tournai Road. From these casualties IR 54 was able to take weapons and ammunition - the drivers of our munitions transport are so tired that they have been given 24 hours rest.

On this day the 18 ID suffered its heaviest losses throughout the entire campaign: 5 Officers, 19 NCOs and 107 men killed, 15 Officers, 51 NCOs and 339 men wounded, 8 men missing, a total of 544 casualties.

By their own admission, the Germans had made a tactical error in sending IR 51 and 54 across the 'Schelde' without sufficient artillery support. In the words of the 18 ID official history, 'Owing to previous successes we were becoming over confident'. Although IR 51 also managed to cross the river, it only succeeded in seizing several advance positions. Supported by just one battery, elements of IR 54 forced a strong bridgehead at Calonne which it held for some time in spite of strong counter-attacks. Losses were high, however, and fatalities included Major Lengerke, commander of II/IR 54.

Opposing II/IR 54 was the 2nd Bn Royal Norfolk Regiment, the War Diary of which states:-

There was heavy shelling all day. The whole Bde being closely engaged. The forward houses on the river were heavily shelled with trench mortars and the Bn suffered numerous casualties. Bn HQ was established in a large chateau and it was here that the CO, Lieutenant Colonel NP Charlton, Major FR Marshall and 2nd Lieutenant PS Buckingham were all wounded by mortar shell which fell in the porchway of the house. All were evacuated. The enemy continued to put over heavy mortar, artillery and MG fire.

The Bn had difficulty in getting ammunition and food supplies.

Throughout the day, II/IR 54 and the 2nd Royal Norfolks were engaged in bloody attacks and counter-attacks. Private Ernie Leggett, 20 years old at the time, remembers:-

My company was posted along the right flank of the Bn and on the morning of May 21st, just after dawn, all hell and fury of war seemed to break loose. We were bombed and shelled and heavy mortar fire caused heavy casualties and havoc within our ranks.

My Section was in a concrete building which I thought to be an old cement factory, or at least a factory of that type. We were on the second floor overlooking the river with sparse woodland and shrub looking out. There was a balcony type wall about four feet in height which gave us good coverage. At the rear of the building ran a railway line. We could see the Germans at about 150 - 200 yards forming ranks and we played havoc with them with rifle fire.

Twice during the day the Germans attacked but were driven back and it appalled me to see the numbers of enemy soldiers lying dead and wounded. My Section was later down to just four of us, a Lance Corporal, two others and myself.

From our position we could see along to the right flank which was occupied by 'A' Coy HQ. During one quiet spell I heard the unmistakable sound of bursts of machine-gun fire from a *Spandau* (MG 34). About just over a hundred yards away I saw a solitary figure crawling towards a machine-gun post set up on the other side of the river. I saw the figure stop and raise his rifle. I heard shots ring out and almost immediately afterwards saw the machine-gun post blow up. As this was happening I saw another machine-gun post being set up on the soldier's right-hand side, this without doubt out of his view. It opened fire and the soldier lay still. I then had to turn away as action flared up on my front.

The lone British infantryman was Warrant Officer Class II (Company Sergeant Major) George Gristock; his citation, in part, reads:-

After a prolonged attack, the enemy succeeded in breaking through beyond the Company's right flank, which was consequently threatened. Company Sergeant Major Gristock, having organised a part of eight riflemen from Company HQ, went forward to the right flank.

Realising that an enemy machine-gun had moved forward to a position from which it was inflicting heavy casualties on his Company, Company Sergeant Major Gristock went on, with one man acting as connecting file, to try to put it out of action. While advancing he came under heavy machine-gun fire from the opposite bank, and was severely wounded in both legs, his right knee being badly smashed. He nevertheless gained his fire-position, some 20 yards from the enemy machine-gun post undetected, and by well aimed rapid fire killed the machine-gun crew of four and put their gun out of action. He then dragged himself back to the right flank position, from which he refused to be evacuated until contact with the Bn on the right had been established, and the line once more made good.

Company Sergeant Major Gristock was grievously wounded but, like Lance Corporal Nicholls, his initiative and 'conspicuous gallantry' had saved his comrades. Unlike Nicholls, however, Gristock was evacuated home where, as we shall see, his story was to end the following month.

Although both Company Sergeant Major Gristock and Lance Corporal Nicholls were later to receive VCs, there were many other brave deeds performed that day - such as the counter-attack made at Esquelmes led by Major Matthews of the 2nd North Staffordshires - which received no public recognition. Collectively, however, such august deeds and selfless sacrifice enabled the BEF to hold its line.

CSM George Gristock VC, 2nd
Bn Royal Norfolk Regiment.

In what was essentially a battle between infantry supported by artillery (but with no armour engaged on either side) the BEF successfully defended the Escaut line and defeated the German river crossing operations along the entire length of their front. Only one small bridgehead - 1000 yards deep and 3000 yards long - at Peteghem, two miles South West of Oudenaarde, remained in German hands by nightfall.

By late afternoon, in fact, Headquarters VI *Armee* decided, due to mounting and already heavy losses, to withdraw its forces from West of the Escaut and to shift the next attack, intended to surround Lille itself, to a new axis further North, via Courtrai and Ypres. The strongly held Escaut line would be thus be outflanked.

According to the Germans, the task of von Reichenau's VI *Armee*, which fought the BEF on the Escaut, was to divert the enemy from impeding the main offensive by Army Group 'A' in the South. The German intention had been to effect a breakthrough to the North and South of Tournai before advancing West to Seclin, six miles directly South of Lille. Further North, divisions were to advance from

A German infantry column halts just South of Tournai, May 21st, 1940.
Via Peter Taghon.

the area of Oudenaarde in a South Westerly direction towards Armentières. General von Kortzfleisch, commanding XI *Korps* (VI *Armee*) had little intention, however, of playing a subsidiary role and ordered his 19 and 30 IDs to make a determined attack on the high ground at Anseghen, between Oudenaarde and Courtrai. The effect of this move was, in fact, to start driving a wedge between the British and Belgian Armies. This, the Germans maintain, is why the emphasis of their attack was changed to Roulers, to the North West of Courtrai. The Commander-in-Chief of Army Group 'B', *Generaloberst* von Bock, maintained, however, that the role of VI *Armee* was unchanged:-

It is not to defeat the enemy but to contain him without running [VI *Armee's*] head against the Lille fortifications.

These views are complementary but the evidence arising from the attacks in this sector on May 21st suggests that the Germans were repulsed in their attempt to seize crossings over the River Escaut - with significant losses. This delayed the advance of the centre of Army Group 'B'. The attack by XI *Korps* towards Anseghen may have drawn off some Army resources from the Escaut operations, but was within the latitude that the doctrine of *Auftragstaktik* (discretion to command according to a general mission) gave German commanders. Having begun to achieve success along the BEF/Belgian Army boundary, Army Group 'B' began to reinforce this success with (later) spectacular results.

Elsewhere, on the night of May 20th/21st, elements of 2 Pz Div reached the Channel coast near St Valery-sur-Somme; their Corps Commander (XIX *Panzer Korps*), Guderian, spent the following day in Abbeville. Further back, and to the North, Hoth's XV *Panzer Korps* were South and West of Arras.

The counter-attack to the South West of Arras by British tanks from the 1st Army Tank Brigade, with two British infantry battalions and about 70 French tanks in support (commanded by Major General Giffard Martel, a pioneer of armoured forces and associated tactics before the war) achieved local success. The attack caught part of Rommel's 7 Pz Div and the motorised SS *Totenkopf* (Death's Head) Division in the flank.

Hearing of the initial success, Lord Gort passed the message to his troops on the Escaut:-

News from the south reassuring. We stand and fight. Tell your men.

Nearly 400 German prisoners were taken at Arras but eventually the British tanks were halted by Rommel who had to galvanise all the artillery he could find, including his 88mm anti-aircraft guns firing in the ground role, to break up the attack.

Basil Liddell-Hart (later known as the 'Captain who teaches Generals') commented that the mental and moral effect of the British counterstroke at Arras was marked: *this was out of all proportion to the material results*. It imposed a sense of caution on von Runstedt, and on his senior subordinate commanders, including von Kluge of IV *Armee* and even von Kleist.

At 1645 hours on May 21st, Lord Gort met with his three Corps Commanders on the Escaut Front. They made it clear that they would be unable to hold the Escaut line for more than about 24 hours. Lord Gort:-

We discussed a withdrawal to our old frontier defences, where advantage could be taken of the existing blockhouses and trenches, and of the anti-tank ditch. This move would have little effect on the French on our right since it would pivot on the junction point where the Escaut crossed the frontier, but would seriously affect the Belgians, who now held the line of the Escaut from Audenarde to Ghent and of the canal from Ghent to the sea at Terneuzen.

A provisional decision was reached, therefore, for the BEF to withdraw to the prepared defences of the Gort Line along the Belgian frontier. Before doing so, however, Lord Gort had first to reach an agreement with his French superiors - and also the Belgians.

And so, despite the brave efforts of the 1st Army Tank Brigade and their supporting troops at Arras, and despite the gallantry on the River Escaut - which would later see two Victoria Crosses awarded - the BEF was forced to consider another withdrawal. Nevertheless, considerable losses and delay had been inflicted by the BEF on Army Group 'B' in the North, and a salutary check administered to part of Army Group 'A' near Arras.

Consequently those most important options regarding the BEF's withdrawal to the coast remained open. Ultimately this would have a significant effect on the survival of Gort's Army.

CHAPTER NINE

Flames & Bayonets

O n May 22nd, the 3rd Bn Grenadier Guards re-occupied the River Escaut
with two composite companies led by Captains Starkey and Brinkman.
According to the Regimental History 'Every effort was made to bring back the
wounded still lying out and in this Drill Sergeant Randall did particularly heroic
work under heavy fire from across the river'. All such activity, however,
immediately drew heavy machine-gun and artillery fire from the east bank.

For some Guardsmen it was the end of their first day in captivity. Guardsman
Smith, Lance Corporal Everitt and five other Grenadiers joined a number of Welsh
Guardsmen (the latter captured during their heroic defence of Arras) and after
interrogation all were sent by train to Mewe (Weichsel) prison in Poland. They
would later be reunited with Lance Corporal Nicholls in Stalag XXB; it was the
start of five long years behind the barbed wire.

3rd Bn Grenadier Guards War Diary:-

May 22nd:-

2100 hours: Again a heavy arty, mortar and MG barrage came down on the Bde front on our right.
The situation at times appeared critical as reports received stated that the enemy were again
across the canal at the point of junction with 2nd Bn Coldstream Guards, but although enemy
elements crossed the canal and penetrated possibly as far as the main road, the line held. The
casualties during this attack were fairly slight.

During the evening an enemy reconnaissance aircraft appeared over Pecq and seen
to fire a white flare. According to the 1st Guards Brigade War Diary, the same
signal had been noted on May 19th, when the Brigade was spotted whilst on the
move. Although on this occasion eight German bombers soon appeared overhead,
surprisingly no bombs were dropped. Towards dusk, however, pressure increased
on the front of No 1 Company, 2nd Bn Coldstream Guards, which consequently
withdrew, at midnight, from the riverbank to the line of the main road.

At 0200 hours on May 23rd, the 2nd Coldstream started its withdrawal to the
Gort Line in the order Nos 4, 3, 2 then 1 Company. The Carrier Platoon, now
commanded by Lieutenant The Earl of Devon, remained in Pecq as a rearguard.

Corporal Christie:-

Our Carrier Platoon was left as a rear guard whilst the Bn marched off. We were left in Pecq for two hours and when we could pull out one of the carriers would not start. Trying to fix a tow rope *silently* was nerve-wracking!

At 0300 hours on May 23rd, the 3rd Grenadiers also withdrew; War Diary:-

The Bn was lifted behind the defence line prepared by II Corps after its arrival in France. The Bn went into billeting areas, being in Bde Reserve, rested, cleaned up and dug in.
The Bn by now had collected a number of men who had got mixed up with the units on either side during the fighting of the 21/22nd. It was found that (Grenadier) losses amounted to 186, and the Bn was again organised into 4 Coys each of 2 Pls.

Lance Sergeant Constantine:-

We had not marched far when we saw a convoy of trucks stationary under cover of trees. We were told to halt close by and soon after received orders to mount up. It was a real luxury, after all the miles we had walked, to be carried in the trucks but it was not long before we were told to get off after what was a comparatively short journey. I think the trucks must have come up loaded with troops and ammunition so instead of going back empty they gave us a lift before proceeding on a different route.

As the Allies retreated, many bridges across the River Escaut were demolished, including this one at Escanaffles.
Via Peter Taghon.

Later that day, the IV *Armee* was able to cross the River Escaut in safety, the BEF having withdrawn before daybreak. II/IR 12 crossed once more at Esquelmes; *Hauptmann* Ambrosius:-

German *Pioneere* had to work quickly to construct temporary bridges; here such a bridge is crossed by a German Army lorry, again at Escanaffles.
Via Peter Taghon.

Oberleutnant Michael discovered about 60 English soldiers killed during our bridgehead battle of two days previously. Amongst them was a Major West and the Duke of Northumberland. Never before have we found so many Tommies lying out after a battle which proves that the enemy failed to re-occupy the riverline in strength despite our withdrawal. The dead were buried over the next few days in the embattled small wood near the Scheldt in separate graves.

Whilst II/IR 12 buried the 3rd Grenadier casualties from the fighting on May 21st, the Grenadier survivors found themselves manning the Gort Line near Roubaix, some 15 miles North West of their winter position. The 2nd Bn Coldstream Guards had to march six miles West from Pecq to their allotted sector between Leers and Roubaix. This was just North of the positions previously prepared by the 1st Bn Coldstream Guards (of the 7th Guards Brigade) but, according to the War Diary, 'was not in a very advanced state of preparation. 3 Pill Boxes existed and there was an incomplete anti-tank ditch, and that was all'. The Commanding Officer, Lieutenant Colonel Bootle-Wilbraham, 'felt profoundly depressed and apprehensive. In our previous positions we had had a substantial anti-tank obstacle in front of us, but here we had very little protection and would be overlooked at close quarters by the enemy'. Likewise the 2nd Hampshires,

May 23rd, 1940: Pecq, pictured by the Germans from the East bank. Note the low water level caused by the French having opened sluices of Valenciennes (to create inundation's in front of their own positions).
Via Peter Taghon.

British casualties in the Esquelmes sector, as discovered by the Germans on May 23rd, 1940; a mortar barrel appears to protrude from the rearmost weapons pit. This graphically illustrates the tragedy and debris left in the wake of such fierce combat.
Via Peter Taghon.

The original cemetery at Esquelmes contained 49 British soldiers and 69 Germans, the majority of whom fell on May 21st, 1940. The right-hand of the three foremost graves is that of Major FG Matthews, 2nd Bn North Staffordshire Regiment; to his right lies Guardsman WP Meade, 3rd Bn Grenadier Guards (these names being legible on the original photograph). The German graves (the markers of which are styled on the Iron Cross) can be seen running down the right-hand boundary of the cemetery. In September 1940 (when this picture was taken), the Belgian authorities gathered together more BEF casualties from the Escaut and other battles and brought them to rest in this peaceful place. Those burials took place behind the photographer.
Via Peter Taghon.

The wartime marker of Guardsman Hayes' grave, which appears to be situated at the extreme left, back row, in the original cemetery. Such photographs were sent to bereaved families via the International Red Cross.
Mr D Clark.

Der Chef of 5/IR 12, *Oberleutnant* Michael; it was he who supervised burial of both British and German dead at Esquelmes on May 21st, 1940.
Via Peter Taghon.

IR 82 crosses the River Escaut at Pecq, May 23rd, 1940; the 2nd Bn Coldstream Guards had withdrawn just hours previously. Again the low water level can be clearly seen.
Via Peter Taghon.

Men of *Panzer Jäger Abteilung* 31, attached to 31 ID, negotiate the River Escaut on May 23rd, 1940, with a *Pak* 37 anti-tank gun.
Via Peter Taghon.

now in the Gort Line at Vert Bois, also found poorly prepared defences. Considering the hard work undertaken by the 1st Guards Brigade in preparing defences on its own section of the Gort Line throughout the winter, the frustration at finding these inadequate defences can be understood.

General Weygand had met General Pownall, Chief of Staff of the BEF, and the King of the Begians in several conferences at Ypres on May 22nd; Lord Gort also gained a measure of agreement from the Belgian King that he should withdraw his Armies to the Yser. Weygand was determined to develop a major counter-attack, with strong BEF participation, to the South of Arras. The overall situation faced by Lord Gort, however, who shouldered responsibility for Britain's only major expeditionary force, on May 23rd was thus:-

1.   The main strength of the BEF was now withdrawing to the defences prepared during the winter along the Gort Line (from Halluin in the North to Bourghelles, from where the French 1st Army continued to Maulde). The front now held by the BEF was significantly shorter than on the Escaut, thus enabling three divisions to be withdrawn for tasks elsewhere.

2.   Although he was aware that the Belgian Army - situated on the BEF's Northern flank (from Halluin/Menin to Courtrai and Ghent) - was tired, comprised troops of variable quality, and lacked both tanks and aircraft, Lord Gort resolved to maintain contact to continue the defence of Belgium and to protect his left flank.

3.   To the South the French 1st Army was holding a salient from Bourghelles through Maulde, then down the Escaut to Condé and Valenciennes, then swinging West to Denain and Douai. Further West, the flank of Pz Grp Kleist's advance was covered only by improvised forces (from both the BEF and French Army).

4.   Both Churchill and General Weygand (who had succeeded Gamelin on May 20th) were increasing pressure for the BEF to attack Southwards as a part of the French offensive. With very little armour left after the action at Arras, and diminishing hope of reinforcement from the 1st (British) Armoured Division, however, Lord Gort was aware that the Allies would not, in reality, be able to mount such an operation.

The Battle of Arras, in fact, continued until the evening of May 23rd, when it became clear that both PETREFORCE and MACFORCE would have to be withdrawn. Lord Gort:-

Thus concluded the defence of Arras which had been carried out by a small garrison, hastily assembled but well commanded, and determined to fight. It had imposed a valuable delay on a greatly superior enemy force against which it had blocked a vital road centre.

The *Panzer* Divisions had started to swing Northwards, outflanking Arras. In fact, Guderian's XIX *Panzer Korps* was advancing up the Channel coast and starting to invest Boulogne, Calais and even Gravelines - just 10 miles West of Dunkirk itself.

The lesson drawn from the defence of Arras was that, since the number of effective tanks available were now very few, canal lines, if defended, could provide obstacles to delay the *Panzer* Divisions threatening the BEF's right flank. Consequently the canal line running from La Bassee (12 miles South West of Lille) North West to Béthune, Aire, St Omer and thence to the English Channel at Gravelines began to assume great importance. The defence of this canal line was assigned to small *ad hoc* groups of infantry, with some artillery - sometimes just a single gun - in support.

During the evening of May 23rd, the 2nd Bn Coldstream Guards, occupying the Gort Line between Leers and Roubaix, was in contact with the enemy. All civilians had already been evacuated from the area and so rations were supplemented from garden produce and the absent native population's pet rabbits! Drill Sergeant Robinson rounded up the local cattle and collected together a herd of 40 cows which were milked twice daily. At dawn the following morning, each forward Company was ordered to send out a platoon some 600 yards to act as a temporary outpost. 2nd Bn Coldstream Guards War Diary:-

No 4 Coy's had no adventures. No 3 Coy's was commanded by Platoon Sergeant Major Maloney who, mistaking some Germans for a part of his own patrol, was captured, the rest of the patrol getting safely back. No 2 Coy's was commanded by Platoon Sergeant Major Simpson, which, after advancing some 400 yards, got caught in German machine-gun cross fire and suffered heavy casualties. Only three survivors got back.

On May 25th, the Germans resumed their attack in strength. With the enemy driving a wedge through the Belgians between Haluin/Menin and Desselghem (12 miles to the North East of Menin). Lord Gort became increasingly concerned that the Belgian right would become separated from the British left and be forced to withdraw North rather than West. This would permit VI *Armee* to break through to the coast or join up with Pz Grp von Kleist - either way the BEF would be encircled.

During the day, a BEF forward patrol ambushed a German staff car. The occupant, the German Commander-in-Chief's Liaison Officer to Army Group 'B' escaped, but the vehicle contained vital intelligence documents concerning the attack of VI *Armee*. An analysis of this unexpected intelligence indicated that IX *Korps* was detailed to attack towards Ypres, and VI *Korps* towards Wytschaete (six miles further South). VI *Armee* was to be reinforced by both X *Korps* and 61 ID, all of which suggested that this attack was the *Schwerpunkt*.

Lord Gort:-

I considered it vitally urgent to prolong the British front without delay northwards to Ypres, along the old Ypres-Comines Canal, now practically dry, and round Ypres itself to the line of the Yser Canal..... By 6 pm that night I was convinced that the steps I had taken to secure my left flank would prove insufficient to meet the growing danger in the north. The pattern of the enemy pincer attack was becoming clearer. One movement from the south-west on Dunkirk had already developed and was being held; the counterpart was now developing on the Belgian front. The gap between the British left and the Belgian right, which had been threatening the whole day, might at any time become impossible to close: were this to happen, my last hope of reaching the coast would be gone.

With the Belgian front crumbling to the north, close to the boundary with the BEF, Lord Gort realised that to save his Army there was no alternative but to abandon plans for a counter attack to the South, and withdraw behind the Ypres-Comines Canal and those positions covering Ypres. The 50th Division was ordered to join II Corps immediately, and 5th Division followed soon afterwards.

Lord Gort was not alone in fearing a Belgian collapse. General Blanchard, appointed to replace General Billotte (who died following a road accident on May 21st), agreed that the opportunity for a successful counter-attack Southwards had passed, and that the situation on both flanks now made a further withdrawal towards the sea imperative. The joint decision was made, therefore, to withdraw behind the River Lys. *The unilateral decisions made by Lord Gort on May 25th, and the subsequent defence of Comines, effectively laid the foundations for the successful withdrawal to Dunkirk, and indeed the preservation of the BEF.* Lord Gort:-

The layout of the BEF was now beginning to take its final shape. Starting from what could be described as a normal situation with Allied troops on the right and left, there had developed an ever lengthening defensive right flank. This had then become a semi-circular line, with both flanks resting on the sea, manned by British, French and Belgians. Later the position became a corridor in shape. The southern end of this corridor was blocked by the French 1st Army; and each side was manned, for the greater part of its length, by British troops. Next to the sea were French troops on the west, and French and British troops on the eastern flank.

The immediate problem was to shorten this perimeter. British and French forces were together holding a front of 128 miles of which 97 miles were held by British troops, though some sectors were held jointly with the French. The virtual closing of Dunkirk as a port of entry was making a supply situation ever more difficult, and the ammunition situation permitted only of very restricted expenditure.

By the following day, the military situation had deteriorated further still. At 1030 hours on May 26th, Lord Gort had received a telegram from the Secretary of State, The Rt Hon Anthony Eden:-

I have had information all of which goes to show that French offensive from Somme cannot be made in sufficient strength to hold any prospect of functioning with your Allies in the north. Should this prove to be the case you will be faced with a situation in which the safety of the BEF will predominate. In such conditions only course open to you may be to fight your way back to west where all beaches and ports east of Gravelines will be used for embarkation. Navy will provide fleet of ships and small boats and RAF would give full support. As withdrawal may have to begin very early preliminary plans should be urgently prepared.... Prime Minister is seeing M. Reynaud tomorrow afternoon when the whole situation will be clarified including the attitude of French to the possible move.

Lord Gort responded to the effect that a withdrawal North-Westwards had already been agreed with the French, and that news from the Belgian front was 'disquieting'. He concluded:-

I must not conceal from you that a great part of the BEF and its equipment will inevitably be lost even in best circumstances.

A further telegram arrived from the War Office during the afternoon:-

Prime Minister had conversation with M. Reynaud this afternoon. Latter fully explained to him the situation and resources French Army. It is clear that it will not be possible for French to deliver attack on the south in sufficient strength to enable them to effect junction with Northern Armies. In these circumstances no course open to you but to fall back upon coast.... M. Reynaud communicating General Weygand and latter will no doubt issue orders in this sense forthwith. You are now authorised to operate towards coast forthwith in conjunction with French and Belgian Armies.

The enormity of these instructions should not be missed. A week before, in fact, Lord Gort had foreseen that such a course of action might prove necessary, but at that time this was met with disapproval by both Churchill and the Chiefs of Staff. Some might detect a certain irony in Lord Gort's order to withdraw to positions near Ypres: from October 1914 until 1918, this area was held by the British Army at immense cost of human life; Lord Gort himself, in fact, had fought in those battles with gallantry and distinction. A generation later, however, after just <u>16 days</u>, the BEF was being forced to make urgent arrangements for an evacuation back across the Channel to England, leaving most of its equipment behind.

It has been said that between May 23rd and 26th, 'the fate of entire empires was at stake', but ironically the 1st Guards Brigade Sector was hardly disturbed; for the first time in over two weeks these well disciplined but very tired soldiers had been able to rest.

3rd Bn Grenadier Guards War Diary:-

May 26/27th:-

Considerable enemy air activity. Bombs were dropped all over the Bn area including two very near misses at Bn HQ which was in the cellar of a carpet factory. Orders were received during the afternoon for the Bn to be relieved at 2230 hours by 2 Hamps and to move by route march across the River Lys, and in company with the reserve Bns of 1 Div to cover 1 Div front on that river. The Bn marched out at 2315 hours and after a tiring march of 18 miles, the roads being crowded with troops, transport and guns, the Bn crossed the Lys at Le Touquet [not the coastal holiday resort but located three miles North of Armentières] and Coys marched onto their positions at about 1600 hours. At 1630 hours a written message from 1 Gds Bde was received to march at once to Dunkirk and embark for the United Kingdom.

At this point a Gunner Battery Commander arrived at Battalion HQ of the 3rd Grenadiers with most alarming news: the 5th Division's line along the Ypres-Comines Canal, north of Comines, had broken. The Germans were apparently already pushing towards the high ground at Messines. This was disastrous, as if the northern arm of the German pincer had pushed Westwards from this point, the ports of Ostend and Dunkirk might have fallen and the BEF encircled. General Alexander's *Aide de Camp*, Captain George Thorne, Grenadier Guards, then arrived on a motor cycle and sought out the Commanding Officer, Major Allan Adair:-

I found the Bn having a much needed 10 minute halt, looking supremely confident but dog tired and covered by a layer of dust. I was filled with some trepidation being only a Supplementary Reserve Officer and having heard of the fierce and successful fight on the River Escaut. My reception at Bn Headquarters was mixed. Major Adair was his usual cheerful, optimistic self, lying in a ditch with his feet up. He told me he was delighted to see the son of his 1917 Commanding Officer doing his bit, and of course the Bn would set off at once to plug the gap. The Bn Second-in-Command, Major Osbert Smith, took a different line and said it was a pity I had not fallen off my bike miles away!

3rd Bn Grenadier Guards War Diary:-

May 27th:-

..... information was received.... that the line held by 5 Div .... had broken. The Bns of 1 Div in the area were put under command of 5 Div and ordered to go at once to restore the situation which was very serious. The enemy in their westward drive were threatening Warneton. Therefore the Bn quickly collected at the Brickery and marched through Ploegsteert to Ploegsteert Wood.

Once again the 3rd Grenadiers were in familiar territory: 'Plugstreet Wood' was known, of course, to their forebears, to most of the Senior Officers, and to some of the older soldiers who had fought there in the Great War. During the day, the men of the 1/7th Royal Warwickshires were also reminded of the First World War; Corporal Hawkins:-

At Comines we came down a track alongside a 1914-18 British War Cemetery - 'Sanctuary Wood', I think it was. Beyond the cemetery wall was this old wrecked canal, the embankment being about level with the cemetery wall. On this corner we started digging in, preparing a position which overlooked both the canal and countryside on other side of same. In places the canal was almost blocked, in fact, by large lumps of masonry and debris from the Great War, during which the canal was all but destroyed in the heavy fighting there. As we dug our trenches through the roots of trees and bushes, we came across many macabre or rusting artefacts of the 'War to End All Wars'. There were bullets, cartridge clips, Lewis gun ammunition pans, shell fragments, helmets, personal equipment, barbed wire, parts of weapons and even the odd bone! We all knew that another battle lay ahead, and indeed recognised the importance of it.

At 1730 hours, Major Adair attended a briefing at Headquarters 5th Division, located in 'Plugstreet Wood', in company with Lieutenant Colonel Butterworth, Commanding Officer of the 2nd North Staffordshires (alongside whom the 3rd Grenadiers had fought on May 21st). The Divisional Commander, General Franklyn, gave his orders to the Officers present: throughout the day, the 143rd Brigade had been hard pressed, and the Germans had eventually established a bridgehead between Comines and Houthem. The bend in the canal at Comines was vital, the General explained, as if the Germans were able to make progress beyond it then the entire Dunkirk perimeter would be in great danger. The only reserves available to him were the 3rd Grenadiers and 2nd North Staffordshires, the Commanding Officers of which General Franklyn ordered to retake the canal line between Comines and Houthem.

3rd Bn Grenadier Guards War Diary:-

.... 13/18 Hussars and the Black Watch had already moved down south of the Armentières - Comines Rly, but were held up on the outskirts of Comines. The two (counter-attacking) Bns were to form up facing east on the line of the road La Basse-Ville - Messines and advance forward across country to re-take line of Ypres - Comines Canal. This road was to crossed at 2000 hours. The Comd Officer pointed out the improbability of getting there in time, but the Bn was told to go on as quickly as possible.
The line was crossed at 2030 hours, the Bn in square formation with No 1 Coy right, 2 Coy left,

4 Coy right rear and 3 Coy left rear. Bn HQ and Carriers in between and behind the rear Coys advanced across the open. 'A' Echelon and the Mortars under Major OWD Smith and the remainder of HQ Coy with Major ASP Murray and Lieutenant FJRP Needham followed by road and established themselves in Warneton. Efforts made to get touch with North Staffs on the starting line subsequently failed. As it was growing dusk the Bn came under SA [Small Arms] and shell fire, but in spite of casualties pushed on to the objective. However it was soon found that the Bns on our right and left had been ordered to hold the line from Mai Cornet - rd junc (627536) and therefore the Bn consolidated on the line of River Korketeer. Owing to the very wide frontage, large gaps existed on the flanks of the Bn.

As previously indicated by Captain George Thorne, the 3rd Grenadiers had already won respect and admiration for the action on the Escaut; others watched in awe, as reported by an Officer of the Royal Artillery:-

I saw the Grenadiers form up in perfect order, and then advance towards the enemy calmly and cheerfully. I watched them disappear over the ridge in the setting sun - it was a most comforting and inspiring sight.

Lance Sergeant Constantine:-

After another long march we arrived in darkness at the area where our No 4 Company had to start its part in the attack. After a short period the order came to "Fix Bayonets" and to spread out into extended order. We then advanced forward into country that was mostly flat with some fields separated by hedges. We went forward a mile or two without contacting the enemy.

Major Adair's Grenadiers evoked the highest admiration amongst all the soldiers that they passed on the way in, the Guardsmen showing no sign of exhaustion. The ferocity of their attack, however, would later be confirmed by Lance Corporal Kenning of the 1st Bn Oxfordshire & Buckinghamshire Light Infantry; wounded and captured during the enemy's initial attack, he had yet to be evacuated when the Grenadiers arrived on the scene, bayonets fixed.

The counter-attack was preceded by a bombardment fired by some 100 guns drawn from 97 Army Field Regiment, four Medium Regiments and one battery of Heavy Artillery from I Corps. Soon many buildings around the canal were ablaze, which unfortunately silhouetted the Guardsmen against the flames, and the whole front was vividly illuminated by glowing tracer ammunition. At 2050 hours, the enemy, IR 176 of the 61 ID, reported that violent hand to hand fighting had broken out. As if scenting danger, however, the Germans had withdrawn from Maurice Bonte's farm just before the Grenadiers arrived, and soon Major Adair's men were pressing on beyond that of Emile Ghesquière, the buildings of which were burning fiercely.

As the Grenadiers moved up to the Canal, German activity caught Captain

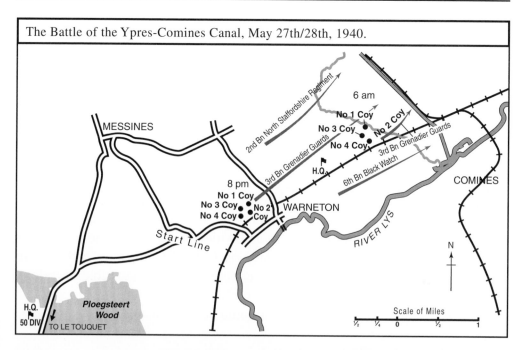

The Battle of the Ypres-Comines Canal, May 27th/28th, 1940.

Brinkman's attention in the Woestyn's house; some well aimed grenades had the required effect, after which Brinkman and his Sergeant Ryder watched wounded enemy soldiers being evacuated across a makeshift bridge. Before they could open fire, both men were wounded when a shell exploded nearby. Brinkman and Ryder were subsequently captured and taken by the Germans to their First Aid Post, situated in the house attacked.

By 2300 hours, the Grenadier leading companies were well forward, so Captain Starkey's No 3 Company was moved up in close support of No 1 Company, which had suffered many losses. No 4 Company, now led by Captain CW Norman Barnett, consequently filled the gap now existing between the leading companies. Lance Sergeant Constantine:-

We were told to get down in a field and be prepared should an attack come our way. Everyone lay there silently in almost continuous rain, for hours, waiting for the next orders to come. So passed the rest of what was a most miserable night.

The Grenadiers still had no contact with the 2nd North Staffordshires, however, and the Grenadier patrol sent to try and communicate with Lieutenant Colonel Butterworth was, according to Major Adair, 'heavily shot at'. Second Lieutenant Lance Aubrey Fletcher's platoon was moved to protect this flank, but also ran into trouble: Aubrey Fletcher himself was wounded and captured. Also wounded was Second Lieutenant Lane-Fox, who was safe but evacuated later the following day. Lieutenant Crompton Roberts, sent to recover wounded from in front of the burning Collie-Baelen farmhouse, was killed during the night.

German losses were also high. In front of the bitterly fought over Woestyn's house lay the bodies of Major Riedelsdorfer, *Kommandeur* of III/IR 176, together with his adjutant, *Leutnant* Ganske, and *Oberleutnant* Gorg. The latter had considered it unworthy to lie down during a battle and took a bullet in the chest; dragging himself upright he told his men "*Oberleutnant* Gorg announces his death", then collapsed and died.

The counter-attack by the 3rd Grenadiers stunned the enemy who consequently over-estimated the Battalions' strength and withdrew. In fact, Major Adair was beset by communication difficulties and Nos 1 and 2 Companies had been so reduced in numbers as to be almost non-effective. It was impossible, therefore, for the weakened counter-attacking force to summon further support and reinforcements, meaning that their gains could not be consolidated.

At midnight on May 27th/28th, the Belgian Army surrendered. The immediate effect upon the BEF was that its Northern flank was now open. General Montgomery's 3rd Division was consequently ordered to 'side-step' to the North, thus extending the BEF's line to Hondschoote on the Yser.

3rd Bn Grenadier Guards War Diary:-

May 28th:-

Repeated enemy attacks throughout the early morning were supported by accurate Mortar and Arty shelling. Ammunition in the forward Coys started to run out and was sent up under great difficulties by Carrier over appalling country. One Carrier was ditched and lost. One Carrier of the 13/18 Hussars was salved by 3 Coy, but was almost immediately hit and set on fire by an A/Tk Gun. The Mortars were brought up to Bn HQ in a farm about (631512). The men had had no rations since a short hard ration tea on May 27th.
Enemy infiltration, very skilfully carried out, and was supported by continual accurate Mortar and MG fire. This caused the reserve Coys and Bn HQ to take to the ditches and start the fight which lasted all day. Casualties were heavy but the posts never wavered. Rations and tea were brought up to Bn HQ in a truck by Drill Sergeant Randall, but it was impossible to get them out to Coys. A direct hit by a bomb on a Carrier set fire to same at about 0900 hours which set fire to the buildings, and a half dozen casualties were sustained amongst the personnel of Bn HQ. The casualties were evacuated on the truck which brought the rations.... During the day Lieutenant PF Thorne [brother of Captain George Thorne, both Officers being sons of General Andrew Thorne, Commanding 48th (South Midland) Division] was wounded and evacuated and the Adjutant was slightly wounded.

Lance Sergeant Constantine:-

As dawn approached an order was received from Platoon HQ to the effect that I was to take my Section forward and occupy what looked like a small brick built barn a short distance ahead; the enemy were behind the hedge in the field beyond it.

We crawled very cautiously to the barn and managed to get in by the single door on our nearside. We had got there before the enemy. The barn had been used as a storeroom and was empty except for a pile of potatoes against the far wall. I told the men to equal themselves around the walls and to knock out a brick or two for firing positions. I set an example myself by knocking a slot hole just above the pile of potatoes. It was a great help that some of the bricks were loose and in places there was only one layer. We had just prepared ourselves when the enemy put in a big attack. I had got myself in a good position, lying at an angle on the potatoes, and could see the firing had started from the far hedge of the field about two hundred yards to our front. We saw plenty of movement and returned the fire; much to our satisfaction we saw several enemy soldiers go down, not to move again. They had started coming forward and some had managed to get into the long grass and small hollows in different parts of the field and were trying to surround us. Bullets were penetrating the brickwork of the old barn and one or two would ricochet amongst us. Now and again one would come through the wall and specks of white would appear where the bullets had gone through the potatoes.

We were all occupied firing at different movements and targets of what we knew were the enemy. The Bren gunner was standing up and firing through a hole in the wall to my left when suddenly he screamed in agony, his weapon falling to the floor - he had been hit in the eye and was in a terrible state. I got to him quickly and held him to see what could be done. I tried to get his hands away from his eye to inspect the damage but he broke away from me screaming in pain. He ran to the end of the barn where two of the Section tried to hold him but again he broke away. Before we could stop him he ran out of the door in sheer agony, out of his mind. He disappeared from sight and I felt badly, but because of the situation there was nothing further I could do. I then picked up his Bren, intending to use it myself, but found that a bullet had penetrated the mechanism and gone half way through the metal casing then out again. As it could not therefore be fired I hurried back to my position with my rifle. Instead of things looking better, however, I found that they were worse. Light mortar bombs were falling in our area and I could just pin-point where they were being fired from - behind the hedge at the end of the field. Once they got the range on the barn I knew that we would not stand a chance.

When the Bren gunner was wounded and I was away from my post, one of the enemy got into some cover some 25 yards away. I had not been back two minutes when suddenly he got up as though from nowhere and ran towards the barn raising an automatic weapon, preparing to fire. I fired instantly and saw him fall with the weapon beside him. At the same time I saw a movement to my right. In a split second it passed through my mind that once I had taken my eyes off him and was doing something else, if he was only slightly wounded he could still do considerable damage with that gun beside him. To take no chance I fired another shot then concentrated again to where I had seen the other movement, putting a few quick rounds into that area.

The attack went on well into the afternoon, when it looked as though they were giving up the attempt. At last we were able to light up a cigarette, something we had not managed to do these last few hours. By late afternoon it had become very quiet, although the normal artillery gunfire was still in progress, so all we could do was keep good observation everywhere. I found my gaze continually returning to the man I had killed who was lying in the grass about a dozen yards away. I could see half of his face which was turned as though looking up at the sky. Also I thought of our Bren gunner, for whom I had great admiration but never did find out how he fared; naturally I sincerely hope that he ran into our own lines and received medical attention in time.

It had started to rain heavily whilst we continued looking out. My eyes searched the far hedges of the field and likely cover where the enemy might remain, but still my gaze returned to and eventually settled on this dead German. It had become so quiet after all that had happened and now I could see the rain falling on his upturned face. I know that I had hit and probably killed many others but I had not had to look so close at their faces as I had with this man. Because of the silence I got thinking of his parents, whether he was married and had children, or perhaps a girlfriend. At that moment I could not get these thoughts out of my mind. A tear came to my eye and I knew then that I must force myself to think of something different.

We remained in our positions and it was getting near darkness when word got through to us that the enemy had been held by our Bn. It was not long afterwards that we got orders to leave and we learned that the Bn had suffered many casualties.

Some members of the Battalion had, in fact, worked courageously to bring in wounded left lying out during this battle. Later, Sergeant Norton Bullock of the No 4 Company Stretcher Bearer Section would receive the Distinguished Conduct Medal. His citation reads:-

Sergeant Norton Bullock DCM,
3rd Bn Grenadier Guards.
Mrs. I. Bullock.

On the 27/28 May 1940 on the Lys Canal this NCO was in Command of a squad of stretcher bearers. He was continuously in the front line and succeeded in bringing in a number of wounded under heavy fire. His work was invaluable throughout the battle.

At 2200 hours on May 28th, Major Adair received orders from 143 Brigade HQ, under whose orders the 3rd Grenadiers now came, to withdraw on Messines. The transport of 'A' Echelon moved up from Warneton to collect the Battalion, the Guardsmen dashing from their positions and mounting up whilst the Anti-Aircraft Platoon provided a rearguard. The Grenadiers were proud that they had not lost a single inch of the ground they had been ordered to hold. Whilst collecting at Messines, the Bn was shelled, suffering two casualties. Having embussed, the Bn travelled via Poperinge to Eikhoek, arriving at 1000 hours on May 29th. Eikhoek lay to the North of the Yser, the next canal line, behind which lay only the Basse - Calonne Canal and the Dunkirk - Furnes Canal. The 3rd Grenadiers were met at Eikhoek by the GOC 5 Division, Major General Franklyn, who (3rd Bn Grenadier Guards War Diary refers) '... thanked them for restoring the position and holding the line of the River Lys at a most critical moment on 27/28 May'; when later addressing Officers in Northern Ireland, he said:-

I give this example of the highest form of discipline. Last May, when my Division was being hard pressed on the Ypres-Comines Canal I was given a Bn of the Grenadier Guards as a reserve. After marching well over 20 miles on a very hot day they arrived at my Headquarters at 7.30 pm. An hour later they were put into a vital counter-attack in the half light, over unknown ground. They advanced as efficiently as if on a field day at Pirbright - and their efforts were completely successful.

The German 61 ID history states that:-

The British succeeded in making a breakthrough during the night of May 27th/28th amongst III/ IR 176; bitter hand to hand fighting ensued.... As a result of losses, 61 ID took III/176 back across the Ypres Canal. The Regiment was relieved by IR 151. The Division ordered a renewed attack in the same direction for May 28th. The great battle in Flanders reached its peak.... From hedges and houses, from haystacks and roofs, the admirably camouflaged opponent, well organised for defence, maintained fire. Snipers behind trees with automatic weapons swept the meadows with their fire, British armoured cars standing well hidden behind hedges were adapted as strong points. Lying on the flat slopes our *Kompanies* were exposed to heavy enemy fire and soon had to dig in. Unceasing rain hampered vision and made it even more difficult to attack.

Enemy artillery fire systematically strafed the front line right up to the top of the Regimental Command Post. Our own aerial reconnaissance had noticed the concentration of enemy armoured forces near Poperinge, and soon the enemy armoured attack was under way. A few tanks were wiped out but, on the other hand, our own losses mounted: *Oberleutnant* Christofzik, *Leutnant* Mendritzki (both of IR 151) and numerous junior Officers and men were killed. Amongst the fallen was also the son of the Divisional *Kommodore*. The increasingly heavy rain had thoroughly

After much bitter fighting, and having been held at bay for several precious days, German
troops eventually cross the Ypres-Comines Canal.
Via Peter Taghon.

soaked the clay soil. The men stood knee deep in water. Flanders mud clung to the whole body and made weapons and equipment filthy.

In between the forward IRs of the Division a gap had been torn, which III/151, whose 10 Kp had been sent back to Advanced HQ of VI *Armee*, could no longer close. This task was taken over by I/151, under heavy enemy fire; during this attack *Leutnant* Nitzky fell. Yet another attack ordered by the Division, for 2200 hours, was given up. The *Kompanies* spent a bitterly cold night in the muddy shell holes and ditches. Losses were high, and essentially our attacks had won no ground whatsoever.

On May 29th, the Germans were once again determined to destroy British resistance so that the VI *Armee* could link up with Hoth's *panzers*, then only 15 miles away between Cassel and Hazebrouck. Three infantry divisions were called in: 18 ID to attack Ypres, 31 ID to capture Hollebeke, and 61 ID Mont Kemmel (which rose some 100 feet above the surrounding countryside, dominating the area between Poperinghe and Bailleul). When enemy scouts cautiously probed forward early in the morning, according to the 61 ID history:-

...they met no resistance. Warneton was reached by assault troops of 10/151 and the remaining weak enemy defenders, a rearguard of the English Grenadier Guards from 5 Division, were captured. By 0900 hours our Bns were advancing on Messines and Warneton. They gathered together in Messines and now the Division, in marching column, pushed westwards in sunny, windy weather. On the Kemmel, so much fought around in the Great War, British ammunition dumps blew up. The hilly countryside lay yellow in the afternoon sun. To the left the French town of Bailleul was smoking. The Belgian-French frontier was crossed at last.

Although the BEF had left behind around 1,000 dead during this battle, something which must also be emphasised is the importance of this line having held. The Official History of the War in France and Flanders states that:-

The 5th Division's staunch defence of the Ypres-Comines Canal front had defeated the assault of three German divisions and certainly saved II Corps and equally the BEF.

The strength of the 3rd Grenadiers, however, had been reduced to just nine Officers and 270 Other Ranks.

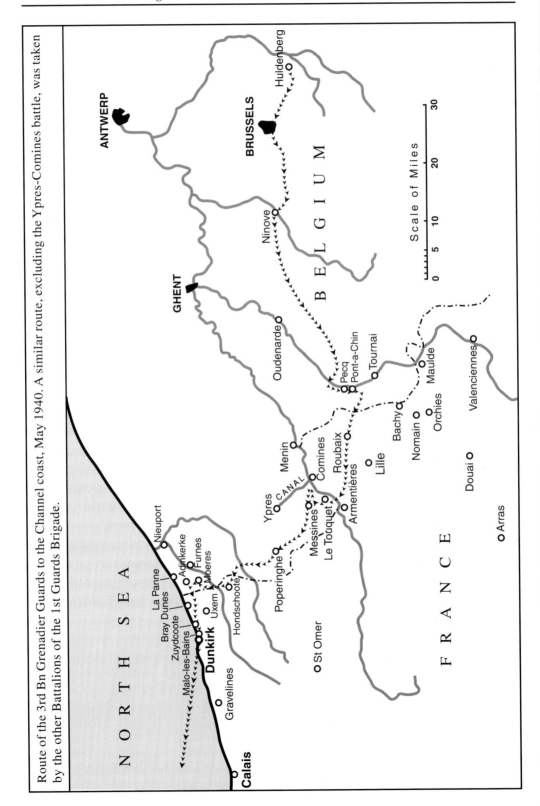

Route of the 3rd Bn Grenadier Guards to the Channel coast, May 1940. A similar route, excluding the Ypres-Comines battle, was taken by the other Battalions of the 1st Guards Brigade.

NORTH SEA

Calais

Gravelines

Dunkirk

Malo-les-Bains

Zuydcoote

Bray Dunes

La Panne

Adinkerke

Nieuport

Furnes

Moeres

Uxem

Hondschoote

St Omer

Poperinghe

Messines

Le Toutquet

Armentières

Ypres

CANAL

Menin

Comines

Roubaix

Lille

Bachy

Nomain

Orchies

Douai

Arras

Valenciennes

Maulde

Tournai

Pont-a-Chin

Pecq

Oudenarde

GHENT

Ninove

BELGIUM

ANTWERP

BRUSSELS

Huldenberg

FRANCE

Scale of Miles

0   5   10   20   30

CHAPTER TEN

Dunkirk

The first British troops to be evacuated from Dunkirk were administration units and certain key personnel, this being to ease the increasingly acute supply problem. All units not needed to continue the battle, in fact, were sensibly ordered to withdraw. The fighting troops were naturally required to stay until the very end. To facilitate the embarkation of the BEF, it was clearly necessary to arrange a robust defence of the bridgehead; Lord Gort:-

The perimeter was to extend from Gravelines south-eastwards to the Canal de la Colme, along the canal to Bergues and thence by Furnes and Nieuport to the Belgian coast. In fact, the French were by now evacuating Gravelines and the western part of the perimeter, and in the process of going back to the line of the Mardyk Canal from the sea to Spyker, on the Canal de la Colme. The French were to be responsible for the defence of the western half of the perimeter as far as Bergues inclusive, and the British the eastern half.

Lieutenant General Sir Ronald Adam had been given the task of organising the Dunkirk perimeter, the troops defending it being known as ADAMFORCE. Corps boundaries, assembly areas and the layout of beaches were rapidly organised. It was important to avoid traffic congestion within the bridgehead, so no British transport, other than that required for tactical, supply or medical purposes, was allowed North of the canal line. Lord Gort:-

The British Sector of the Dunkirk perimeter had its right at Bergues, and thence followed the canals to Furnes and Nieuport. These places were old-fashioned fortified towns, easy to defend but affording good bombing targets. The destruction of the bridges presented no difficulty, and all were in fact blown in time by British or French troops except that in Nieuport which was wide and solid, and could not be demolished before the arrival of the enemy. Two natural switch lines were available: the canal from Bergues to Dunkirk and the Canal des Moeres from Dunkirk south-east towards Hondschoote.

Immediately north of this line came the inundations, extending from Bergues over the district of Moeres to a width varying from one to three miles. Except in a few places, they did not cover the roads but were designed to leave them clear, while preventing deployment.

To the north of the inundations was more low-lying land; then came the Bergues-Furnes Canal, and the main lateral road from Furnes to Dunkirk. Finally there was the narrow strip of dunes giving way to a wide, open beach running the whole length of the position and shelving very slowly out to sea. There were no quays or piers whatever except those at Dunkirk itself. At intervals of about a mile along the shore lay the seaside resorts of Coxyde, La Panne, Bray Dunes and Malo-les-Bains.

The position was then divided into three Corps areas, each including a collecting area outside the perimeter, a sector of the canal line and a sector of beach.

The Admiralty had placed Naval arrangements for embarkation - Operation DYNAMO - in the hands of Vice Admiral Sir Bertram Ramsey, Flag Officer Dover. Rear Admiral WF Wake-Walker was sent to Dunkirk to work out detailed plans, and steps were taken to collect a large number of small ships and boats for taking troops from the beach out to the waiting ships. Although at first the military improvised its own beach parties, Naval Ratings eventually manned and organised the beaches at La Panne, Bray Dunes and Malo-les-Bains (one beach to each Corps). For some days Dunkirk itself had been heavily bombed. During a particularly heavy attack on May 27th, lorry columns had been set on fire within the perimeter, and a pall of black smoke from burning oil tanks hung continuously over the town and docks. For many Spitfire pilots taking off from such forward aerodromes as Manston and Hawkinge in Kent, this pall of black smoke was immediately seen and would remain an enduring memory. The damage to Dunkirk harbour itself, however, was such that it was only accessible to small ships. As a result, all troops were sent to the beaches east of the town to there await embarkation.

3rd Bn Grenadier Guards War Diary:-

May 30th:-

The Bn lay in a wood and rested during the day. At 1500 hours the Commanding Officer was sent for and ordered to come under Comd 50 Div to be ready to move and support 151 Bde which was giving ground under enemy pressure.
The Adjutant was evacuated.
A recce was made by the Comd Officer and Coy Cmdrs of the area over which the Bn was likely to counter-attack. The area was west of Bulscamp. The Bn was promised the support of two Fd Regts and a lot of MGs to help the counter attack. The Bn was not, however, called upon to do this.

Lance Sergeant Constantine:-

In Belgium we had seen many vehicles abandoned, but now in France it was hard to believe the number being left on the road side. Most of them had been left and made completely immobile so that they could be made no use of by the Germans. Nevertheless there were many we had to deal with by putting a bayonet through the tyres and petrol tank. Many had been set fire too and smoke was drifting all over the area.

After the Ypres-Comines battle I remember how everyone seemed tired, both physically and mentally. I must add that everyone still had a high sense of morale, and a great feeling of comradeship existed amongst the few survivors of our company. The men in my section had all been exceptional.
We had all got on well and there had been no disagreements. Everything had been taken very calmly, including the hardships, shortage of rations and changes of orders received from time to time.

3rd Bn Grenadier Guards War Diary:-

May 31st:-

Certain amount of Arty fire which fortunately did not reach the Bn. Much air activity in the afternoon. The Comd Officer was again summoned to 50th Div HQ. The Bn was ordered to go to Moeres by MT (3-ton lorries) to support 151 Bde, part of which had been driven back in some disorder from the canal at Bulscamp. A dangerous gap had occurred on the Bde front and the Bn took up a posn to fill this gap in failing light. However the enemy did not press forward and at 0230 hours the 1st Bn was ordered to withdraw to the outskirts of Dunkirk. This withdrawal was carried out without difficulty. GOC 50 Div (Major General Martel) met the Bn at Zuydcoote and thanked all for the part they had played in restoring the situation.

Lance Sergeant Constantine:-

After a brief period of rest we carried on marching towards Dunkirk, artillery fire increasing. Frequently we passed units which were disorganised, or they were passing us when we halted. Most rations had been finished and the last day or two we were lucky to even have a packet of Army ration biscuits left. When we passed abandoned trucks and other vehicles we would often look to see if there were any rations within.

As we approached the town of Dunkirk, everything looked like a mass of destruction. Heavy shelling was prominent and there was a complete state of bombardment. Soon we were able to see the damage ourselves caused during the previous couple of weeks or so. It was pitiful to see the buildings - shops and houses all blown apart. Private belongings, such as furniture, beds and mattresses, were hanging from different parts of buildings that had taken the full force of bombs and shells. Going through one street we stepped over bricks and rubble covering the ground. Just ahead, on my right, I could see a soldier sitting on the ground with his back resting against a low wall with a cigarette in his mouth. I thought at the time that he didn't much look like he cared less about what was going on, taking it easy there having a smoke. I was just going to say something when I realised that he was dead. We continued through the town, passing several bodies - a sight to which we were now accustomed - but a sight that turned me most was a horse, the side of which was blown away.

At last we got through the town and reached the dunes at the rear of the beach. We then had orders to wait until such time as arrangements could be made for a ship to transport our 3rd Bn - or what was left of it - back to England.

The scene was recorded in the 61 ID KTB:-

The BEF was fleeing to the sea. The roads were blocked with columns of British vehicles: lorries with munitions and all kinds of equipment, motorised supply and baggage vans, radio cars, guns of all sizes from armoured anti tank guns to the 21 cm heavy guns had run helplessly into each other in the narrow lanes. For miles around, all major and minor roads were blocked in this way. In between was a gigantic abandoned vehicle park. In the middle of this chaos, after eliminating some weak resistance, the Division rested. By night there was lively enemy aerial activity; numerous flares lit up the wretched vehicle graveyard.

The remnants of Major Adair's 3rd Bn Grenadier Guards reached the beach at Zuydcoote on May 31st. Lance Sergeant Constantine recalls the evacuation as experienced by those Grenadiers lucky enough to get that far:-

British troops await embarkation at Zuydcoote.
Grenadier Guards.

Very heavy gunfire was going on and explosions could be heard close by. Orders were given to dig in, which was easy because the ground was mainly sand and tufts of grass. Nevertheless it represented a means of cover and protection, and we lost no time in getting down to a depth that would get our heads below ground level. During the night a shell landed close to our trench and those of us in it got covered almost to the waist by the loose sand which had given way and fallen in. We managed to remove it but spent an uncomfortable time until daybreak.

From where we had made our rough trenches we could look along the beach and out to sea, and observe the damage that had been done. There were three or four ships which had been destroyed, with the nose of one vessel sticking up out of the water; how many had been sunk no-one could say. Along the beach were bodies of the men who had been killed and died there. Some had been covered with pieces of tarpaulin or some other type of cover. Troops were in scattered groups and queues waited for any type of ship or craft that would get them off the beach. Some were wading out to anything that floated, large or small, that would take them across the Channel.

During the day we were informed that it had been arranged for our Bn to be picked up by a ship when it managed to pull alongside the Mole, which was the name of a long wooden pier that stretched out to sea from the beach at Dunkirk.

We left what I called our trenches, but which in reality were no more than holes in the sand, then made our way along the beach towards the Mole which was a few hundred yards to our left. I don't think we had gone much more than 100 yards when we were told to wait because the ship had not been able to get in yet. There was a great many of us together there, waiting, when a *Stuka* appeared travelling in the direction of the beach. Another was making a dive a little further away, releasing its bombs. I think every one of us in that large group said a little prayer when the first plane was directly overhead; if they all felt like myself then they must have felt it was our last. It looked as though our prayer was answered when the aircraft carried on over our heads, turned and flew out to sea where it dropped its bombs. The relief could be seen in every face, and we thought that the German aircrew concerned must have had some sympathy for us. Soon afterwards we received orders to return to where we had started from as another attempt would have to be made later.

On the way back to our makeshift trenches we passed some of the unfortunates lying there in the sand. I noticed one whose face was covered and his webbing buckled round his waist; his ammunition pouches were crammed full. I unfastened the pouches and was, in addition to ammunition, a full tin of 50 cigarettes and an emergency ration. I said "God Bless you", and I really meant it.

When we arrived back at our sand trenches, I opened the sealed tin of emergency rations, broke up the hard chocolate and shared it with those near me, then handed around the cigarettes. These were the first we had smoked for a very long time. From then on it was a time for waiting. The next attempt to get a ship would be made in darkness. There were also many French troops in the area, and we heard that many more were hoping to get to England but all we could do was wish that a miracle would happen, thus enabling the ships and smaller craft to get in and get them away safely.

What there was of our artillery was being kept very busy, and because of the cover required it looked as though they would be amongst the last to leave. We had heard, however, that due to the extra amount of firepower they had had to use throughout the last day or two, the gunners were practically out of ammunition.

It was just after darkness had set in when orders were given that we were ready to start moving towards the Mole, and it was hoped that we would be taken off this time. Gunfire was still ongoing as we slowly made our way along the beach and finally got to the wooden structure of the pier. We walked very carefully over the planks that made up the flooring of it, and at certain points there would be someone to warn everybody of parts that were damaged, to be aware of missing flooring timbers. Enemy aircraft had clearly scored hits to the pier and in several places we had to jump across gaping holes. I noticed many loose rounds of .303 ammunition on the left-hand side of the flooring whilst we carefully moved along, and was very careful not to step on too many in case of a heavy fall in the darkness.

Some wounded had been taken on the ship (the *Newhaven*) and there had been delays. Since being taken on board one or two of the severe cases had died so had to be taken off again to make more room for the living. I can remember getting on the ship, being directed towards an opening, walking along a passageway and seeing a vacant space I put down my rifle, helmet and small pack. I got down beside them and, after placing my head on the small pack, the next thing I remember was someone shaking me and telling me that we were pulling in to Dover harbour.

The 3rd Bn Grenadier Guards had, due to having reinforced the 5th Division, made its way to Dunkirk independently of the 1st Guards Brigade.

Back in 'Blighty' an impressive logistic operation was underway to receive the BEF evacuated from France. Although Major Adair's men were now faced with problems of a different nature at the Port of Dover, they were nevertheless safe and had lived to fight another day. The rest of the 1st Guards Brigade, however, remained in France and was still in danger.

On May 26th, the 1st Guards Brigade had received orders to withdraw from Roubaix to behind the Lys Canal. Given that the *Luftwaffe* enjoyed aerial superiority for much of the time, troop movements by daylight tended to provoke a violent response: at 1900 hours 12 bombers attacked the 1st Guards Brigade area before making off in an easterly direction; an hour later, nine *Stukas* dive-bombed the road along which the column was travelling West. The Royal Artillery remained active, however, and responded by destroying the identified enemy Observation Post and adjacent mortar position. The Brigade's destination was the staging area North West of Neuve Eglise (NNE of Bailleul, some 18 miles away), preparatory to withdrawing onwards to Hondschoote (10 miles South East of Dunkirk). Bringing up the Brigade's rear were the Carrier Platoons of both the 2nd Coldstream and 2nd Hampshires, under the command of Major WS Stewart Brown, Coldstream Guards, together with 'A' Company of the 2nd Bn Cheshire Regiment. By 2130 hours the Deule Canal had been reached, held by the 42nd Division, and at 2200 hours the Brigade started the march to Hondschoote. As the convoy moved slowly south of Armentières, over the old Neuve Chappelle (1915) battlefields, firing was heard on both sides and the Brigade only just managed to get through what was in effect a bottle-neck; it only narrowly escaped being cut off.

By 0100 hours on May 28th, the Staging Area was reached, and at 0400 hours 1st Guards Brigade Headquarters struck out for Hondschoote. 1st Guards Brigade War Diary:-

During the morning enemy bombers were active up and down the column. Although the column was blocked and held up many times, the bombers seemed to make very little of their chances, and very few bombs dropped near Bde HQ vehicles.

1230 hours: At Killem Linde [2 miles South of Hondschoote] vehicles were turned into different fields, with the exception of those carrying arms, food and ammunition, and ordered to be burnt. Personal kit only was taken, the rest, including signal, intelligence and cypher kit was burnt and ditched. The ORs were taken on to Hondschoote in 3 ton lorries of the Signals.

1500 hours: After resting in a field at Hondschoote for about one hour, the ORs, including Signallers, were formed into a platoon under Captain Nelson (A/T Coy) and 2nd Lieutenant Morrison (Signals) and sent as an outpost patrol. The object of this platoon was to guard a bridge at Hoymille, to remain in position until all the 42 Div had withdrawn, and give warning of enemy approach. No enemy was seen.

2130 hours: Sections were withdrawn and taken back in the two 3 ton lorries to Les Moeres [3 miles North of Hondschoote], where HQ 1 Div and HQ 1 GB were situated. Owing to the ditched vehicles around Les Moeres, the lorries were abandoned and the last mile or so covered on foot. About half-a-mile from Les Moeres we came across Captain TRD Batt directing French troops and vehicles one way and British troops the other.

The Bns on the night 28/29 occupied fighting positions south of canal Hondschoote - Bergues. 3 IB were on 1 Div left, 1st GB on right.

2nd Bn Coldstream Guards War Diary:-

The one o'clock news this day told of the submission of the Belgian Army which provided the first explanation of our withdrawal.

During the Bn's 4 hours rest, the enemy's shelling of surrounding villages showed that he was not far away.

At 1400 hours the Bn continued its withdrawal towards Dunkirk via Dranoutre and Locre [both North East of Bailleul], where a very heavy thunderstorm broke, the noise of which entirely drowned that of the German arty, and again soaked the men to the skin. The conditions were now very bad. Only a few small scale maps were available. The routes seemed choked not only by French vehicles but by hundreds of French horses...

The Poperinge by-pass could not be found and so again the Bn passed through this town so well known in the last war and again badly battered by the Germans.

1st Guards Brigade War Diary:-

May 29th:-

French and British troops were moving through all day on their way to Dunkirk and Bray Dunes. Vehicles and even equipment and clothing etc were dumped en route.

1130 hours: 1st GB Op Order No 11 issued. This gave information of the enemy threat appearing to come from the direction of Nieuport, the situation on the south was uncertain. 1st GB to hold line of Canal de Bergues and Furnes from including bridge north of A in Warhem to including bridge NW of first 'H' in Hondschoote. Forward Defence Line north bank of canal held by 2 CG with in support one pl A/T Coy. Reserve Line stream Digue de Glaises, held by 2 Hamps.

During the day enemy bombers appeared over the Bde area quite often but no bombs were dropped on 1st GB HQ.

In the morning 2 Hamps supplied burial parties for men killed by bomb (direct hit on house).

1830 hours: Advance HQ moved to Uxem and was established in a school. Rear HQ moved off soon after by march route to the beach at Bray Dunes. Soon after the move out the village was heavily shelled. Advance HQ en route was held up by stragglers, British and French, who were making their way to the beach. Enemy aircraft were active but caused no damage.

The amount of clothing and equipment dumped, damaged and destroyed was enormous, kit of all description was to be had for the taking from the vehicles etc lining the road to Dunkirk. Documents and Army manuals were left without being destroyed. Ammunition, in many cases, had been left on ditched lorries and trucks; only in a few cases was it dumped on one side. The Bns not being able to get ammunition from regular sources went around picking up whatever they wanted.

2nd Bn Coldstream Guards War Diary:-

There was appalling confusion on the roads due to the complete lack of control of French columns which were lined up three deep and the lack of organisation on the perimeter at Dunkirk. All day long exhausted British and French troops poured across our bridges and back the remaining 10 miles to the sea, whilst enemy bombers passed overhead to deal with the situation on the beaches.

As the Germans closed in, BEF rearguard units maintained a staunch defence of the perimeter. Amongst the British soldiers fighting in such unenviable circumstances was Lance Corporal Mike Coyle of 'D' Company, 1/6th Bn East Surrey Regiment:-

We took over front line trenches from another infantry unit at the Brickfields near Nieuport. Our orders were to hold up the German advance. We didn't take too much notice of the German spotter plane flying to and from overhead but we guessed that the pilot was watching us. Later on an occasional shell would land either in front of our trench or behind it. What we didn't realise was that these were mortar shells being fired as rangers and being directed onto our position by the spotter plane in preparation for a box barrage to come later.

Our Platoon Commander and his runner had dug themselves a slit trench half way between us and the Company HQ which was set up in an old farm house. Their position was very exposed, just a few shrubs for cover. In retrospect it was like sitting out in the open. The plan in those days was the same as that used in the Great War, i.e. the Platoon Commander would send his runner to Company HQ with messages etc and the Company Commander in return would send his runner back to the Platoon Commander with orders or whatever. Unfortunately for us the enemy had long since abandoned such thinking and rightly so, what a waste of time.

As soon as dusk arrived the Germans, having prepared the ground, opened up with heavy mortars, machine-guns and anything else they could find. They kept up this prolonged attack until after midnight. An exploding mortar on the parapet above smothered me with sandbags and stopped my watch at the same time. We were able to keep firing back at them because their bullets, which included a lot of tracer, were just high enough to allow us to fire through slits in the sandbags. A couple of lads had narrow squeaks, one had the magazine shot off his Bren gun right beside his ear; another had a bullet go through his helmet just above the rim, it came out through the top! Had it gone the other way he would not have survived to joke about it later.

Finally the attack ceased and soon it was dawn. We then started looking around. The ground behind the trench was pock marked with shell holes and there were several unexploded shells lying around as well. We had a lad by the name of Carrol, Christmas we called him, and as he walked about in a daze he tripped over one of those shells. Realising the danger he was in he froze like a statue, he couldn't move. He called me: "Hi Corp". I went over and pulled him away, warning him about his carelessness. Had he touched the nose cone we would both have been killed instantly. Another lad went over to the neighbouring trench where he could hear laughter and talking, he soon came running back to tell me that the trench was occupied by Germans! I then found our first casualty, a young Welsh lad who had unfortunately wandered out of his trench. Next I found our Platoon Commander and his Runner: both dead, they had been killed by mortars. We then discovered that the Company HQ in the old farmhouse had been evacuated, just our platoon left, all the others gone.

After discovering the abandoned HQ, the obvious thing to do was get out fast and this we did. We were practically surrounded, our escape being assisted by that morning's very heavy mist. This, combined with smoke from recently exploding shells, reduced visibility to just a few yards. As we wearily trudged along, our one thought was to keep ahead of the advancing Germans. We knew they were never very far behind Exhaustion through lack of sleep began to set in and the lack of food and drink didn't help either. The old Belgian farmhouses which we passed were empty too, so were the larders.

Without maps or any other form of guidance we were completely lost, still we plodded on wearily, never a friendly face in sight. Towards evening we came across one of Belgium's famous canals, we called it the Albert Canal, that being the only name we could think of. As we reached the bank on one side we saw two Officers on the other, but because we came upon them suddenly they drew their revolvers to shoot us. As we should not have been there they, in confusion, thought we were Germans and for a moment things looked ugly. Another problem now confronted us, how to get across the canal. Only one of our party could swim so the British Officer arranged for someone to ferry us across in a boat, there was one in use on the other side. The plan was for us to pile all our belongings bar vest and pants, on the boat. This we did hurriedly, rifles, Bren guns, uniforms etc. I and a few others tied our boot laces together and hung the boots round our necks before sliding into the water to get hold of the boat. This was probably the most sensible thing we did as we soon found out.

Scarcely had we reached the other side of the canal when the cry went up:- "Run for it lads, Jerry's here!" We soon forgot our tiredness as we raced up an open field to safety. As for the boat and our belongings, that was scuttled to prevent the Germans getting hold of anything. For some of us there was a crumb of comfort in having our own boots. We were given a good meal, the first for about 36 hours, by kindly cooks from the Royal West Sussex Regiment - the unit which had rescued us. As there were no battledress uniforms available we were issued with Belgian Army uniforms complete with funny hats, this again nearly proved our undoing. As we marched, or tried to, through some nameless towns, a few hefty ladies mistook us for Germans and, to the accompaniment of shaking fists and shouts of "Bosch prisonair!" we plodded on towards Dunkirk and survived once more.

Certain 1st Guards Brigade survivors recall the withdrawal to Dunkirk:-

Lieutenant Halliday:-

It was an extraordinary scene. On the far bank of the canal at Hondschoote, about seven miles from the coast, as far as one could see in either direction, were abandoned and burning vehicles. Coming out of the ruins of Hondschoote and over the bridge was a continuous stream of formed units, sub-units separated from their parent HQs and obviously lost, and just stragglers. The most shocking sight was an RAMC Casualty Clearing Station which had to abandon its transport except for its ambulances with lying cases. The walking wounded, numbering about 150, came staggering past me, swathed in bandages, with still at least seven miles to go. They were not a morale raising sight.

The 2nd Hampshires immediately settled down to digging new defences along the canal line. James Lee reported that he had had a brush with a Fifth Columnist. The column had been stopped some miles east of Hondschoote by a smartly turned out French Officer who said: "Your column should turn left here". James knew exactly where he was going, however, and realised that he was being deliberately mis-directed. Drawing his revolver he shot the 'French Officer' out of hand.

During the night, as more troops arrived, there was an adjustment of the lay-out and the whole brigade side stepped to the right. The Bn now toiled to make new defences based on the village of Uxem which is five miles ESE of Dunkirk. This was part of the last rear guard position of the BEF which was ultimately held by the 1st Division and here we remained for the final three days. We were on a dead flat low lying plain of pasture and, I suppose, sugar-beet. Such roads as they were, were unfenced and generally built on causeways raised two or three feet above the plain. We began to feel pretty secure from tank attack, as the French had opened the sluices and much of the land was going under water.

Movement on the roads, however, made one feel very vulnerable and we were subjected to pretty continuous shelling. We were not, however, bombed from the air. The reason for this was that the *Luftwaffe* was concentrating on Dunkirk and the beaches between there and La Panne. We could see and hear their efforts, which seemed to be continuous. Many of the German bombers returned low over us and gave us what we regarded good sport. We found lots of abandoned ammunition and let fly with everything we had. Cecil Thomas had actually found an abandoned Vickers MMG and 50,000 rounds of ammunition. By mounting it on a kitchen table, the carrier platoon found that they could use it as an AA gun. On occasions planes came over so low that I even fired my revolver at them. This was all very good for morale!

Willie Wilson saw a section of a Lancashire regiment stumbling past, which had evidently been reduced to a very tired looking Corporal and an even more weary looking private soldier. The private stopped and sat down by the road side. I have found a certain four-letter word to be grammatically flexible, and this was now demonstrated. "Corporal", said the private, "Ah'm fooked". The Corporal was obviously at the end of his tether and threw his rifle to the ground. "Fooked be fooked", he cried, "All the fookers is fooked!"

An outstanding character was our Padre, Hugh Blackburne, who was well known by, and very popular with, all ranks; he was a great asset to the Bn. In Uxem I remember meeting him coming back somewhat shaken from having gone to succour a Brigade Anti-Tank Gun Company detachment which was in the Bn area. The gun had received a direct hit and the Number One was sitting in his firing position with his head blown off. Lying beside him, mortally wounded, was an extremely tall Coldstreamer. The only words Hugh could get out of him were "Oh fook, oh fook". One supposes that the Lord understood.

An account by Corporal Christie of the 2nd Bn Coldstream Guards Carrier Section provides an idea of the stresses and strains endured on the road to Dunkirk:-

On the night march we came under quite a few bomb attacks. My Carrier was halted by a Sergeant of the Royal Artillery who demanded that I should tow his gun quad, to which was attached an

Corporal R Christie, 2nd Bn
Coldstream Guards.
Mr R Christie.

18 pounder field gun, out of a ditch. As this was an impossible task for a Carrier I refused. He then drew his pistol and threatened me. As he kept to one side I was unable to shoot him with our fixed Bren. I nudged my driver to pull away which he did. As we moved the Sergeant fired at me. After 100 yards I uncoupled the Bren and nudged my No 2 on the gun to follow me. He then slumped forward and blood poured from his throat. I went back to avenge him only to find my Platoon Sergeant surrounded by the RA gun crew. It was an impasse and my next job was to get the wounded Guardsman Walton on an ambulance. Consequently he was captured by the Jerries and spent the next five years as a prisoner in Poland. This might sound like fiction but was later confirmed by a fellow ex-sergeant who I keep in contact with. His neighbour was in that Territorial Battery with the Sergeant concerned who was 'bomb happy' from service in India.

After many miles and many thrills we finished up on the canal at Bergues, across which we faced the Germans. Thousands of other BEF soldiers passed by on their way to Dunkirk. My section defended a small bridge over the canal. We were surprised to see a detachment marching at ease in perfect order: it was the Welsh Guards who had so valiantly defended Arras. Their drummers piled their drums near me and I burnt them to deny the Germans the satisfaction of taking such splendid war trophies!

My next job was to support a depleted platoon in a blockhouse at a cross-roads. It was about 15 strong and our Bren was one of the few automatic weapons. The Platoon Sergeant Major sent me to patrol towards the German lines. Trucks were driven into ditches either side of the road - perfect for an ambush. When an A/T gun opened up it was time to retire behind the blockhouse. At 2200 hours the infantry mob marched off but I had orders to wait for two hours before getting out. At midnight on June 1st, therefore, I drove my carrier into a field, put a 36 Mills Grenade into the Ford V8 engine and marched to Dunkirk.

Private Ellingworth:-

On all roads and even fields there were lines of abandoned lorries of all kinds. On one such road Darky and I came across some RE wagons, on which were pontoons. Can't have these falling into German hands, so taps on petrol tanks were turned on, and from a safe distance a couple of Mills grenades did the trick. Soon the whole line was on fire. Of course we two Despatch Riders (DR) could not do the same for the many more vehicles we were to see in such circumstances.

Time arrived for us to head back towards the coast. By this time the 3rd Bn Grenadier Guards were with another Brigade, but we still called on them. We left Hondschoote where we had lost some of our transport. We had to keep the wireless trucks, i.e. No 11 sets to contact forward troops and No 9 sets to stay in contact with 1 Div. The ride to Hondschoote was a little dangerous, as guns could be heard firing on both sides, but we got through okay.

We set up 1st Guards Brigade HQ in Le Moeres, and I went on an early morning run to the Bns. When I returned there was no-one left at Moeres. I was sitting on the steps of a house that was the Officers' Mess having a smoke, when the Brigadier came up to me: "Have you had breakfast?", he asked. I replied not so he told me to go into the Mess and join him for a bite to eat. After that we left the village just before it was attacked by German bombers. We found the Brigade in Uxem, this being our last HQ. We were in the school where there were just two rooms: Signal Office and other Officers in one, the lads in the other.

To get to one or two places we DRs had to ride through an RA position. They had guns on one side of the track and slit trenches on the other. Only one thing - when the DRs rode through Jerry put a few shells after them. On one run an Officer stood in the path of the DRs, pistol drawn. "You're not coming through, you put my men in danger", he shouted. My mate Darky drew his pistol and said "Oh yes we are, and I can shoot as well!" The Officer then put his pistol down and we had no more problems.

Things were getting rather bad, there were a lot of people passing through Uxem on their way to either Dunkirk or Bray Dunes. We stayed at Uxem. One morning I returned from a run when a call came out for the Guardsman runner to take a message to 2nd Bn Coldstream Guards. He was too scared, he said "I can't do it, I'll get killed". As I was nearby I said that I would take this message, which was for the CO of 2nd Coldstream. So once more through the RA lines to Bergues. I found the CO and Adjutant in the square. The CO said "You were brave coming through, its bad out there". Then, to the Adjutant "Take his name".
"Oh, it is written here", he said looking at the order. A name was there alright but not mine, it was the Guardsman's!

We then had to move 1st Guards Brigade HQ out of the school because Jerry had its range. Orders came for anyone not required to be sent to the coast. There were just a few of us left behind - we did not expect to get out.

1st Guards Brigade War Diary:-

May 30th:-

1 GB Op Order No 12 issued. This gave information of enemy Armoured Fighting Vehicles in the area of Rexpoede. Later it was found that the Welsh Guards were heavily engaged by tanks and infantry at this place. They withdrew during the early morning north of canal after suffering heavy casualties..... One of the two roads leading back from 2 CG positions are made extremely dangerous by bursting shells on burning artillery ammunition lorries on the banks of the canal. The ditched lorries on the far side of the river are affording excellent cover for enemy snipers who are able to approach the canal easily as they can only be observed from a few places.
1230 hours: Enemy patrol of 12 men seen south of the 'S' in Hondschoote.

1315 hours: Enemy vehicle seen on road near La Maison Neove.

Enemy arty was active during the day and at 1320 hours the forward posts on the extreme left of the Bde front were heavily shelled.

1330 hours: Shelling, believed mortar, of area 347796.

1700 hours: Shelling of village of Uxem.

A few enemy recce planes were seen over 1 GB area during the day. Company Sergeant Major A/T Coy with small party went into Dunkirk and salvaged ammunition, weapons, cigarettes and food.

Dunkirk was bombed early morning and again at dusk by aircraft. The arty shelling was systematic, the Mole heavily shelled at night (whilst troops embarked) and the beach by day.

On May 31st, the shelling increased in intensity. The Battalion Headquarters of both 2nd Coldstream and 2nd Hampshires were heavily bombarded throughout the afternoon. Company Quarter Master Sergeant Eastwood and Sergeant Sowerby of the 2nd Coldstream Carrier Platoon were severely wounded. Later in the day the 2nd Coldstream Battalion HQ was hit, killing the Armourer Sergeant and wounding Company Sergeant Major Hewitt of HQ Company. The companies deployed along the canal bank also suffered casualties. Enemy bombers continually pounded the beaches and some HE was dropped near Brigade HQ and the 2nd Hampshire HQ.

On this day, despite having vainly tried to get permission to remain in France until the end, Lord Gort was ordered back to England. His last operational order was to the effect that I Corps would stay to fight beside the French. General Alexander was appointed to command I Corps and also the last remaining elements of the BEF. Brigadier Beckwith-Smith was appointed to command 1st Division and Lieutenant Colonel Bootle-Wilbraham of the 2nd Bn Coldstream succeeded him in command of 1st Guards Brigade; Major Stewart-Brown then took command of the 2nd Coldstream. Doubtless these changes, however, were of little interest to those British soldiers still fighting for their lives in and around Dunkirk. Towards evening, four German tanks with supporting infantry were seen on the 1st Guards Brigade front, just 500 yards from the canal. During the night, the Brigade dug a defensive position around the school and an artillery ammunition carrier full of shells was very sensibly moved some distance away.

1st Guards Brigade War Diary:-

June 1st:-

During the night 31st May - 1st June, the enemy crossed the canal and attacked on the left of the 3rd Infantry Brigade east of Les Moeres, and got into some woods at about 0300 hours. These 100 men or so were soon ejected and driven back to the swampy ground just north of the canal. The morning started with more heavy shelling at Uxem at 0600 hours.

HQ 1 GB collected kits and moved to a farm about 300 yards along the road to Dunkirk, the civilians still in occupation. The enemy arty appeared to have the range on the school (Bde HQ) and the church at Uxem (previously 2 Hamps HQ), this received two direct hits. While Bde HQ were moving, enemy bombers appeared and, moving slowly around overhead, bombed anything that looked important. During the move the Adjt 2 Hamps and one driver (Guardsman Wilkes) Bde HQ were hit by shrapnel.

During the morning an advance party, Brigade Transport Officer [BTO], Royal Army Service Corps Officer [RASCO] and 10 Other Ranks moved on to Dunkirk to prepare for embarkation of 1 GB. This party collected food and blankets from abandoned vehicles and prepared for issuing of same.

During the afternoon, the 2nd Bn Coldstream Guards suffered further casualties: at 1400 hours, Lieutenant EL Gibbs, commanding No 1 Company, was killed, as was Second Lieutenant CA Blackwell (the Regimental Signals Officer, attached to No 1 Company). At about 1600 hours, instructions were received to the effect that as the French were to hold the canal line that night, 1st Guards Brigade was to withdraw to Dunkirk and embark at the Mole and beach to the west end of Malo-Les-Bains. The Rear Companies and HQ 2nd Hampshires finally withdrew and abandoned their positions at 2030 hours. At 2100 hours, Brigade HQ left the farm in which it was established. It was then that the 2nd Bn Coldstream Guards received further bad news; War Diary:-

...the news arrived that Major McCorquodale, commanding No 3 Coy had been killed, and also 2nd Lieutenant RDE Speed, the remaining Officer in No 1 Coy. Lieutenant JM Langley, the remaining Officer with No 3 Coy was wounded, and only Captain Bowman, the Mechanical Transport Officer, survived to bring out the remnants of Nos 1 and 3 Coys. No 2 Coy had up to now suffered less casualties but on the beach an unlucky German shell hit the head of this Coy's column. Several men belonging to Coy HQ were killed and Major ET Wyatt and Lieutenant RT Combe were mortally wounded. No 4 Coy which was the last out of the line still had all its Officers and thus the Bn reached the sea covered by the Carriers which took up a position on the Dunkirk canal until 0200 hours, when, in accordance with his orders, Lieutenant The Earl of Devon abandoned his vehicles and immobilised them.

During the night, part of the 1st Guards Brigade managed to embark for England, but the following, according to its War Diary, were left on the beaches:-

(a) Brigadier MB Beckwith-Smith DSO MC (Div Cmdr), Lieutenant Colonel L Bootle-Wilbraham MC (Brig Cmdr), Brigade Major [BM], Brigade Transport Officer [BTO], Staff Captain [SC], RASC Officer (wounded) and skeleton HQ.
(b) Approx 150 Officers and Men 2 CG.
(c) Major WSS Sanguinetti's Coy 2 Hamps and detachment of Hamps carriers.

(b) & (c) were dug in on the slopes of Naval Fort.

A shell which landed between two companies 2 CG killed Lieutenant Coombe and injured Major Wyatt and Lieutenant Hon GL Hamilton Russell (HQ 1 GB). Both died on their way to England.

The party which failed to embark on the night 1/2nd all embarked at 2145 hours, from the Mole, except Brigadier MB Beckwith-Smith DSO MC, SC, BTO and eight Other Ranks who controlled traffic in entrance to Mole till evacuation was completed at 2330 hours. The Brigade Report Centre under Captain PPH Flower managed to board a sailing boat at 0400 hours, and after being afloat for some 12 hours were picked up by a destroyer and landed at Dover 1900 hours.

The survivors tell their stories:-

Corporal Christie:-

We spent the day near the break-water under bomb and mortar attack, with neither water or food since June 1st. At about 2200 hours on June 2nd, we joined the Bn and marched to the East quay to board HMS *Sabre*. No Coldstreamer was allowed on board without his rifle, or in my case a Bren gun. Once on the destroyer we were packed into a room below and had our first drink for 24 hours, cocoa in big buckets made by the matloes, wounded served first. Our destroyer had made many trips to Dunkirk and was second only to HMS *Wakefield* in terms of quantity of men rescued. My admiration for the Royal Navy is second only to my Regiment, the Coldstream Guards: *Nulli Secundus*. We landed at Dover in the early hours of June 3rd.

Sergeant Court:-

When we waded out into the sea towards a fishing vessel, I had in my possession the 1st Guards Brigade War Diary. Unfortunately a wave caught us and the document floated away. I swam after it and successfully recovered the War Diary which thereafter returned with me to England without further mishap.

Private Ellingworth:-

On the night of 1st/2nd June, along with the Intelligence Officer, a No 11 set and No 11 set with drivers and wireless operators, with my old soldier pal of a DR, we were told to man a check point on a crossroad. The 2nd Coldstream and 2nd Hampshires were to have taken that route to the beaches at Bray Dunes. As we lay in a rather deep ditch, we could hear and feel the rather large shells heading for the German lines. I don't know how many fags I smoked, quite a lot, but no sign of the troops, so the Intelligence Officer decided to go and look for them. Next thing we knew was a 15 cwt truck coming towards us at rather a high rate of knots, and the Officer standing up in the front seat: "Jerry's coming", he shouted! We had no need for orders: wagons and bikes were started up immediately and we were on our way. We got to a bridge over a canal where a sapper sergeant asked who we were; "Guards Brigade" we shouted, and when the last vehicle was clear the bridge went up in smoke.

We could not take the wireless trucks any further so did our best to make sure that all wireless equipment and engines could be of no use to the Germans. By this time the road to Bray Dunes was - to say the least - a shambles. Trucks of all sizes, motor cycles etc were just abandoned. Their contents had just been thrown all over the place. Some trucks were burning, some torched by our soldiers, others by the bombing. When we finally got to the beach there were few troops to be seen. If I looked towards burning Dunkirk, or the other way towards La Panne, I could see some movement. There were no boats leaving the beach. An aero-engine was heard and the shout "Take cover!" Those who were able did what they could. There were big ships coming offshore and some brave soldiers were trying to swim and reach some of the sunken hulks. There were bodies all over the place and there was nothing to eat.

Of the party I had been with at the checkpoint, there was now only four of us still together: a Grenadier Guardsman who had been the Brigadier's driver, Taffy Hawkins, an old soldier wireless operator, and two DRs (Darky Phipps and me). We found some shelter and took it in turns to go to sleep. German dive-bombers kept up a steady stream of bombs. One thing about being on a sandy shore was that that the sand kept the damage down. The worst thing was when the planes' machine-guns got going - the safest place then was inside a tank!

After a quiet night, our group of four walked along the beach in the hope of finding a cup of tea and something to eat, but there was nothing to be found. Still the brave were in the sea swimming, or holding on to ships floating by.

We saw a beached barge, with a number of soldiers on board. We climbed on and saw that it was loaded with tins of what looked like petrol. Tied up alongside, however, were two river craft - most soldiers were climbing on to the one pointing out to sea. As that appeared full, our group decided to get on the second boat. Just then a flight of *Stukas* appeared. The Midshipman in charge of the front craft started the engine and pulled away. It was then that we saw a tow rope, as this was only a thin rope it soon parted leaving us still tied up to the barge. A sailor who was on board said "The engine doesn't work". Darky told me that we should try and repair it. We found a few tools but worked away without any luck. Whilst working in the well of the boat we could not see what was happening. Suddenly a voice rang out: "Why is this boat not moving?" We looked over the stern and there was a Major of the Royal Artillery. Darky said "Can't get the engine started".
"What do you want, a battery?", asked the Major.
"Yes", said Darky.
So the Major waded back to shore, up to his waist in the sea. A while later he returned with six soldiers, each carrying a battery. "Try these", he said, and the batteries were passed over the transom.
"Have you got room for these men?", the Major asked.
"We'll get them in", I said, but the Major himself turned to go back to the shore and the six soldiers followed him. What happened to them all I have no idea. Meanwhile Darky and I got to work again but the engine was in a poor state.

All this time waves were pushing the small boat against the barge. This upset the Brigadier's driver. I gave him a drink from my water bottle; the Guardsman just tipped it up and I had to stop him - it was neat rum! The lad was so beside himself that he could not tell the difference between a strong spirit and cold tea.

Fortunately the engine finally started. Before casting off, Darky asked for a tin off the barge, just in case. The sailor sat in the cockpit and headed out to sea. We had people all over the place, the stern was really full. Where the bunks were there were more people than the boat was made to carry. We head for England, no compass, so we just kept the sun on our right and a little behind. I think we got about four or five miles out when the engine stopped. Darky and I went to put things right, but without success this time. Darky thought it was lack of fuel, so I asked someone to put some in the tank, from the tin taken off the barge. Still no luck, then someone called out "That's not petrol - its water!". So there we were out in the Channel just drifting with the tide. Hopeless.

In the distance a dark rectangle was seen, heading our way. Darky and I were convinced that this was Jerry coming out for us. We told the only Officer on board, who was in the RAMC, to tell everyone with arms to load, so we could make a fight of it as no-one wished to become a POW. We need not have worried, as it turned out to be a Landing Craft, one of the first anyone had ever seen. It was packed with French soldiers. The Midshipman in charge of the Landing Craft asked us what was wrong and if we wanted a tow. To the latter we said "Yes", so a Chief Petty Officer came to us with a tow rope. He made fast and we were soon under way.

Then we saw waves in the distance, these were made by a speed boat coming from England. The leading boat slowed down and the speedboat came alongside our boat. When we looked in it, there was just one sailor - packed around him was bread, butter and corn beef! We asked where he was going, he said to the beaches to see if he could pick anyone up. We told him that we could do with some food, some of us had not eaten for two days. He said that he would swap some food for a Bren gun and all the .303 ammunition we had! This we did, off he went, never to be seen by us again. We gave each boat enough for a bite to eat, then got under way again.

As we got nearer to England, we saw two ships heading towards us but then one went left the other right. We could follow them by the smoke. They made a square pattern, coming back towards our two boats. Taking no notice we went straight to Ramsgate. At least we got home, but were not a pretty sight. A Red Cap sergeant told us to hurry up as there was a train just about to leave. After picking up a mug of tea, a sandwich and some fags, we boarded the train.

When I got home, I told my father of our adventures and he said "You were lucky - you came over a minefield!" Someone must have been watching over us.

Lieutenant Halliday:-

The first of the companies appeared, followed at various intervals by the rest. They were closed up in threes, clearly carrying all their weapons and equipment, and marched to attention past the CO. I was not particularly moved at the time but, in retrospect, it was clearly a marvellous demonstration of the *espirit de corps* of a totally undefeated regiment.

Eventually we reached the outskirts of Dunkirk town and found the Brigade check point (manned by the Bn Transport Officer). This was in a shattered warehouse near the base of the Mole. We duly reported the passing of the Bn and were told that all embarkation was now under control of the naval beach parties. The Brigade Order had stated that commanders would embark when two thirds of their units had done so. The BTO indicated that Cadoux should now go on to the Mole. He was reluctant to do so but there was nothing else he could do, so Bn HQ duly moved on. A large shell had blown a huge hole in the near end of the Mole so we had to cross over it via a long sagging plank. The queue ahead of us slowly thinned out as people were got off.

Finally a Naval Officer came along collecting the complement for what turned out to be LCA No 4. This was one of the proto-types of what later became the standard infantry platoon assault craft and had been sent over hanging from the davits of the *Clan MacAllister*, which was now a bombed and burnt out hulk on the beach.

The Commander of our craft was an RNVR Sub-Lieutenant, who at least looked the part with a large black beard. We clambered down a steel ladder into what looked to us to be a pretty odd sort of craft. The boat filled up with about 30 others while Bn HQ remained clustered round this little sort of conning compartment on the starboard side. Into this stepped our Captain, when he had decided that we could cram in no more people, and we cast off. He took us out of the harbour and some way to sea and then, turning to Cadoux, he said "I will now set compass course for Dover".

"Well done", said we and looked with relief over the stern at the receding outline of Dunkirk, silhouetted in flames and smoke. The sea was flat and calm and we settled ourselves for a long haul. To our dismay, however, our stern began slowly to swing and pretty soon our bows were pointing straight back to Dunkirk. Cadoux touched the skipper on the shoulder and said "I say, do you mind leaving your compass for a moment and taking a look over the bow?". This happened twice more then Cadoux said "Forgive my interference, but we would all be much happier if you forgot your compass and just kept Dunkirk over the stern". Our skipper then confessed that the compass had only been installed the day previous and there had not been time to check it!

Dawn of June 2nd, was then approaching and we could aim at England by the sun. About an hour later we were overtaken by a paddle mine-sweeper in which, amazingly, was our X Company, commanded by Willie Wilson. The paddle steamer took us all off the LCA and we left our late skipper to carry on with his own crew. The paddle steamer was very over-crowded and all I can remember about her is falling asleep on the floor at the foot of the main companion way. We were taken into Harwich, where we arrived about mid-day, and were given a hot meal in the station. How I enjoyed that meal, and the irony was that we had bread and butter pudding which, before, I had absolutely abhorred. The Bn arrived home much dispersed, but complete with all its weapons.

The 1st Guards Brigade were actually amongst the last British troops rescued from Dunkirk. Although the evacuation continued throughout the night on June 1st/2nd, Admiral Ramsay had called off daylight operations to avoid further heavy losses. At 1700 hours on June 2nd, the evacuation re-started. During the early hours of June 3rd, however, Major General Alexander and the Senior Naval Officer ashore at Dunkirk, Captain WG Tennant, toured the beaches in a motor launch. Satisfied that no-one was left behind, they then set sail for England.

From the British viewpoint the Dunkirk evacuation was a great success: a stupendous achievement arising out of defeat. Although assisted by calm seas - which some consider a miracle - the efforts of both the Royal Navy and crews of the 'Little Ships' were to become legendary. According to War Office figures published in 1941, 211,532 fit men, 13,053 wounded and 112,546 Allied troops were rescued: a total of 337,131 men.

If the BEF had not been saved but captured, the remaining elements of the British Army at home might not have been able to resist a German landing. The *pre-requisite* to such an ambitious operation was aerial superiority, but RAF Fighter Command - the Few - remained determined to maintain control of British skies, and the Royal Navy still commanded the seas. As General Weygand said, "The Battle of France is over: the Battle of Britain is about to begin."

The capture of the BEF would have given Hitler a major diplomatic advantage in that, with so many British prisoners, Germany would have been, in theory, in a strong position to force Britain into a peace settlement - under Nazi terms. Without a war to fight against the West, Hitler's subsequent invasion of Russia might then have had a very different outcome.

Allied vehicles and equipment left behind
on the beach at Zuydcoote.
Via Peter Taghon.

The BEF survivors safely returned to England would be re-formed into fighting units which, given their combat experience and lessons learned, became the foundation of a new Army. Eventually that Army would re-cross the Channel - this time together with Allies from across the Free World, including the United States. Failing to capture or destroy the BEF at Dunkirk, therefore, ultimately had far-reaching and shattering consequences for Nazi Germany.

Veteran Joe Nixon, of the Dunkirk Veterans' Association's Medway Branch:-

Surviving Dunkirk Veterans, who lived to fight another day, have no illusions: quite simply, had Britain been defeated in 1940, World History would have been drastically different.

Dunkirk Veterans, in fact, were to fight on in all theatres throughout World War II. In the case of our 2nd Bn Coldstream Guards we experienced savage and bitter fighting in both North Africa and Italy; we suffered hundreds of sad losses, none sadder than on Christmas Day 1942: 'Long Stop Hill', Tunisia ('Christmas Mountain' to the *Afrika Korps*).

For thousands of Dunkirk Veterans, surviving the Fall of France and being safely evacuated was the start of the road back. We must not forget, however, those of our number who were captured and consequently endured five long years in captivity as a result of desperate rear-guard actions.

It must be remembered, however, that the Allies were defeated in this campaign of 1940; as Churchill himself said, 'Wars are not won by evacuations'. Nevertheless the 'Dunkirk Spirit' has become a British watchword for defiance and successfully struggling out of disaster. Indeed 1940, again as Churchill said, was, after all, the British people's 'Finest Hour'.

German soldiers examine a downed Me 109 of JG51 on the beach at Dunkirk.
Via Peter Taghon.

It is appropriate here to quote Lord Gort himself regarding the BEF:-

Most important of all, the campaign has proved beyond doubt that the British Soldier has once again deserved well of his country. The troops under my command, whatever their category, displayed those virtues of steadiness, patience, courage and endurance for which their Corps and Regiments have long been famous.

In addition to the fighting troops, the rearward units, as well as the three divisions sent to France for pioneer duties, all found themselves, at one time or another, engaged with the enemy although often incompletely trained and short of the proper complement of weapons.

Time and time again, the operations proved the vital importance of the good junior leader, who has learned to encourage, by his example, the men whom he leads, and whose first care is the well-being of the troops placed under his command. Firm discipline, physical fitness, efficiency in marching and digging, and skill at arms, old fashioned virtues though they may be, are as important in modern warfare as ever they were in the past.

CHAPTER ELEVEN

Aftermath

A lthough the BEF's story ended at such British ports of Dover, Folkestone, Ramsgate, Margate and Sheerness, I think it fascinating to learn more of events affecting certain of our heroes in the aftermath of this traumatic campaign.

For some families there was the worst kind of news, a terse telegram informing next-of-kin of their loved one's death in action. For others life hung in limbo: Missing in Action. With so many thousands of casualties and prisoners it took time to tie up the loose ends. Some casualties would never be identified, so although after a certain period of time death was presumed for official purposes, those families would never have a tangible full stop upon which to focus their grief. The Worcester *News & Times* of June 20th, 1940, headlined 'Worcester Guardsman Missing', and reported that 2611042 Guardsman HH Smith was Missing in Action. Similar reports appeared in newspapers throughout the country.

British prisoners, including Guardsman Bert Smith, and German guards, working on a sports ground in Poland, in September 1940. It is quite possible that others in the photograph were also captured by II/IR12 on May 21st, 1940.

For the family of Lance Corporal Harry Nicholls, the situation was somewhat different, however. Given the evidence of Guardsman Nash, Nicholls was 'Missing Presumed Dead', although Guardsman Lewcock did not share this view:-

I was the only one who insisted that Harry Nicholls was still alive, but Percy Nash took the opposite view. When we returned to England he wanted me to go with him to visit Harry's 'widow' in Nottingham, but I refused on the grounds that I said he was still alive.

Mrs Irene Hazeldine, Harry Nicholls' sister, adds:-

The family was distraught at the news that he was missing and believed dead, but we never gave up hope. Mum even went to a spiritualist to try and confirm he was still alive.

Percy Nash himself was later promoted in the field to Sergeant and was mentioned in despatches. He survived the war, throughout which he served as a fighting soldier in various theatres. He did not receive a gallantry decoration for his part in the River Escaut action, which was perhaps a disappointment since his actions appear worthy of such recognition. Before Percy died in 1989, he went 'missing' and arrived, unannounced, at Wellington Barracks. He just wanted to come 'home' for the last time: Once a Grenadier, *always* a Grenadier.

The bravery of Lance Corporal Harry Nicholls was recognised, however, through the award of a 'posthumous' Victoria Cross, notification of which was given in the London Gazette on July 30th, 1940; as former Guardsman Les Drinkwater says:-

The War Office announced that the highest British decoration for valour had been awarded to Harry Nicholls, this for such conduct in the field as was outstanding even at a time when brave deeds and heroic sacrifices were of an hourly occurrence.

The citation was written by Major Allan Adair, Commanding Officer of the 3rd Bn Grenadier Guards:-

On the 21st May, 1940, Lance Corporal Nicholls was commanding a section in the right-forward platoon of his company when the company was ordered to counter-attack. At the very start of the advance he was wounded in the arm by shrapnel, but continued to lead his section forward; as the company came over a small ridge, the enemy opened heavy machine-gun fire at close range.

Lance Corporal Nicholls, realising the danger to the company, immediately seized a Bren gun and dashed forward towards the machine-guns, firing from the hip. He succeeded in silencing first one machine-gun and then two other machine-guns, in spite of being severely wounded.

Lance Corporal Nicholls then went on up to a higher piece of ground and engaged the German infantry massed behind, causing many casualties, and continued to fire until he had no more ammunition left.

He was wounded at least four times in all, but absolutely refused to give in. There is no doubt that his gallant action was instrumental in enabling his company to reach its objective, and in causing the enemy to fall back across the River Scheldt.

Lance Corporal Nicholls has since been reported to have been killed in action.

Former Guardsman Eric Pounder, a member of Lance Corporal Nicholls' No 9 Platoon in No 3 Company, paid tribute to both the VC and Guardsman Nash:-

I remember talking to Harry in billets before the offensive started and he always said that he was determined to go down fighting if ever there appeared a possibility of being taken prisoner. What you have to understand is that Harry Nicholls and Percy Nash were big men - in every sense. For Harry to do what he did on May 21st, 1940, was no surprise. He was so physically strong that for him carrying a Bren - which weighed 23 pounds - was like carrying a peashooter. For an ordinary chap it would have been an amazing feat.

Mrs Hazeldine adds:-

Harry certainly wasn't thinking of himself was he? No, he was thinking of his mates and his country, and that's what he put first. *People today would do well to remember that.*

On August 6th, 1940, Mrs Connie Nicholls, together with her baby daughter Carol, parents-in-law and sister-in-law, Florence May, attended Buckingham Palace. There Connie received her husband's Victoria Cross from King George VI. His Majesty was impressed by old Mr Nicholls' pride in his family: "You're a family Britain is proud of", said the wartime King of England, adding to Connie "I only wish it was your husband himself I was giving the VC." After the investiture, nine month old baby Carol was photographed outside the Palace wearing her father's VC. The story could have ended there, but it was actually far from over.

The Victoria Cross of Lance Corporal
Harry Nicholls.
*Photograph by Andrew Long, courtesy
Regimental Adjutant Grenadier Guards.*

Throughout the Second World War, the International Red Cross, based at Geneva in neutral Switzerland, worked with both the Allies and Germans in respect of the interests of Prisoners of War. Consequently in September 1940, news was received that many BEF soldiers officially 'Missing' were actually prisoners held by the Germans. Mrs Nicholls was staggered to receive a telegram from Regimental Headquarters:-

Very pleased to inform you your husband safe and reported a prisoner of war.

Upon receiving this news, the overjoyed Connie Nicholls returned the VC for her husband to collect personally after the war.

At the same time, word was received that my Grandfather, Guardsman Bert Smith, was also a prisoner, having suffered a head wound. This well received news came in the form of a small brown Field Service Post Card indicating 'I am quite well, wounded but hope to be discharged soon; letter follows at first opportunity'. It was signed 'HH Smith', which must have seemed to his family as coming back from the dead.

On October 3rd, 1940, the Regimental Adjutant Grenadier Guards wrote to my Grandmother:-

I thank you for your reply to my letter of the 23rd September, 1940, and for loaning me the card sent to you by your husband.

The Lieutenant Colonel and myself are very pleased indeed to hear that your husband is now safe, and we hope that he has recovered from the wound in his head. If he should disclose to you the exact nature of this wound I shall be glad if you will let me know, as this information is required for official purposes, and for recording upon his documents. He has now been officially posted by the Regiment as a Prisoner of War.

I am returning your husband's card and the Red Cross letter.

On October 28th, Lady Lort-Phillips, wife of Captain Lort-Phillips of the 3rd Bn Grenadier Guards, also wrote to Mrs Smith:-

I have just heard that your husband has been reported prisoner of war. I am so glad that you have had news of him at last. It must have seemed an awful long time that you were without any news. Have you heard from him since he arrived at the camp? I am told that they are treating the prisoners very well on the whole. My brother in law is also a prisoner, but he writes quite cheerfully and is very well.

How are the children? I do hope that have been keeping well all summer. Are you still at Worcester? Please let me know if there is anything you want, or if there is anything I can do for you. My address is now as above, as I have had to move into a smaller house.

My children are all well, and the baby is getting lovely, nearly eight months and getting on very well.

Both Lance Corporal Harry Nicholls and Guardsman Bert Smith (Prisoner of War Numbers 20473 and 57035 respectively) ended up in Stalag XXB. Popular legend - which survivors swear is true - suggests that when Adolf Hitler learned that a Lance Corporal of the Grenadier Guards in German custody had been awarded the VC, he offered to present the medal to Nicholls personally! So the story goes, Hitler, himself a Corporal in Flanders during the Great War and awarded the Iron Cross, felt an affinity with Nicholls on that basis. In fact, Hitler's award was made for his distinguished actions as a Company Runner at the Battle of Gheluvelt (on the Ypres-Menin Road) in 1914, where his Bavarian Reserve Regiment XVI fought against the 1st Guards Brigade! Lance Corporal Nicholls, however, is said to have rejected the offer out of hand, but many maintain that conditions improved in that particular camp for some time afterwards!

On October 22nd, 1941, the *News of the World* published the following article:-

VC LEFT AS DEAD IS BOXING AGAIN

Behind the wire but still fighting!
Lance Corporal Nicholls VC
strikes a familiar pose at Stalag
XXB, April 9th, 1943.
Mrs I Hazeldine.

Lance Corporal Harry Nicholls VC, Grenadier Guards, who is a prisoner in Germany, has so far recovered from his wounds that he is able to box again when there is anyone to box.

In a letter from Stalag XXB, a Lance Corporal Robert Woods of the Royal Norfolk Regiment, a fellow prisoner, writes "Last night we had a boxing tournament. Harry Nicholls VC is in the camp with us but he doesn't box. There is no one here big enough, let alone experienced enough to meet him. He hit one chap only lightly. I don't think the chap knows to this day what hit him!"

The years of captivity were long and appeared endless. On May 21st, 1943 (three years exactly after his capture), Bert Smith wrote to relatives in Coventry:-

Thanks for your letter, pleased to hear that you are well. It is very hot here and I shall soon be black from the sun! Glad you know I had the cigs, that's all I want here is cigs. Without a smoke days are long and we work 11 hours a day. I'm down on the farm now and we have been working in a forest felling trees. How's Dick's roses now? Wish I could have a walk on the 'Rough' now [woodland near the River Severn at Ombersley]. Don't see any bluebells here but we did see some blue frogs in the wood - the first I have seen. I need two gym vests for hot weather - I have four good shirts now. Glad Mother is well, and that Tom and Walter are still in England. We only hope it will finish soon as I have been here three years now, a long time to be a prisoner. I think we shall all go mad when it does end! I had a parcel of cigs today from the factory.... I don't suppose I shall know Jan and Joan when I get back as Jan will be 10 this month and Joan seven. I bet they like going to their Gran at Ombersley. It will be a treat to get back. So Mum still works, it's about time she packed it in. I fetched Red Cross parcels with two horses last week from a big town. Shall be busy this summer I bet. Tell Floss I have her letters OK and glad she sees Dorothy. Remember me to all the others, we will have a real knees up and a good drink when this is all over - tell Dick we will be going fishing!

Eventually those long years behind the barbed wire would come to an end. In a panic, however, in January 1945, the Germans moved their Prisoner of War camps in Eastern Germany and Poland to the West in a determined attempt to escape the Russian advance. On January 22nd, 1945, the inmates of Stalag XXB started a long march to Brunswick. Their clothing was inadequate given the bitterly cold winter conditions, and food was in extremely short supply. The daily ration was less than one sixth of a small loaf of bread per man per day. Once a week hot, watery soup was provided at the prisoners' own expense. Many men were soon in need of medical treatment due to frost-bite; none was ever provided. According to one survivor, Private Frank Norbury of the Worcestershire Regiment:-

The condition of the men's feet was terrible. Some had no boots left at all and marched with socks tied round their feet. One of our prisoners lost both legs from frost-bite. If we tried to go to the assistance of a fellow prisoner in desperate straits the guards always kept us off with bayonets. Quite a number of the prisoners died in the course of the march, from dysentery. Whilst at one village there was a search of all prisoners because some food had been stolen. I saw the *Kommandant*, *Oberleutnant* Heering, take a rifle from one of the guards and break it over the neck of a prisoner who had annoyed him.

On one occasion some prisoners went missing. When Heering got to hear of this he kept us standing on parade from 0800 hours until 1300 hours. We were standing in the open and it was raining heavily at the time. Heering gave orders to the guards who went in search of the missing prisoners that they were to shoot them if found. During the march Heering was always jumping off his bicycle and striking members of the marching column with his revolver.

Similar conditions prevailed throughout the march until we reached Brunswick towards the end of March 1945. There we were billeted in a brewery which had been bombed. We were made to use a cold concrete floor as sleeping quarters. No straw was provided. There were holes in the roof and if it rained the floors were flooded. Several of the men's faces swelled up very badly as a result of these conditions. After we had been at Brunswick for about four days we were made to go to work on the railway on bomb damage clearance. None of the men were in any way fit for such work after the privations of the march.

I am still suffering from the effects of the horrors of this march. My memory is very bad for names, even those of my friends. I have great difficulty in sleeping at night and I suffer severe pains in the head.

These prisoners - who must have been a pitiful sight - were finally liberated by the Americans in May 1945. It can only be considered appalling that having already endured so much, these men were subjected to this tortuous march. The *Kommandant*, *Oberleutnant* Arno von Heering, - was later found in a British Prisoner of War camp in August 1945. He was interviewed and charged with the ill-treatment of British and Allied nationals. The trial was held at the Hanover Law Courts over three days in January 1946. Heering, a 48 year old former laundry worker, was found guilty and sentenced to just one day's imprisonment, the Court taking into account the period already spent in Allied custody.

Fortunately both Lance Corporal Nicholls VC and Guardsman Smith survived the 'Death March', but the latter returned home not to the celebrating he had craved so long, but to a broken marriage and further heartache.

On June 22nd, 1945, Lance Corporal Nicholls attended Buckingham Palace and, fulfilling His Majesty's wish of five years earlier, personally received his VC from King George VI. This marked the only occasion since the inception of the Victoria Cross in 1856 that the Cross has been presented twice.

Over the years, there has been much confusion regarding this particular VC award, often described as the 'First Army VC of World War Two'. This is not actually the case. In chronological order, the first 'signal act of valour' to be so recognised occurred on the 15th-16th May, 1940, and concerned, as we have seen, Second Lieutenant Richard Annand of the Durham Light

Guardsman Bert Smith shortly after repatriation, May 1945.

Infantry. The next two awards arose as a result of valour on May 21st: Lance Corporal Nicholls and Company Sergeant Major Gristock. Captain Harold Ervine-Andrews, of the East Lancashire Regiment, received his VC 'For most conspicuous gallantry on active service on the night of the 31st May/1st June, 1940'. Finally, the citation of Lieutenant The Hon. Christopher Furness of the Welsh Guards covers a whole week: May 17th-24th; sadly Furness remains posted Missing in Action to this day. Gallantry awards were announced by the War Office in the *London Gazette*, and the first of the five BEF VCs to be approved were those of Ervine-Andrews and Nicholls, both of which appeared in print on July 30th, 1940. Chronologically, therefore, Nicholls' VC was actually a joint second (with Company Sergeant Major Gristock) in terms of the date on which his 'signal act of valour' had taken place, and joint second in respect of the date Gazetted. It may have been, however, the first to have actually been awarded by the King, and, as previously explained, is the only VC to have been presented twice. The little bronze cross concerned therefore justifies the financial figure for which the Regiment now has it insured (the medal was a gift to the Regiment from the VC's second wife, the now late Mrs Grace Nicholls). Is it possible, however, to put such a price on supreme courage?

It is worth putting the Victoria Cross into perspective when compared to German gallantry awards. To the layman the most obvious equivalent is the so-called Iron Cross (*Eisernes Kreuz*); indeed, a recently published work on the VC by an academic historian makes this comparison. The fact is, however, that there were some 300,000 awards of the Iron Cross Ist Class between 1939-45, and many more of the Iron Cross 2nd Class! On September 1st, 1939, a new Nazi gallantry award was instituted: the Knight's Cross of the Iron Cross (*Ritterkreuz des Eisernen Kreuzes*). The Knight's Cross became Germany's highest gallantry award. On June 3rd, 1940, Hitler instituted the Oak Leaf Cluster (*Eichenlaub*), which was the next step up from the Knight's Cross. On June 21st, 1941, came the *Eichenlaub mit Schwerten* - Oak Leaves with Swords - and the following month saw the RK upgraded further by the *Eichenlaub, Schwerten und Brillanten* - Oak Leaves, Swords and Diamonds. Finally, on December 29th, 1944, came the *Goldenem Eichenlaub, Schwerten und Brillanten* - Gold Oak Leaves, Swords and Diamonds. The quantity of these awards were as follows:-

Knight's Cross:	7,300
Oak Leaves:	890
Oak Leaves & Swords:	159
Oak Leaves, Swords & Diamonds:	27
Gold Oak Leaves, Swords & Diamonds:	1

By comparison, there were but 106 Victoria Crosses awarded in total throughout the Second World War. This rather puts the VC, and in particular the five received by the BEF, in perspective as a *supreme* gallantry award.

'Civvy Street', however, proved difficult for Harry Nicholls VC, the man of action. For a while he worked as a boxing instructor at Butlin's in Filey, but, still suffering from the effect of his head wound, he struggled to hold down regular employment. Although examined by an Army Medical Board in October 1946, which assessed that he was not in any way disabled, a few years later newspapers reported that this valiant Grenadier had applied for a pension. Nicholls claimed that he was compelled to seek public assistance due to dizziness caused by his head injuries preventing him from continuing his work with a ball-bearing company. His plight won sympathy from the general public, some of whom sent financial gifts. It was typical of the man, however, that every penny was returned. The publicity did bring a welcome job offer in Rhodesia, which Harry accepted. Together with Connie and young daughter Carol, Harry set off for a new life. Happiness seemed determined to elude him, however, and Harry was taken ill on a visit to England. Unable to return to his new home, his marriage failed. Although he married a second time, to Grace, ill health prevented him from working again. Fortunately the Grenadier Guards Association was able to support him as he neared the end of his life, when the former boxing champion became confined to a wheelchair. Les Drinkwater:-

Harry Nicholls VC now lies buried with his parents at Wilford Hill Cemetery, Nottingham.

I met Harry Nicholls again in December 1974, during which I spent a week close to the British Legion Flats where he lived near Leeds. We talked about old times, including the River Escaut business where his body was found on higher ground. He told me that when the last bullet hit him he collapsed, blood pouring out of his mouth. He didn't remember anything else until regaining consciousness in a German hospital.

Harry Nicholls VC died, aged 60, on September 11th, 1975. His funeral took place at Wilford Hill, Nottingham, the coffin being carried by eight Grenadier Guardsmen from Chelsea Barracks, London. Senior Grenadier Officers and civic dignitaries joined grieving members of the Nicholls family at the graveside; the Rev. Walter Beasley spoke of Harry's "very great courage which brought honour to the Country, the City and his Regiment." A lone Grenadier Drummer sounded the evocative Last Post as Harry Nicholls VC was finally laid to rest in peace.

Despite his problems, Harry Nicholls considerably outlived the other May 21st, 1940, VC - Company Sergeant Major George Gristock - as explained by former Private Ernie Leggett:-

I was wounded myself during the fighting on May 22nd. As a result I was evacuated. On May 28th, I was admitted to the Royal Sussex County General Hospital at Brighton; I was to remain there for almost a year. My operation over, a few days later a nurse came to my bed and said I was to be wheeled through to the next ward where someone had asked, or so she said, politely ordered that he should see me. I there saw Company Sergeant Major George Gristock, his lower half covered with steel cages: his legs had been amputated. Unable to use one arm he asked that I should take the top off a bottle of ale, several of which were lined up on a ledge beside his bed. I managed to do this and poured the beer into one of the old drinking pots with a handle one side and a spout on the other, and held it to his lips. We talked for several minutes. A visit to see him was arranged and made every day, during which times we talked about everything and sundry. I learned from him that during the fighting on the River Escaut, Captain Barclay had suffered a leg wound and had been evacuated from front line action. HQ section was being over-run and a machine-gun post had been set up, causing many casualties. He told me it was he who had crawled out, with covering fire, and had disposed of the machine-gun but was then hit himself. I was wheeled through to him and spoke with him almost everyday. The coincidence was that we were the only members of the 2nd Royal Norfolk Regiment in the hospital, and, surprisingly enough, were both from 'A' Company.

Sad news was given to me on June 16th, 1940, when I asked to be wheeled through to see the Company Sergeant Major: he had passed away early that morning. Unfortunately he died without knowing that he had won that most coveted of all gallantry awards; the Victoria Cross. This was the first of five awarded to the Regiment. His father and sister, she being a serving member of the Auxiliary Transport Service, were at the investiture at Buckingham Palace and received the medal from King George VI.

I prided myself as being in the unique position of having glimpsed the action in which that particular VC was won, and having been the only member of the Regiment to have spoken and been with him before he died. Fate, I think, plays a significant part in a soldier's life. 'A' Company was virtually wiped out, except for about seven men. One of these was Private Pooley, a Signaller who was transferred to HQ Company. On May 27th, he was one of the two survivors of the Le Paradis massacre, an unprovoked and unforgivable atrocity committed by the SS *Totenkopf.*

Company Sergeant Major George Gristock VC, aged 35, lies buried in Brighton Cemetery, situated on a hill overlooking the sea. His headstone, into which is carved the VC, is inscribed: 'In Loving Memory of My Dear Son. Gone But Not Forgotten'.

At 1130 hours on Sunday, 2nd June 1940, a flag was flown at half mast from the keep of Alnwick Castle, Northumberland. People leaving church nearby could see that the flag was that of the Duke of Northumberland, a blue lion rampant on a gold field. It could only mean one thing: the Duke was dead; the battlefield had claimed him too as it had so many of his august ancestors. Soon more flags were lowered to half mast on such buildings as Alnwick Parish Church and Northumberland Hall in the town centre. The community went into mourning. The Archdeacon of Lindisfarne, the Ven. RR Mangin, said:-

The grave of CSM George Gristock VC at Brighton.

The loss to Alnwick is immense. He was a regular attender and communicant at the parish church and was, in fact, a true Percy - a most devoted Churchman.

He was a good landlord and had great interest in his estates. He was developing into a fine character and was beginning to take an interest in public work. He was a fine sportsman, a very good shot and beautiful rider, and a very true friend.

The late 9th Duke also owned estates at Albury, near Guildford in Surrey. All of Albury's 2,000 inhabitants were tenants of the Duke; all knew him well and held him in high esteem. A newspaper reported the reaction of 93 year old Will Barber:-

The young Duke was such a chivalrous, gallant gentleman. Six years ago at his coming-of-age celebration I presented him with a token of congratulation on behalf of all the tenants. His loss will be deeply felt by us all. The last time I saw him was on the village green joining in a cricket match. I shall always remember his jolly laugh and his friendly manner towards us.

It is noteworthy that only the Percy family shares with Royalty the right of burial in Westminster Abbey. The 9th Duke's father, in fact, was taken to the Abbey in 1930, the Grenadier Guards - his old Regiment - playing a prominent part in the service. The 9th Duke, however, lies with his comrades who also fell on May 21st, 1940: not at Westminster Abbey but at Esquelmes British War Cemetery. His Grace's headstone is simply inscribed *Esperance En Dieu*. Information regarding the action in which the 9th Duke had fallen was apparently provided to the *Journal & North Mail* newspaper by a Mrs Elizabeth Burnett of Ravensworth Terrace, Gateshead, Newcastle: her husband was amongst the Duke's Guardsmen, but 26 year old Lance Corporal Burnett was reported 'Missing' by the War Office on May 25th. Sadly his grave can also be found at Esquelmes.

Lord and Lady Falmouth too faced great sorrow when news was received that their son, 23 year old Lieutenant the Hon. Evelyn Boscawen of the 2nd Bn Coldstream Guards had also been killed. On June 6th, 1940, the *West Briton* newspaper reported this sad loss to 'an ancient Cornish family':-

The Hon. Evelyn Frederick Vere Boscawen, heir to the Tregothnan Estates, has been killed in action in Flanders. He was a Lieutenant in the Coldstream Guards. Mr Boscawen came of age three years ago, when about 900 of the tenantry and employees of the estate participated in the rejoicing at Tregothnan, and beautiful presents were handed to the young heir.

Welcoming the assembly, Viscount Falmouth made reference to the Great War, saying that little did they think in April 1909, when his own coming of age was celebrated, what terrible trials lay before this country - that a whole generation was going to be wiped out in the furnace of the greatest disaster that had ever happened to the world. Viscount Falmouth told the tenants that he liked to look back on the great traditions which had held them all together through all the centuries, and in his speech of thanks for the gifts, the Hon Evelyn Boscawen assured the company that he would try to do his part in keeping up that fine tradition. He was also sure that the younger generation represented there would also do their part....

A member of an ancient Cornish family, Mr Boscawen had perhaps the most famous ancestor in Admiral Boscawen, whose fearlessness won him the title of 'Old Dreadnought'. The second Viscount was Yeoman of the Guard to George II, and he formed in Cornwall an Association of 6,387 [volunteer soldiers], who pledged themselves to appear armed at his command to defend the King and the Government.

Guardsman Joe Nixon, Lieutenant Boscawen's soldier servant who had been amongst the wounded evacuated from Pecq, made it home after a fraught journey on a Red Cross train, which was repeatedly attacked by *Stukas*, to Calais. Whilst in hospital at Epsom, Joe was visited by Lady Falmouth to whom he was at last able to hand over his Officer's Coldstream Capstar. Joe himself survived the Second World War, throughout which he was a fighting soldier. Before eventual retirement he served in both the Metropolitan Police ('Nick' of Notting Hill) and the Prison Service. Having only recently become a Grandfather for the first time, Joe maintains a keen interest in the Dunkirk Veterans' Association, The Coldstream Guards Association and the Royal British Legion. A remarkable man, it is a privilege to know him.

The saddest thing about the tragic incident in which Lieutenant Boscawen was killed, however, was that he was later buried in Pecq cemetery as an 'Unknown Lieutenant of the Grenadier Guards'. On Easter Day, April 1954, however, St Michael Penkevil Church, near Truro, was crowded on the occasion of the dedication and unveiling of a memorial to Lieutenant the Hon. EFV Boscawen. Set in a pillared alcove, the bronze memorial depicts the figure of the Archangel Michael kneeling in prayer upon a vanquished dragon. The figure's face is the likeness of Lieutenant Boscawen. The story, however, has an even more satisfying sequel.

The Grenadier Guards attribution on the original headstone at Pecq was probably due to the discovery of an epaulette with two elongated Garter rank stars in brass. At the time this was believed to indicate a Grenadier Guards Officer. Although Lord and Lady Falmouth corresponded with the Commonwealth War Graves Commission (CWGC) in the 1960s, no conclusion were reached due to the fact that Lieutenant Reynell-Pack of the 3rd Bn Grenadier Guards remained missing from the main action. According to the CWGC:-

When the case was re-opened in 1989, it was pointed out that these stars also applied to the Coldstream Guards. As a result, the information contained in the exhumation report of 1946 was compared with the service particulars for Lieutenants Boscawen and Reynell-Pack. Boscawen was found to be the best fit.

A new, named, headstone was erected on May 8th, 1990, which was dedicated during a small, essentially private family service. Also present, however, were Mr Joe Nixon and his brother Jim (the latter also a former Coldstreamer), and six serving Guardsmen from the 1st Bn Coldstream Guards. The latter included Lieutenant Boscawen's nephew, Major (now Lieutenant Colonel) Hugh Boscawen; the Frock Coat he wore that day, in fact, once belonged to his uncle (and the Capstar recovered by Joe Nixon is also now in his proud possession). The moving service was conducted by the former Bishop of Dover, Bishop David Say, a great friend of Evelyn Boscawen's at Cambridge. Upon conclusion of the service, Drummer Taylor of the 2nd Bn sounded the haunting notes of the Last Post, which could probably be heard across most of the old battlefield itself. No doubt Joe, and the other members of the Coldstream Guards there present, also remembered many other comrades who perished during what became a long and bitter war.

Another Cornishman was in the news back in June 1940: Guardsman Les Drinkwater. *The Western Morning News* reported:-

One of the most striking tales of valour is that about Leslie Hamilton Drinkwater of St Mawes,

Dedication of new (named) headstone to Lieutenant The Hon. EFV Boscawen, Coldstream Guards, Pecq, May 1990. From left to right: Guardsman Douglas, Drummer Taylor, Sergeant Knight, Bishop David Say, Viscount Falmouth, The Rt Hon Robert Boscawen MC, The Hon Mrs Mary Verney, The Hon Edward Boscawen, Major Hugh Boscawen, The Hon Mrs Robert Boscawen, The Hon Evelyn Boscawen, two representatives from the Commune de Pecq, Major Hugo Barnett (Coldstream Guards). Although not pictured here, Mr Joe Nixon and Mr Jim Nixon, both former Guardsmen, were also present).
Lieutenant Colonel HGR Boscawen.

The Coldstream Capstar once worn by Lieutenant The Hon EFV Boscawen, saved by Guardsman Joe Nixon and now in the proud possession of the original owner's nephew - Lieutenant Colonel HGR Boscawen, Coldstream Guards.
Lieutenant Colonel HGR Boscawen.

who, with another Guardsman was holding a position on the bank of a river canal.

His companion, Guardsman Arthur Rice of Worcester, fell wounded in head, arm and leg. Drinkwater hauled him up and onto his back, and carried him two miles through the fire to a farmhouse, himself getting a shrapnel wound on the way. By the time he reached safety, Rice was unconscious. Drinkwater's comradely labour undoubtedly saved his life.

This is the stuff of which the young BEF is made. It is stuff that cannot be beaten, whatever reserves and suffering it may have to endure.

So, after breaking out of the barn used as No 4 Company HQ, what exactly happened to these two Grenadiers? Les Drinkwater:-

After we broke out of the barn, we carried on for a mile or so until we found a Belgian farmhouse constructed in a square with a yard in the centre. The letters RAP (Regimental Aid Post) could be clearly seen. Someone gave me a hand with Arthur on the stretcher, we placed him in the first barn on the left of the entrance. My assistant promptly disappeared - I heard the vehicle accelerating and ran out in an effort to stop them but was too late. If there wasn't a Medical Officer at this post then Arthur and I were back to Square One - on our own!

Shells were falling in the area, they were getting increasingly accurate. I could see a ridge of higher ground to the north, it being obvious that they had an OP up there. Apart from Arthur and me, and the bellowing cattle, there was no other sign of life. The whole area appeared deserted. It was obvious that Arthur required urgent medical treatment - I must find the Medical Officer. On moving across the farmyard to the main living quarters (situated on the right-hand side past the entrance) a shell demolished a section of buildings to the rear. I entered the living quarters, crossed a room and found an open trap door with steps leading down into a cellar. There stood the MO, around him lay Officers and men all seriously wounded. I reported Rice's condition. The MO replied "I have ordered ambulances to take the wounded out but it doesn't look as if they can get through. I would like you to collect all walking wounded, if any, and get them out. There's no point in us all being captured."
I replied "Sir", and commenced to walk up the cellar steps. He called after me,
"Oh, before you go, farther up the road you will find two houses, recently vacated, would you see if they have left any food? These chaps haven't eaten for some considerable time."
Again I replied "Sir" and continued up the cellar steps. I crossed the room towards the door, which I had entered earlier. In my right hand I held my rifle, with my left I reached towards the door catch. Suddenly a terrific explosion, it felt as if the whole world was on top of me. I had severe pain in my left arm, my ears were ringing like hell, and a thick yellowish-brown dust made it impossible for me to see. Somewhere in the distance I could hear muffled voices. Someone dragged me out into the sunlight.

Where was I going? The ground around me appeared to be rising and falling. I moved on. Something ahead of me appeared to be bobbing up and down. A strange sensation came over me, a feeling that nothing would matter any more. They could take my arm, my leg, what the hell was the difference? Again something was bobbing up and down. I felt for my rifle. Where was it? Where was my equipment? Where was my steel helmet? Where in the hell was Arthur Rice? What was wrong with my arm? Christ, I wish this roaring in my head would stop!

What was this crawling along a ditch? A Grenadier minus his boots and battle-dress trousers! What a strange dress for action - I look again - part of his heel had been shot away and further up his leg was a nasty flesh wound. I found a shell dressing and tossed it down to him. We were slowly moving along, one supporting the other. He had spotted, up an incline, a stationary PU. We found it riddled with bullet holes. We moved on, finally being picked up by a returning ammunition truck. At the Field Ambulance Station we parted company.

At the main hospital in Lille, after my medical examination, I received treatment for my fractured left arm. They led me across the ward to a group of five men (one a PSM). All were suffering from shell shock. Then came the ambulance train which was bombed to a standstill. We eventually made Dunkirk, then Newhaven and Wharncliffe Emergency Hospital, Sheffield. At Dunkirk I felt very depressed indeed. Somewhere back there was Arthur Rice and No 4 Company without a snowball's chance in hell of getting out. You can imagine my jubilation when the chap in the next bed to me read a press report confirming that Arthur was safe and doing well! Little did I realise that 35 years would pass before we made contact again. So far as medals go, I was delighted to get a little mention in the local paper.

Ironically, the chances are that Arthur and Les could even have been on the same ambulance train and boat home; Arthur Rice:-

There is just one part of Les's story that I have to correct. It was not actually me firing the Bren but Guardsman Button; he is still 'missing'.

Just after we left the field hospital in a convoy of 12 ambulances, *Stukas* attacked and destroyed the building. I was lucky to get out of Dunkirk on the last ship to Newhaven. When we were half way across the Channel we were attacked by an enemy aircraft which dropped a stick of six bombs alongside the ship. The vessel rocked violently and those on deck reckoned that the bombs missed the ship by but a very narrow margin. After landing in England I was sent on a hospital train to Bristol Infirmary. We were held up en route at Cirencester because of an unexploded German bomb.

Whilst I was at Bristol I received a questionnaire from the Regiment requesting information regarding when and where I last saw whoever doing what. The list of names naturally concerned the 'Missing', but I knew that some must surely have been killed on the hospital train.

When I left hospital and eventually arrived home at Pershore, near Worcester, bombs were dropped in the area that night. This convinced me that Hitler was specifically out to get me!

The wounds they had each received saw to it that Arthur and Les were both invalided out of the Army. Even today they are affected: Arthur chuckles when he says "I still have five pieces of shrapnel in my knee, and another in my left eyebrow; I can't go swimming in case I go rusty!" Naturally there is an unmistakable bond between these two men. Arthur admits quite simply "Les saved my life".

On November 9th, 1998, the Lord Lieutenant of Hereford & Worcester, Colonel Sir Thomas Dunne, presented, at Her Majesty's Command, Arthur Rice with the

Mr & Mrs Arthur Rice MBE with Colonel Sir Thomas Dunne, Lord Lieutenant of Hereford & Worcester, November 9th, 1998.

MBE. The honour was bestowed in recognition of this 83 year old's work in respect of the Royal British Legion. My wife and I were amongst the guests at this proud occasion. Arthur's response was typically modest: "Thank you very much, thank you all for coming. I accept this not just for me but for the Pershore & Eckington Branch".

Les Drinkwater on the Escaut battle:-

The only thing I would add regarding the events of May 21st, 1940, is that I am surprised, in retrospect and with the benefit of hindsight, just how far back our reserve Company, No 3, was located; had they been closer to the main Pecq - Pont-à-Chin road, instead of a mile back, then they could possibly have been brought in quickly to help stop 'Jerry' getting across the Escaut, or, at the very least, stop him penetrating so far inland. Having said that, it would not have affected the final result! Those of us who survived were very lucky men, believe me.

The wounded Lord Forbes was also fortunate to escape from the carnage along the Escaut on May 21st, 1940. Whilst being treated in the Regimental Aid Post of an adjacent unit, this was hit by a mortar bomb. From there his Lordship was taken to a Casualty Clearing Station situated in a school, and eventually onwards to Dunkirk courtesy of a hospital train:-

As dawn broke we arrived at Dunkirk and were shunted to the quayside, where we could see a ship tied up. We all thought that we would shortly be transferred on board to cross the Channel, but this proved to be wishful thinking. The train just remained on the quayside and nothing happened, except that during the space of two hours we were dive-bombed three times by German planes. Each time we heard the *Stukas* screeching down, followed by the port and ship's AA guns going into action. Then the dreaded whine of the released bombs. As the bombs hit the ground and exploded, the whole train would shake. It was a miracle that we did not receive a direct hit.

Eventually the occupants of the hospital train were taken aboard and later landed at Folkestone. Having been transferred to a train bound for St Albans Hospital, Lord Forbes found himself in the same coach as his Company Second in Command, Captain Radford-Norcop; sadly this Officer died in hospital on July 14th, 1940.

A number of families, I found, uphold long traditions of Service in the Foot Guards Regiments; some have had forebears in these fine Regiments for over 200 years. Although more recent history, at least two generations of Courts have served the Regiment well, as related by Captain (former Sergeant) LHT 'Mac' Court:-

Our father served in the 1st Bn Coldstream Guards from 1898-1911. My father-in-law was a 3rd Bn man during the 1900s, my brother-in-law joined in 1943 (but was sadly killed whilst fighting in Italy), and my nephew was in 1st Bn Drums in the 1960s.

My brother Frank, always known to all as 'Peter', and I enlisted as Coldstream Drummer Boys on December 11th, 1928, and did our training in Victoria Barracks, Windsor. During 1936, Peter was sent as Sergeant i/c Corps of Drums at the Guards Depot, Caterham. In 1937/8 he was promoted to Drum Major, 1st Bn.

During the action on May 21st, 1940, Peter was i/c of the right-hand platoon of No 1 Company, 2nd Coldstream Guards, and was therefore our closest unit on the River Escaut to the 3rd Grenadiers when the attack came in. As previously recounted, he was found dead in his trench later that day. After I came home via Dunkirk, I was entrained for Aldershot where two days later I was able to visit my sister-in-law. She had rented a house there and so I went to give her the sad news which she found hard to accept, although I gave her Peter's personal effects. Having two children she found life very difficult from then on as she had to exist on a very small widow's pension.

And what of the enemy? We know that *Hauptmann* Dr Lothar Ambrosius, the *Kommandeur* of II/IR 12 received the *Ritterkreuz* (Knight's Cross of the Iron Cross) when serving as an *Oberst* on February 15th, 1944; at that time the 31 ID was still fighting the Russians. Like the rest of the *Wehrmacht*, IR 12 suffered extremely high casualties on the Eastern Front. Figures provided by the *Kameradschaft* (Comrades' Association) indicate that by May 8th, 1945, IR 12 had lost 6,000 men *Gefallene*. The *Kameradschaft* is run by 91 years old Dr Albert Bollmann, himself a *Leutnant* who fought with II/IR 12 on May 21st. As he says, given the heavy losses in Russia (where the 31 ID served with Army Group Centre and fought with particular distinction during the Battle of Kursk in 1943), coupled with the natural march of time, there are very few of *'Die kamerad von der Schelde'* still alive today.

The 31 ID casualties left behind on the River Escaut were eventually exhumed after the war and taken to the *Deutscher Soldatenfriedhof* (German War Cemetery) at Lommel, near the Belgian-Dutch border. Some 39,000 German Servicemen lie therein, which gives some idea of the scale of fighting in what is a comparatively small country (these casualties are mainly from 1940 and 1944). At Lommel, in section five, block 594, can be found the grave of 23 year old *Leutnant* Hans Engel, the II/IR 12 Adjutant killed on Poplar Ridge and spoken so highly of by *Hauptmann* Ambrosius. Yet another wasted life, just one more victim of what is now referred to in Germany as 'Hitler's War'.

Given that both Lance Corporal Nicholls VC and my Grandfather both served in the 3rd Bn Grenadier Guards, this account has naturally featured the day-to-day experiences of that Battalion. The emphasis throughout, in fact, has been upon ordinary Guardsmen and NCOs. But what now of the 3rd Battalion? On March 31st, 1961, it was placed in suspended animation, although Her Majesty The Queen directed that a composite company should be formed from all ranks of the 3rd Bn in order to keep its traditions alive. This new company is still known as Inkerman Company, the Company Call of which is formerly that of the 3rd Grenadiers. Having met several serving members of Inkerman Company, there can be no doubt that the 3rd Bn's proud traditions are in good hands.

Obviously throughout the course of my research I have been fortunate indeed to receive tremendous co-operation from many veterans. Just two, in fact, felt that these were memories best forgotten. I can both understand and respect that view. I nevertheless feel passionately that unless such traumatic experiences are unlocked and published, then future generations will have little idea of what suffering and sacrifice their ancestors endured; the past, of course, will always shape the present and future. Also, Dunkirk and 1st Guards Brigade veteran 'Elly' Ellingworth told me that he just could not understand why so little has previously been written about the 1st Guards Brigade in 1940, especially given that a VC was awarded. I can only hope that together we have now done the subject justice.

Fifty years after the Fall of France, in 1990, I attended an airshow at the Imperial War Museum, Duxford Airfield. The Dunkirk Veterans Association (DVA) had a stand there and I spoke with the Veteran in attendance - a former Royal Artilleryman

- and mentioned that my Grandfather had served with the 3rd Bn Grenadier Guards. "The Guards?", he said in a provocative manner for some reason, "Were they there then?" It was not even worth my breath to reply, but oh yes, the Guards were there alright, and the 3rd Grenadiers, given their success on both the River Escaut and Ypres-Comines Canal, certainly played a most distinguished part in 1st Guards Brigade during the campaign.

The Lord Forbes:-

From the time the 3rd Bn Grenadier Guards had joined the BEF and fought its way back to Dunkirk, eventually to reach the shores of England, it had suffered 40% casualties. That the 3rd Battalion returned to England with honour, to fight again, was in no small measure due to their discipline and indomitable spirit; this had enabled the Battalion to overcome overwhelming odds. British and Allied forces had been outmanoeuvred, both strategically and tactically, by the Germans.

A newspaper cutting from the time sums it up, making any further comment superfluous:-

---

HEROES OF THE GUARDS

This story of the supreme courage shown by the Guards during the retreat in Belgium and Northern France was told in London yesterday.

When our troops were ordered to retire from the Dyle positions at Louvain, the garrison of one of our pillboxes, manned by Guardsmen, did not come back.

An Officer went out to see why they had not retired. He found that all the occupants were so badly wounded that they could not move.

He had no possible means of helping them, but he asked if he could do anything in the way of obtaining morphia to alleviate their sufferings or sending them anything else they might need.

But, wounded and helpless though they were, the Guards were sticking on heroically.

Their answer was "We don't want any morphia, but we are rather short of small arms and ammunition. If you could send us that we should be grateful."

POSTSCRIPT

The War Pilgrim

After the death of my Grandfather in 1983, it was actually my Mother, Janet Sarkar, who obtained details of his Service. It was discovered that the Honorary Secretary of the Worcester & Hereford Branch of the Grenadier Guards Association, Ray Seale, had paid regular visits to Bert Smith, and shortly before his death the following notes were published in the Branch's sixth Newsletter:-

Early May 1940, saw Guardsman Herbert Henry Smith and his colleagues of No 4 Company of the 3rd Bn in Belgium near to the Escaut Canal, fighting a rearguard action. His two companions were killed, one being Guardsman Hayes. He was captured at that point by the Germans and marched to a nearby barn. En route he met Lance Corporal Harry Nicholls VC being brought out of a cornfield. He spent the night with Harry and dressed his wounds. He was afterwards taken by train to Mewe (Weischal) prison, Poland, with Lance Corporal Everitt and about five other Grenadier prisoners together with some half-a-dozen Welsh Guards. There he was put to work re-building the prison, which became his home for the next three-and-a-half years. He was later taken to East Prussia to work on a state farm at Theirgarth, then marched into Austria. On being threatened by the Red Army, the prisoners were marched again over the Vistula river to NW Germany and the town of Hagennue. There he was finally released by the American Army and eventually released from his second period of service with the Regiment in May 1945 (having first joined in 1928). His memory is a little hazy over times of events but well remembers, during his forced march from Poland to NW Germany, spending a comfortable night in a church until one of the prisoners started playing the organ; this was all in order until he played modern dance music - they were then thrown into a saw mill for the rest of a bitterly cold winter's night. At Hagennue he had the foresight to paint in large letters on the roof 'POW' - just in time to prevent the USAAF mistaking the camp for German barracks. This story is naturally much longer but I have insufficient space for more.

Records show that Guardsman Smith was posted Missing Believed Killed in late May 1940, and in hospital in Germany as a POW in September 1940.

Unfortunately Ray's original notes no longer survived. Nevertheless the foregoing actually created the baseline of data which made this book possible, so all I can say is "Thank God" that someone took the time and trouble to talk to my Grandfather and record at least the most basic details for it was too late.

Sadly, as previously indicated, my Mother's parents divorced shortly after the war ended, but nevertheless my Grandmother had kept the telegrams which Bert had sent her from Pirbright in 1939, along with some letters, photographs and his Soldier's Pay Book. These she gave to me in 1983, welcome additions to the medals and brass locker plate given to me by Bert himself some 10 years previously. There the matter largely rested, however, until 1988; having time on my hands during a period of convalescence, I resolved to discover more. Naturally an essential point of contact was Regimental Headquarters, at Wellington Barracks, and a real bonus was that the Archivist, Major (sadly now the late) Eric 'Sam' Weaver was himself a former 3rd Grenadier and veteran of the action on May 21st, 1940. He kindly provided much general information, adding that:-

The episode of Harry Nicholls winning the VC with Percy Nash, his No 2 on the Bren gun, is of course vivid in my memory. It was at a time of tremendous fighting against overwhelming odds. How so many of us managed to live and tell the tale remains a mystery to me. Sadly many did not, and many others were wounded and taken prisoner, amongst them, of course, your Grandfather.

The road soon led to the Worcestershire home of Arthur Rice, who was able to introduce me to the man who had saved his life that fateful day: Les Drinkwater. The latter had, in fact, written an account of his experiences, published in the 1982 *Grenadier Gazette*; this made for inspiring reading. Unfortunately, however, former Sergeant Norton Bullock, in charge of the No 4 Company Stretcher Bearer Section in which Les had served, was deceased, but his widow kindly saw me and provided what information she was able. Mrs Bullock told me that:-

None of us knew that Norton had been awarded the DCM until we read it in the paper along with everyone else. It was typical of him.

Indeed I was to find such modesty typical of these men generally.

In March 1989, my brother, Neil, and I visited Percy Nash at his home in Bournemouth. I made notes, most of which have been reproduced where appropriate in this book. He was a fine man, his memory sharp; it was a great privilege to meet Percy who died in 1994. I hope he would have been pleased with this book.

There matters were to rest a while, however. Since childhood I had been absorbed in a fascination for the Supermarine Spitfire and the pilots who once flew this amazing fighter during the Second World War. By 1989, I had decided to write a series of books dealing with various aspects of this subject. The first was published in 1990, followed by a second in 1992, and one per year up to and including 1998. Naturally given that I have both a demanding full time occupation and a young family, this schedule left little time for any further Grenadier related research. In any case, I had learned sufficient to satisfy both my own and the family's curiosity, so to all intents and purposes the story had been sufficiently recorded - or so I thought!

During 1995, I started work on the first of two books detailing the wartime flying career of the legless air 'ace' Group Captain Sir Douglas Bader. The research process included an analysis of the action fought high over the Pas-de-Calais on August 9th, 1941, during which Bader was brought down and captured. It was a confused fight involving around 100 twisting and turning Spitfires and Me 109s. Exactly how 'DB' had been brought down had never been established. My friends and I decided, therefore, to try and locate the crash site of Bader's Spitfire with a view to recovering any remaining items for conservation and display. This naturally led to numerous trips across the Channel to work alongside my close French friend Dr Bernard-Marie Dupont. At that time he lived in Armentières, just North West of Lille, and I realised that we were not too far away from Pecq and the scene of the Grenadiers' battle on May 21st, 1940. Lack of time always contrived against a foray across the Belgian border, however, but, as we travelled around the area between Calais and Lille, I became increasingly inspired. Overall the countryside in that part of France and Flanders has changed little (although naturally towns have been re-built). Driving along it was easy to imagine meeting a German column on the move around the next bend. I resolved that soon I would visit the Pecq area and undertake further research into the events of the day in question. The problem was that I was already well committed with wartime aviation research and publishing projects; it was 'Catch 22' as I knew that concurrently time was rapidly running out due to the advancing ages of survivors.

In July 1997, Anita and I took our children, James (then aged five) and Hannah (two), for a short break on the South Coast. Impulsively we decided to dash over the Channel for an overnight stay in St Omer before going over the Belgian border to the battlefield. As usual time was short, so the sortie was really no more than a reconnaissance armed with a camera. The sketch plans provided over the years by survivors such as Les Drinkwater were indelibly etched on my memory, so off we went.

It was a warm but dull day, as I recall, and the site was both surprisingly accessible and easy to find: straight down the A27 out of Lille, east towards Brussels, then, at junction 34 (near Tournai), North on the N50 towards Kortrijk (Courtrai). The N50 is actually the road to which 1st Guards Brigade withdrew on May 21st, 1940 (although it has since been elevated and widened to create what is now a busy dual carriageway). The countryside is very, very flat, the openness emphasised by the almost total lack of hedgerows. Driving along through Belgium that day, I experienced an almost overwhelming feeling that I was answering a long overdue part of my personal destiny. I kept thinking back to the day spent researching old copies of the Worcester *News & Times* at the City Library; these are now on micro-film and I was looking for any reference to my Grandfather's home coming in 1945. I spun the machine at random, stopping it on the same basis: there was my Grandfather's picture, circa 1945, staring at me. Sheer coincidence very likely, but nevertheless for a second I felt a freezing sensation at the back of my neck! I was aware, however, that as opposed to all of my previous projects, this trip represented a very personal pilgrimage.

Whilst still travelling North along the N50, there were suddenly sign posts indicating places which had been on my mind for a decade: Pont-à-Chin, Ramegnies-Chin, Bailleul and Esquelmes. To the east, two miles or so away, was the magnificent Mont St Aubert: a wooded hill crowned by a Medieval church. It was almost too much to take in. My large scale map (National Geographic Institute, Estampuis-Pecq 37/1-2) indicated that at Esquelmes there was a British War Cemetery, and, by cross-referencing this plan with the sketches of survivors, it was possible to work out the site of 'Poplar Ridge' itself, this wooded strip actually being indicated on the map. Arriving at the right-turn to leave the N50 opposite the Château d'Esquelmes, first impressions of the battlefield were stunning: the fields still stood high with corn - much the same, therefore, as it would have appeared on the fateful day.

It was an incredible experience to stand on the site of my Grandfather's capture, very consciously in the shadow of the dominating Mont St Aubert. Not all of the fields were corn, in fact, some being maize and others sugar beet. It was intoxicating to view this site, the avenue of poplars - so unmistakably 'Poplar Ridge' - rising from about 200 metres North of the cemetery up to the N50. Several farm buildings were dotted around the area - which one, I wondered, had been No 4 Company HQ from which Arthur and Les had escaped under fire? Here was a head on collision with powerful living history.

Having parked off the track near the British War Cemetery at Esquelmes, situated within a large cornfield, whilst I prepared my camera Anita and the children went on ahead through the gates. The cemetery is an oblong containing the graves of 233 British soldiers, all of whom were killed defending the Escaut in May 1940; 32 are unidentified by name. These casualties were gathered together here in September 1940, by the Belgian authorities. A Cross of Sacrifice mounts a silent vigil over the perfect rows of white headstones in this immaculately kept and peaceful spot: 'some corner of a foreign field that is forever England'. As I entered the gate, Anita called from the plot at the Northern end: "You'd better come over here", she said. As I walked down the regimented lines of stone I guessed that she had found the 3rd Grenadier casualties. "There you are", Anita said: "Guardsman SJ Hayes, Age 28; isn't that what you came for?" It was indeed. Ray Seale's notes had mentioned that my Grandfather's two companions were killed, one being Guardsman Hayes. And here he was. It was a moving moment which made me think: although my Grandfather had been wounded and captured, consequently enduring five years as a prisoner which culminated in the 'Death March', he had nevertheless survived to die as an old man, aged 76. The lives of Guardsman Hayes and the other Grenadiers here, however, had ended abruptly on that now far off May morning: they had been here ever since. Read that last sentence again, and dwell a moment on the word 'ended'. The tragedy of it all struck me hard and brought a tear to my eye. It was interesting to find all of the Grenadiers together, but apart and a little aloof, as is their privilege, from the other regiments represented. Joining them in Plots I - IV, however, was a Coldstreamer, date of death May 22nd, and three soldiers of the North Staffordshire Regiment. I reasoned that these too must also have been killed on this field of battle.

Walking around the headstones was very sad to say the least. Here lay the 9th Duke of Northumberland and Captain Abel-Smith, both killed during No 3 Company's counter-attack, and Second Lieutenant Boyd of No 4 Company, who had been with the 3rd Grenadiers for less than a month. The youngest here was Guardsman RJ Cook at 19 years. Some of the inscriptions, chosen by the families concerned, were tragic in the extreme:-

Guardsman EJ Portsmouth, Age 24:-

We think of him in silence but all we have are memories and a photo in a frame.

Guardsman WW Rowland, Age 28:-

In Ever Loving Remembrance of Daddy.

Warrant Officer III (Platoon Sergeant Major) SW Jenkinson, Age 28:-

He died to save us all. In silence we remember. Sadly missed by wife Olive & twins Maureen & Celia.

I would defy anyone - from any generation - not to be moved whilst standing in such a cemetery. Indeed, I believe that a tour of Flanders' cemeteries should be a compulsory part of the National Curriculum.

We then made our way towards the River Escaut, the line of which could be seen several hundred metres east of the cemetery. East of Poplar Ridge we found a

The remains of Poplar Ridge, Esquelmes, in July 1997. Appropriately, wild poppies grow profusely in the cornfield. The River Escaut is about 200 metres behind the photographer.

Poplar Ridge looking from the South. The main Pecq - Pont-à-Chin Road can be seen to the left. One hundred yards in front of the photographer is the shrine, to which Major Matthews' counter-attack penetrated before he was killed. The main counter-attack, starting at 1130 hrs, mounted by No 3 Company, 3rd Bn Grenadier Guards, crossed the main road and approached the poplars across the cornfield and in open order.

The British War Cemetery at Esquelmes as it appears today. This photograph is taken from behind the plot containing those who fell here (i.e. in the opposite direction as that in which the picture of the original cemetery was taken). As can be seen, the site has been completely re-landscaped and now some 250 British soldiers are at rest here. After the war, most German casualties in Belgium were exhumed and taken to Lommell near the Belgian-Dutch border, so none now remain buried here.

straight and featureless canal some 60 yards wide. I took photographs from the West bank, at what appeared to be, given my information, the position occupied by No 4 Company of the 3rd Grenadiers. Some 500 metres to the North was Pecq bridge, the town itself screened by trees. Quickly moving back inland we came to the base of 'Poplar Ridge'. Appropriately, I found numerous wild poppies growing in the cornfield there - the very cornfield in which had perished so many Grenadiers of both No 3 Company and the Carrier Section. It was at some point along these poplars that the MG 34s had been located, ultimately destroyed by Lance Corporal Nicholls and Guardsman Nash. It occurred to me that, given the uniqueness of the Nicholls VC, I was actually standing on a most important historical site. Far from

Hannah and James Sarkar (then aged two and five) at the graveside of their Great-Grandfather's comrade, Guardsman Sam Hayes.

being included on the itineraries of commercial battlefield tour operators, however, this was a forgotten battle. I certainly had much food for thought as we re-joined the N50 and drove the hour back to Calais.

That brief visit to the battlefield was amongst the most moving experiences of my life to date. I determined that the story of these 'forgotten heroes' should be published. In addition to my existing commitments, I began intensively researching the events in question. Ernie Hardy, an old friend, was commissioned to undertake the work required at the Public Record Office, Kew (where the relevant War Diaries and other records can be consulted), and it soon became apparent from the information arising that I could not write about the 3rd Grenadiers without including reference to the 1st Guards Brigade as a whole. In addition to Grenadiers, therefore, I set out to find members of the former 2nd Coldstream and 2nd Hampshires. Veteran Joe Nixon of the former was found in Kent as the result of a newspaper article about the DVA published in 1990, and Lieutenant Colonel Peter

Halliday was located via The Royal Hampshire Regiment Museum. Both men proved invaluable to me, as their accounts published here now testify.

The CWGC provided a copy of their Register detailing burials in Bruyelle, Esquelmes and Gaurin-Ramecroix War Cemeteries and other minor cemeteries in the Belgian province of Hainault. These registers are essential when it comes to tracing the families of casualties. From information contained therein I was able to trace the sister and family of Guardsman Sam Hayes; a sad story, his brother was a 'Chindit' killed in Burma. His Grace the Duke of Northumberland kindly provided much information regarding the 9th Duke, and also put me in touch with the niece of Lance Corporal Hudson, Mrs Ruth Grocott, who had recently visited her uncle's grave at Esquelmes. Young Guardsman Cook, of Ledbury, I also had an interest in, Ledbury being close to Worcester; I traced his cousin, Mrs Seager, who remembered waving him off at Ledbury railway station after his last leave: it was the last time she saw her young kinsman alive. The Register indicated that the 3rd Grenadiers' youngest casualty of all on May 21st, 1940, was 18 year old Lance Sergeant Arthur Rimell of Severn Stoke, near Worcester (about three miles from my own home just outside the city). The Rimells are a well-known local family and were easy to trace; by coincidence, Arthur's best friend, Ken Ball, spends most of his time in the cul-de-sac where I live! From all of these relatives and friends I was able to obtain photographs and other information which, in a way, has breathed life into these long-dead warriors of whom we now have a record of their likeness published for posterity.

The 3rd Bn Grenadier Guards have, in fact, two Officers still officially 'Missing' from the battle of May 21st, 1940. As previously related, one is Lieutenant Reynell-Pack, the other Major Alston-Roberts-West. German records indicate, in fact, that the latter was buried by *Oberleutnant* Michael's men. In the Grenadier plot at Esquelmes Cemetery lie 10 soldiers merely 'Known unto God'; one is an unidentified Grenadier Guardsman, another a Grenadier Officer. According to the CWGC, the latter was identified as an Officer at the 1946 exhumation due only to the discovery of an 'Officer's quality shirt'. The casualty list indicates that the 3rd Grenadiers suffered 47 fatalities on May 21st; 14, including the two Officers, remain officially 'Missing in Action'. Although 10 of them probably lie in this particular plot at Esquelmes, four have never been accounted for. During the course of my research I was pleased to trace Lieutenant Colonel George West, the son of Major West and himself a retired Grenadier Guards Officer; he wrote to me on March 20th, 1998:-

I was fascinated by your research into No 4 Company of the 3rd Bn Grenadier Guards and the battle near Pecq; you were kind to seek me out and to pass on so much information.

I too have visited Pecq and the cemetery at Esquelmes. I also met in Bachy the family with whom my father was billeted during the winter of 1939/40. The head of the family, who was about eight in 1940, remembered my father well and also his orderly Guardsman Meade. I was saddened to discover that my father did not have a grave so the information you have revealed is most comforting. I did know that his body had been found the night after the battle as I once met a Guardsman who had been in the patrol which found him.

As a result of this research, Lieutenant Colonel West has been able to meet the two men who saw his father fall: Les Drinkwater and Arthur Rice.

It was my great desire to establish which German unit had fought the 3rd Grenadiers on May 21st, and in this endeavour I was pointed towards a Belgian solicitor, Peter Taghon. Just as I have published many books about RAF Fighter Command in 1940/41, Peter has equally well researched and published books on the German advance in 1940. Of a similar age, we realised immediately that we had much in common and became friends. Peter was able to provide copies of all surviving German records including the crucial Ambrosius account. Peter's photographic collection was equally impressive, some examples being included in this book. In my business there are many dead-ends, but sometimes a lucky break; contacting Peter was happily one of the latter.

Former Grenadiers were extremely forthcoming and helpful, notably amongst them Charles Constantine, Mr W Lewcock and Bert Middleton. A life-long friend of Harry Nicholls, Ted 'Boxer' Brown, himself a Grenadier and Dunkirk Veteran, was a fount of knowledge and made the introduction to Mrs Irene Hazeldine, Harry's sister. My friend, photographer and assistant Andrew Long and I drove up to Nottingham to meet this remarkable pair in February 1998. Together we visited Bosworth Road Primary School - Harry's old school - where it was heart-warming to see a copy of his VC citation prominently displayed together with a photograph of a painting, commissioned by the Regiment, depicting the action concerned. We then went on to Wilford Hill Cemetery and photographed Harry Nicholls' grave. There were, of course, four Nicholls brothers in the 3rd Grenadiers; as HM King George VI himself once said, the Nicholls are a "family to be proud of". Many years later, Irene the last survivor of that clan, remains quite rightly proud of Harry in particular, and keeps in pride of place his miniature medals and brass Grenadier Guards nameplate.

My 'spare' time in October 1998, was put aside to conclude the research for this book. On October 6th, I was pleased to be a guest at the Worcester & Hereford Branch of the Grenadier Guards Association and was much impressed with the

The Author with the sister of Lance Corporal Harry Nicholls VC, Mrs Irene Hazeldine,
displaying her brother's miniature medals.
Andrew Long.

young serving Guardsmen I spoke to there. All knew of Harry Nicholls and had
an awareness of and great pride in the Regiment's history. The following day,
Andrew Long and I drove to Regimental Headquarters at Wellington Barracks.
There we undertook research under the ever-helpful guidance of the Regimental
Adjutant, Lieutenant Colonel Conway Seymour, Lieutenant Colonel Sir John
Smiley and Mr Alan Kear. A thrill was being allowed to photograph the actual
Victoria Cross awarded to Lance Corporal Nicholls (presented to the Regiment
by his widow, sadly since deceased). It was a curious feeling to hold this little
bronze medal which represents so much history. October 14th saw me travel to
Elizabeth Barracks, Pirbright, where I enjoyed lunch with Lieutenant Colonel
David Hutchison, Commanding Officer of the 1st Bn Grenadier Guards, certain
of his Officers, 'Boxer' Brown and Irene Hazeldine. As we dined in the Officers'
Mess it occurred to me that when re-joining the 3rd Grenadiers at Pirbright, my
Grandfather could never have imagined that nearly 60 years later his fourth
Grandson would be so entertained in 'Officer Country'!

After lunch I spoke to the Corporals' Mess about the project and Nicholls story in
particular; having Irene in the audience made me slightly nervous as I had to

make sure that everything was right! I need not have worried, however, and it meant a great deal when Irene told me afterwards "My goodness, even I had no idea just how much work you have done. Well done!" We joined the Corporals for a drink in the bar before leaving and there was displayed my 'Holy Grail': the red tunic and silver boxing trophies of Lance Corporal Harry Nicholls: very impressive! As Lieutenant Colonel Hutchison told me, "Harry Nicholls remains a great Regimental hero".

In the Corporals' Mess (Grenadier Guards), Elizabeth Barracks, Pirbright, October 14th, 1998. The Author, Mr Ted 'Boxer' Brown and Mrs Hazeldine flank a display case containing the tunic and boxing trophies of Lance Corporal Harry Nicholls VC.
Grenadier Guards.

Afterwards, I received a letter from the Commanding Officer:-

Thank you for coming all the way to Pirbright to talk about Harry Nicholls. The Corporals were hanging on your every word and it was excellent to see how a really good talk can hold an audience. I myself enjoyed the talk enormously as did the other Officers present.

My response was to the effect that it had been a pleasure; indeed whilst providing the presentation it crossed my mind as to whether there were any potential VCs in the audience!

The youngest casualty of the 3rd Bn
Grenadier Guards on May 21st, 1940:
Lance Sergeant Arthur Rimell, aged 18, of
Kempsey, Worcestershire.
Mr C Rimell.

Lance Sergeant Rimell's grave at
Ramignes-à-Chin, Belgium,
November 1998.
Andrew Long.

Drum Major 'Pete' Court, (then) 1st
Bn Coldstream Guards, wearing
ceremonial dress on the occasion of
the King's birthday, 1938, and leading
the Guards' Regimental Band into
Buckingham Palace for the Guard
Changing ceremony.
Captain (Retd) LHT Court.

The grave of PSM FE Court at Bailleul,
Belgium, November 1998.
Andrew Long.

The 2nd Bn Hampshire Regiment's only fatality
on May 21st, 1940, was Private W Butlin, now
buried at Estaimbourg, Belgium.

It was necessary, however, to return to Belgium before I could complete the book. Arrangements were made for a trip at the end of October. I was to be joined by three like-minded friends: Allan White, whose late father was a Royal Artillery BEF Dunkirk Veteran, Antony Whitehead, and, naturally, Andy Long. Friday, 30th October, found us in the Pecq area. First we visited and photographed the grave of young Lance Sergeant Rimell at the tiny village of Ramignes; again, another moving inscription was found on this headstone: *Dear "Bubbles" always in our thoughts, Father, Mother, Charles and Dennis*; it was Charles and Dennis whom Andy and I had visited a year before to talk about their brother, 'Bubs'. From Ramignes we drove the short distance to Bailleul, which we found curiously deserted, and in the cemetery there found, amongst others, the grave of Platoon Sergeant Major Frank 'Pete' Court of the 2nd Bn Coldstream Guards. Afterwards we located Estaimbourg cemetery next to the chateau in which 1st Guards Brigade HQ was situated. In that cemetery lay an unknown airman and five British soldiers: four Gunners and the only 2nd Hampshire fatality on May 21st: 36 year old Private Walter Butlin, a married man of Sparkbrook, Birmingham.

En route to the town of Pecq we passed a memorial commemorating the two battles there: May 1940 and September 1944. Soon we were in Pecq itself and our thoughts turned to the 2nd Bn Coldstream Guards. The imposing tannery, from which Guardsman Swaby shot 14 Germans, is still there, situated on the east side of the N50 and immediately South of the cemetery. The difference with Pecq today is that all windows are glazed; on May 21st, glass crunched

The tannery at Pecq which provided an excellent local vantage point for No 4 Company, 2nd Bn Coldstream Guards. In November 1998, however, we were to discover that at this point the River Escaut had since been moved some 100 metres Eastwards. In 1940, therefore, the German occupied East bank would have been almost adjacent to the tannery.

The grave of Captain Charles Fane, 2nd Bn Coldstream Guards, at Pecq Cemetery.

underfoot as every window in the town had gone in when the bridge was blown! The majority of 2nd Coldstream dead lie in the town cemetery; there 19 British soldiers lie, including 13 identified Coldstreamers. Of the two unidentified soldiers in that cemetery, one headstone records a Coldstreamer 'Known Unto God'; there are, in fact, two Coldstreamers missing to this day from the Battle of Pecq: Guardsman Coope and Guardsman Jones. Amongst the headstones can be found those of Captain Charles Fane, killed when his Carrier was hit near Guardsman Joe Nixon, and the comparatively recently named headstone of Lieutenant The Hon. EFV Boscawen.

On from the cemetery we drove across the new Pecq bridge and down to the River Escaut itself. Peter Taghon had obtained some photographs from a former German soldier, taken on or about May 23rd, 1940, which showed the blown original bridge from the east bank. On the west bank, and <u>immediately adjacent</u> to the river, was a large detached building. Hoping to make a 'Then & Now' comparison for *After the Battle* magazine which had already commissioned an article on our work, we were stunned to realise that although the building was still there, it was now some <u>150 metres West of the river</u>! We realised immediately

Pecq bridge, demolished by the Royal Engineers on the night of May 20th/21st, 1940, pictured by the Germans two days later.

Via Peter Taghon.

It was whilst trying to take a comparison photograph in November 1998, that we realised the canal had been moved Eastwards! A direct comparison is now impossible for that reason and because of the large barn type structure built on the site of the blown bridge! The same large house, however, can clearly be seen. The River Escaut in this area has been particularly straightened and diverted.

Fortunately in the area of the position briefly occupied by No 4 Company, 3rd Bn Grenadier Guards, a section of the original River Escaut remains (visible through the trees on the left). To the right can be seen the 'new' River Escaut which is wider than the original; the West bank of today, would clearly have been on the East bank in 1940, however!

Andrew Long.

This photograph was taken from the dammed South end of the surviving original section of River Escaut. It was the left-hand bank which No 4 Company defended until being over-run. Somewhere along that bank, therefore, occurred many of the dramatic events recounted in this book. Evidence of the heavy German bombardment was found here in November 1998.

what had happened: after the war the River Escaut had been canalised, straightened and widened. This process had clearly entailed *moving* the river eastwards in what can only be described as a major feat of civil engineering! Things rapidly started to fall into place. During my first visit, I had been surprised regarding the width of the River Escaut - around 40 metres. *The Grenadier Guards 1939-45* (Volume I) describes the River Escaut as similar in width to the Basingstoke Canal. Having travelled over that waterway during my visit to Pirbright, I was aware that the Basingstoke Canal was no more than 15 metres wide - probably less. The open, wide expanse of the new River Escaut would be very difficult to cross under fire without a very heavy bombardment indeed and overwhelming numbers. That extra 25 metres would make a great deal of difference. As we studied the ground after this significant discovery, we could see willow trees, and the remains of some original flood defences, along both sides of what was clearly the original river bank. There was another exciting discovery about to be made, but to confirm it we had to re-cross the bridge and drive to the west bank of the new River Escaut.

During that first visit, I had parked my car on the west bank in the area of what appeared to be No 4 Company's position. Immediately to the right was a narrow strip of water running parallel with the river. It was fringed with trees and local anglers fished there. When I returned home with photographs, both the survivors and myself were puzzled by this water, but now the answer was glaringly obvious - it was a section of the original river, the west bank of which really was defended by No 4 Company! What a terrific stroke of luck, I felt like the 'Battlefield Detective'! This section of water, some 200 metres long and 30 metres wide, is clearly marked on most maps and means that, in 1940, today's West bank would actually have been on the German held East bank! This section of original canal also tallied with the dimensions of the Basingstoke Canal and, given the reduced width, a crossing under fire now seemed a realistic prospect - as indeed it had proved to be on May 21st, 1940.

Mont St Aubert still silently dominating the landscape, happily now in more peaceful times. The village is Léacourt, and it was from the road there that II/IR 12 brought their rubber boats across the fields and launched the assault river crossing on May 21st, 1940.
Andrew Long.

The climb by road to the top of Mont St Aubert was impressive. At the summit we found the old church, in the tower of which was a once German OP. Climbing up onto the churchyard wall, looking west, the view was absolutely incredible. We reckoned on seeing, through the zoom lenses of our cameras, at least 30 miles - well beyond the city of Lille. With the high powered magnification available to the military - even in 1940 - that distance would doubtless be increased. In any case a great section of the BEF's line along the River Escaut could be studied with ease - even with the naked eye towns such as Pecq stood out like the proverbial sore thumb. Anyone who visits the area as a result of this book *must* include a visit to the top of Mont St Aubert - only when you have stood there yourself can the benefits of this observatory be fully appreciated. It is awesome.

Pecq seen from the top of Mont St Aubert, which gives a good impression of the height's great benefit to the Germans. Pecq church and bridge can clearly be seen.
Andrew Long.

We then visited Esquelmes British War Cemetery, where more video footage was filmed and 'stills' taken. I had with me a Royal British Legion wreath of poppies, bearing the Royal Cypher, and this was photographed against many of the Grenadier graves. We left it, appropriately, on the grave of Guardsman Sam Hayes. I have often wondered what my Grandfather would have thought of my project but have never been entirely decided on his reaction; leaving the wreath on Sam's grave would, I think, have been a gesture he would have appreciated.

Driving along the track back to the N50 - virtually in the middle of nowhere - another surprise lay in store: the shrine (2nd Bn North Staffordshire War Diary

Photographed at Esquelmes in November 1998, the grave of Lieutenant The 9th Duke of Northumberland.
Andrew Long.

The now famous shrine. Beyond it, to the
West, the N50 can be seen.
Andrew Long.

The grave of Major FG Matthews, 2nd
Bn North Staffordshire Regiment,
photographed at Esquelmes, November
1998.
Andrew Long.

refers, see Chapter Seven) where the wounded Captain Birch and the Grenadier Corporal with whom he was in company had been rescued! There it was, this strange little old structure containing rosaries and a Madonna figure. It is, in fact, situated some 70 metres east of and parallel to the N50, and marked on the map as *Chapel Notre Dame de la Misericorde*; another tangible link with the past.

The following morning, my French 'brother', Dr Bernard-Marie Dupont (a confirmed Anglophile) was meeting us at our hotel in Lille - by coincidence near the main hospital where Les Drinkwater was treated - and we were then travelling on together to meet Peter Taghon at Esquelmes. The day dawned extremely cold, windy and wet. We were just about to discover first-hand what Flanders mud was all about! Having met Peter as arranged, we sheltered from the elements in the small building at the cemetery in which the Burial Register and Visitors' Book is kept. Browsing through the latter I had another bonus: one entry was by a Mrs Pat Jordan, nee Matthews; surely this was the daughter of Major FG Matthews of the 2nd North Staffordshires? He had, of course, led the gallant counter-attack towards the shrine and had fallen at the head of his small force; the Major's grave was right in front of me. This, without a doubt, was a line of enquiry to follow up back in England.

Despite the awful weather we had no choice but to leave the cemetery's sanctuary and head out across the battlefield towards Poplar Ridge. Having obtained the landowner's consent, it was our intention, using metal detectors, to establish whether any tangible link could be found with the events 'under the microscope'. As Andy and Antony started their search in front of the poplars and in what was the cornfield across which No 3 Company attacked, the rest of us studied the ground. Within the poplars was a marsh, this being consistent with *Hauptmann* Ambrosius describing how his soldiers waded through waist high mud and water. We also realised that the poplars standing today are not the originals, being only some 25 years old. The large trunks of the originals can be clearly seen, however. We also realised that 'Poplar Ridge' is now a confusing misnomer. Although the line of trees rises slightly from the river to the N50, it does not provide a sweeping view of the whole battlefield as the name suggests. Looking South from the poplars, the direction which Ambrosius and his men faced their enemies, the view is about 100 metres up a rising field; the summit there does provide a better view of the 'Killing Fields', but that is not where the Germans were dug in. The intentions of *Hauptmann* Ambrosius became clearer standing on the spot his men once occupied. His instructions were, in fact, to seize Bailleul, so his initial intention was to hurry inland and cross the N50, heading east. The line of poplars provided perfect cover to undertake the rush up to the main road. Various elements of the 1st Guards Brigade had withdrawn and gathered in strength along the road, and Major Matthews' counter-attack from the South indicated a strong British presence. What had started as an offensive operation for the Germans had soon degenerated into a defensive battle as Ambrosius tried to hold his small bridgehead. The answer to the Poplar Ridge puzzle of the present day would only later be solved using the 1943 aerial photograph as reference:-

The photograph shows, quite clearly, that the poplars of today run on the same diagonal line, from North East to South West, as indicated by the original trunks. What is not present today, however, is that in 1940 another line of poplars, again visible on the aerial picture, ran at 45° from the South Western end of the aforementioned line, across a large square field, diagonally from North West to South East. Those trees have since been completely removed, but from that location - the relatively higher ground - such a field of fire as indicated by contemporary accounts would have existed, right across the fields to the shrine and River Escaut. The large field concerned and pictured in the aerial photograph, at the Western boundary of which is the N50 and indeed No 3 Company's Forming Up Position, is, in fact, the infamous cornfield crossed by Captain Starkey's men during the counter-attack. This whole exercise provides a classic example and warning to the would-be historian that things in today's world are not necessarily as they appeared in 1940!

As the present day deluge continued unabated, however, the metal detectors bleeped away. In this field was found the screw-cap off a 'flimsy' (a British military fluid can). Other items included various small pieces of shrapnel - probably from the Grenadier mortar bombs which preceded No 3 Company's counter-attack. The prize find, however, was a virtually complete British .303 cartridge case (unfired) dated 1939. A rusting but substantial lever-like handle was found (later found to weigh 12 oz), but its origin is not yet known. It is certainly substantial enough to be from an Armoured Fighting Vehicle, but only further research will provide the answers. By coincidence, some aircraft parts were also discovered. Two pieces since identified pieces being a calibrated instrument edge and a small alloy lever. The parts are believed to be from a *Messerschmitt* 109 which, it appears, has exploded, scattering pieces over a wide area. The details of this incident, however, are as yet unknown.

A small selection of artefacts recovered from the Esquelmes battlefield in November 1998.
From top left: mortar shell shrapnel, two .303 cartridge cases, a 'flimsy' cap, and hefty piece
of shrapnel from a German artillery shell.
Andrew Long.

Close-up of the flimsy cap. If only such things could talk! We will never know for sure, but it is quite possible that this is from the gallant Lieutenant Reynell-Pack's Carrier which was destroyed in the same area as this discovery.

Andrew Long.

We then moved down to search the west bank of the original canal section, although a sign indicated that this had been re-landscaped by the Boy Scouts! In the field behind, however, Antony discovered another .303 cartridge case and yet more shrapnel. These pieces were more substantial than those found on 'Poplar Ridge' and were clearly from heavier calibre German shells. All of this confirmed our plotting of No 4 Company's positions. It was then that Peter became quite animated and said "I know that you appreciate how well the BEF fought in 1940, but the world as a whole does not. Make no mistake, without the bravery and tenacity of these boys here there could never have been a Dunkirk. You have to make people understand that". I really could not agree more, and as we six friends trudged through the Flanders mud I was reminded of a particular speech made by Winston Churchill:-

History with its flickering lamp, stumbles along the trail of the past, trying to reconstruct its scenes, to revive its echoes, and kindle with pale gleams the passion of former days.

There was then one job left to do: the identification of No 4 Company's HQ. We knew that Les had dragged Arthur Southwards, and from a conversation on site

The barn used by Major Alston-Roberts-West as his No 4 Company Headquarters on May 21st, 1940, and from which the wounded were able to escape on the Company Transport. The double-doors, facing the River Escaut, have since been bricked up, but the building remains covered in 'spang' marks from the battle.
Andrew Long.

with an 86 year old former Belgian soldier, we knew that certain buildings had existed at the time. We looked at them all but in the end the barn was obvious given its location and lay out. When we got up to it, lo and behold, there were the double doors facing the canal - albeit bricked up now but the old opening still clearly visible. The whole building was still pockmarked by bullet and shrapnel holes - 'spang' marks to us - which again made me stop and think. The jagged lumps of metal already gathered from the battlefield, now in my soaking wet coat pocket, also made me realise just how dangerous the whole business of war is - these sharp shards of bombs and shells were clearly lethal and my Grandfather was a lucky man indeed. How easily he could have been beneath one of the nearby headstones.

Eventually, however, the freezing rain got the better of us so off we headed into Pecq. In a warm and cosy Belgian bar, we six 'War Pilgrims' re-fought the battle over much needed hot coffee. The consensus of opinion was that, despite the weather, we had achieved the purpose of the exercise and could return home not only with sufficient information to finish the book but also some tangible reminders of the 3rd Bn Grenadier Guards' successful action. We were surprised not to have found more such items, in fact, but as Peter pointed out the ground had been considerably excavated in many places when the River Escaut was canalised. Furthermore, such sites were well cleared by the Belgian authorities and the public: after the war brass and copper commanded a respectable price on the Belgian scrap metal market - making cartridge cases much sought after!

The morning after dawned windy but bright, so we decided to take advantage of the few hours available before our ferry crossing by visiting some other BEF related sites en route to Calais. The first was Cassell, at the top of which hill the 2nd Bn Gloucestershire Regiment had fought a bitter rearguard action. Secondly, the memorial at Wormhoudt dedicated to those men of the Royal Warwickshire, the Cheshire Regiment and Royal Artillery who were massacred in a nearby barn on May 28th, 1940. Their only 'crime' was to have held up elements of the SS *Liebstandarte* - Adolf Hitler's elite bodyguard - for most of the day. Over the years many have tried to justify SS 'excesses' in France during 1944, claiming that in Russia such atrocities had allegedly been commonplace. Given that the massacres of British soldiers at both Wormhoudt and Le Paradis occurred in 1940 - before the Russian campaign - and, the available evidence suggests, were premeditated, such lame excuses have no credibility.

Back home in England I had two tasks left. One to pursue the avenue of enquiry with Mrs Jordan regarding Major Matthews, and secondly to complete the book (the latter proving the more difficult task!). After a call to Directory Enquiries I was soon talking to Pat Jordan who was indeed Major Matthews' daughter. I would like to conclude this book with an extract from the letter Pat consequently wrote to me. This underlines, I think, the importance of this research and the heart-warming value placed upon our interest by many people. From a personal viewpoint I was most encouraged by the British public's reaction to Remembrance Day 1998; this November, at which time I write in fact, marks the 80th anniversary of the Great War Armistice. There was widespread and overwhelming support for the occasion and a revival of interest in the two great conflicts of this century. In this book we heave learned a little of some who fell on the road to Dunkirk; we are about to learn of one more.

November 3rd, 1998

Dear Dilip,

I cannot say 'thank you' enough for contacting me - it was wonderful.

Yes, I was over there in May; I was taken over by my children as a 70th birthday present.

My father and I were very, very close. We did everything together. I could de-coke the car when I was 10, helped with his woodwork, and spent hours with him fly fishing, also at Bisley where he practised his shooting. We were inseparable. In fact I never believed he was dead until I went to the poplar copse (as the cemetery at Esquelmes originally appeared) and saw for myself. That really hit me for six.

I have provided some biographical details relating to my father, Major Frederick George Matthews.

He was born on November 3rd, 1899 (his birthday today!), in Burton-on-Trent. His father, CG Matthews, was the Chief Analytical Chemist for Burton Breweries. His Mother was Clara - nee Goodyer. In early days she was a painter for Staffordshire Potteries. Her brother was the Mayor of Burton.

My father was educated at Trent College where he was once caught by the Headmaster smoking a pipe in the loo - smoke poured out under the door! "Matthews, is that you in there? Come out!"

He was at Sandhurst in 1917, and joined the North Staffordshire Regiment in 1920. He was later sent to Ireland, later returning to Lichfield Barracks where he somehow managed to get the innards of the clock in the clocktower on the parade ground down to ground level - with what consequences I know not!

On May 23rd, 1927, he married Olive Mary Pollett, a pianist of Burton-on-Trent. I, Patricia May, was born on May 7th, 1928, in Farnborough. Believe it or not, I received a birthday present from my father on the right day in 1940 - a very pretty silk pink floral nightie!

I was three months old when the three of us went out to India for the first time. During this time the Headman of a village came to my father to ask him to shoot a man-eating panther which had killed some women and children in the village. So he got a machan built in a tree and arranged to sit up all night - but one of the Officer's wives asked if she could accompany him. Unfortunately she took her knitting too. Several times she dropped her needles, so he had to keep climbing down to collect them for her! A goat was tethered in the clearing - he heard the panther getting nearer. It was nearly dawn by this time and he saw the beast - got it just before it got to the goat. Just one shot, because it was skinned and made into a rug. There was just one hole in the brain. It was carried on poles to our bungalow and placed on the veranda. We then went to Madras, eventually returning home to England in 1936. We lived in Farnham but not for long as in 1938, my father was sent to York on a staff job.

Come the outbreak of war my father wished to be with the Regiment, but was told he had to stay in York to do his job. He badgered and badgered them to let him go, to which, in the end, they agreed. So off he went and met up with the rest of them, I think after Christmas 1939. So he wasn't over there for long

You know what happened then.

Index

Index of military personnel, ranks and status given as per 1940 for purposes of continuity.

Abel-Smith, RE, Capt — 26, 34, 123, 208

Adair, AHS, Major — 24, 26, 33, 35, 37, 42, 43, 50, 60, 61, 65, 77, 86, 87, 121, 129, 152, 154, 156, 159, 166, 168, 185

Adam, Sir Ronald, Lt Gen — 163

Aird, Sir John, Lt. Col — 19, 24, 41, 68

Alexander, The Hon. Harold, Major General — 19, 31, 35, 64, 175, 180

Alston-Roberts-West, WRJ, Major — 20, 24, 74, 75, 101, 102, 110, 111, 114, 212, 228

Ambrosius, Dr L, *Hauptmann* — 107, 111, 112, 117, 121, 123, 124, 128, 129, 130, 144, 201, 225

Annand VC, RW, 2nd Lt — 84, 85, 190

Antony, JE, Lt — 24

Aubrey-Fletcher, LP, 2nd Lt — 24, 68, 75, 156

Bader, Sir DRS, Grp Capt — 206

Baring, P, 2nd Lt — 68, 75

Barker, MGH, Lt Gen — 63

Barthels, *Leutant* — 117, 121

Beaumont-Nesbitt, DJF, 2nd Lt — 24

Beckwith-Smith, M, Brig — 19, 46, 96, 175

Bennett, R, Guardsman — 25, 177

Bethold, *Oberst* — 106

Billote, Gen — 32, 33, 85, 88

Birch, Capt — 119, 120, 224

Blackwell, CA, 2nd Lt — 75, 176

Blackwell, JE, Lt — 75

Blanchard, Gen — 150

Bock, Fedor von, *Generaloberst* — 69, 139

Bootle-Wilbraham, L, Lt Col — 19, 42, 75, 97, 144, 175, 177

Boscawen, The Hon EFV, Lt — 75, 102, 103, 195, 196, 197, 219

Bowes-Lyon, FJC, 2nd Lt — 24

Bowman, JH, Capt — 75, 176

Boyd, AN, 2nd Lt — 68, 75, 111, 208

Brauchitsch, Walther von, *Generaloberst* — 69

Brinkman, RN, Capt — 75, 131, 142, 154, 155

Britton, BG, Lt — 75

Broderick, The Hon MV, 2nd Lt — 75

Brooke, AF, Lt Gen — 63

Brown, Ted, Guardsman — 213, 214

Brown, The Rev, Capt — 32

Buchanan, JD, 2nd Lt — 24

Buckley, Guardsman — 21

Bullock, N, Sgt — 21, 110, 158, 205

Burke, PHA, Lt — 24

Burnett, CQMS — 133

Butlin, W, Private — 217

Butterworth, Lt Col — 153, 155, 156

Cadoux-Hudson, P, Lt Col — 19, 46, 120, 180

Cassford, PSM — 116

Chapman, Guardsman — 20

Chichester, APS, Capt — 75

Christie, Corp — 132, 142, 172, 173, 177

Christie, Guardsman — 21

Christofzik, *Oberleutnant* — 161

Clifton, PT, Capt — 24, 31, 75, 113, 118

Combe, RT, Lt — 75, 176, 177

Constantine, C, Lance Sgt — 17, 51, 52, 55, 74, 76, 77, 81, 83, 87, 107, 108, 111, 116, 117, 121, 129, 130, 143, 154, 155, 157, 158, 164 - 167

Connaught, HRH Field Marshal The Duke of — 23

Cook, RJ, Guardsman — 208, 212

Corap, Gen — 84

Court, F, PSM — 133, 201, 216

Court, LHT, Sgt — 133, 134, 177, 201, 216, 217

Coyle, M, Lance Corp — 170

Crossman, Lance Corp — 20

Devon, The Earl of, 2nd Lt — 75, 142

Dietrichs, *Oberleutnant* — 112

Dill, Sir John, Gen — 63

Dixon, GH, 2nd Lt — 204, 206, 207, 213

Dove, A, Guardsman — 25

Dowding, Sir HCT, ACM — 91

Drinkwater, L, Guardsman — 10, 21, 109-111, 115, 116, 196, 198, 200, 204, 206, 207, 213, 227

Earle, C, Lt — 74

Eastwood, CQMS — 175

Ellingworth, D, Private — 78, 85, 90, 173, 174, 177-179, 202

Engel, *Leutnant* — 107, 113, 117, 123, 130, 202

Ervine-Andrews VC, H, Capt — 191

Everitt, B, Lance Corp — 20, 111, 142, 204

Fane, CN, Capt — 75, 84, 132, 133, 218, 219

Fenwick, CQMS — 83

Fielden, CH, Capt — 75, 133, 134

Flower, PPH, Capt — 177

Follett, G, Guardsman — 23, 90, 95

Forbes, The Master of, Lt — 17, 24, 48, 74, 96, 108, 114-116, 200, 203

Ford, CG, Lt — 75, 129

Ford, EWS, Lt — 17, 33, 43, 54, 74, 92, 129, 131

Foster, Sgt Major — 120

Franklyn, HF, Major Gen — 64, 153

Furness VC, The Hon C, Lt — 191

Gamelin, Gen — 32, 33

Gansk, *Leutnant* — 156

Georges, Gen — 32, 48, 62, 63, 65

Gibbs, EL, Lt — 75, 176

Gloucester, HRH The Duke of — 33, 35, 37, 40

Gordon-Lennox, GC, Capt — 24, 33

Gorg, *Leutnant* — 156

Gort VC, The Lord, — 7, 18, 19, 32, 33, 35, 37, 38, 48, 49, 62, 63, 65, 68, 73, 75, 85, 88, 89, 91, 140, 141, 148-151, 163, 182

Grazebrook, MW, 2nd Lt — 24

Gristock VC, G, CSM — 137, 138, 191, 193, 194

Guderian, H, Gen — 73, 87, 149

Haersler, *Leutnant* — 130

Hairs, Guardsman — 20

Haking, Gen — 26

Halliday, P, Lt — 26, 27, 29, 31, 34, 35, 41, 43, 45, 50, 53, 56, 73, 78, 81, 89, 98, 120, 171, 179, 180, 211

Hamilton-Russell, The Hon GL, Lt — 24, 177

Hasselmann, *Leutnant* — 117

Hawkins, K, Lance Corp — 76, 98, 99, 153

Hayes, SJ, Guardsman — 111, 113, 146, 204, 207, 208, 212

Heering, Arno von, *Oberleutnant* — 190

Hewitt, CSM — 175

Heywood-Lonsdale, RH, 2nd Lt — 24

Hill, ER, Capt — 75

Hozback, *Oberst* — 106, 132

Hudson, J, Lance Corp — 127, 212

Humphrey, RFM, Capt — 73

Ironside, Sir Edward, Gen — 37

Jenkinson, SW, PSM — 208

Johnson, DG, Major Gen — 64

Johnstone, NDM, Capt — 24

Jones, M, Lt — 75

Kaempfe, *Generalleutnant* — 106

Kenning, Lance Corp — 154

Koch, *Hauptmann* — 71

Kortzfleisch, General von — 139

Kuthe, *Leutnant* — 111

Lane-Fox, JH, 2nd Lt — 68, 75, 156

Langley, J, Lt — 75, 176

Leggett, E, Private — 82, 87, 137, 193

Lewcock, W, Guardsman — 123, 124, 127, 184, 185, 213

Linemann, *Leutnant* — 111

Lomer, RH, Capt — 24

Lort-Phillips, PH, Capt — 26, 32, 33, 39, 187

Loyd, HC, Major Gen — 35, 64

Maloney, PSM — 149

Manstein, Eric von, General — 69

Martel, G, Major Gen — 140, 165

Mason-McFarlane, FN, Major Gen — 88

Matthews, FG, Major — 118, 119, 146, 224, 229, 230

McCorquodale, A, Major — 75, 176

Meade, WP, Guardsman — 146, 213

Mendritzki, *Leutnant* — 161

Michael, *Oberleutnant* — 111, 144, 146, 212

Middleton, H, Guardsman — 17, 25, 41, 56, 74, 77, 81, 83, 90, 91, 102, 129, 213

Moor, JNR, Capt — 24

Montgomery, BL, Major Gen — 64, 81, 83, 156

Murray, ASP, Major — 24, 35, 74, 154

Nash, P, Guardsman — 10, 21, 54, 86, 123, 124, 127, 184-186, 205, 211

Needham, FJRP, Lt — 24, 43, 74, 154

Nicholls VC, H, Lance Corp — 7, 18, 22, 23, 52, 53, 57, 123, 124, 126, 128, 131, 138, 142, 185-188, 190-193, 202, 205, 211, 213-215

Nicholls, J, Guardsman — 127

Nitzky, *Leutnant* — 161

Nixon, J, Guardsman — 102, 103, 132, 133, 181, 182, 195-197, 219

Norbury, F, Private — 189

Norman-Barnett, CW, Capt — 155

Northumberland, The Duke of, Lt — 65, 75, 115, 123, 144, 194, 195, 208, 212, 223

Petre, RL, Major Gen — 88

Piggott-Brown, JH, 2nd Lt — 75, 134

Phillips, H, Major — 120

Portsmouth, EJ, Guardsman — 208

Potter, Guardsman — 84

Pounder, E, Guardsman — 186

Pownall, Gen — 148

Price, Rev GH, Capt — 75

Price, S, Guardsman — 25

Radford Norcop, PJC, Lt — 24, 26, 30, 75, 96, 117, 118, 201

Ramsay, AAAD, 2nd Lt — 24

Ramsey, Sir B, Vice-Admiral — 164, 180

Randall, Drill Sgt — 133, 142, 156

Rankin, JG, Lt — 31

Reinburger, Major — 69

Reynell-Pack, H, 2nd Lt — 24, 31, 33, 48, 74, 101, 121, 123, 212, 227

Ribstern, *Oberst*   106
Rice, A, Guardsman   9, 10, 16, 20, 91, 102,
109, 115, 116, 198-200,
205, 207, 213, 227
Riedelsdorfer, Major   156
Rimell, A, Lance Sgt   119, 212, 216, 217
Rommel, Erwin, Major Gen   83, 85
Rowland, WW, Guardsman   208
Ryder, Sgt   155

Schlinke, *Leutnant*   123, 124
Seekt, Hans von, General   14
Seymour, Guardsman   83
Shrumpel, *Oberleutnant*   124
Simpson, PSM   149
Smith, HH, Guardsman   8, 13, 16, 20, 23, 25,
111, 128, 142, 184,
187, 188, 190, 202, 204
Smith, OWD, Major   74, 152, 154
South, DM, Capt   47
Sowerby, Sgt   175
Speed, RDE, 2nd Lt   75, 176
Starkey, LS, Capt   23, 24, 43, 75, 121-123,
142, 155
Stokes-Roberts, Colonel   46
Stucley, LRC, Capt   24
Stewart-Brown, WS, Major   75, 132, 168, 175
Stromsky, Dr   111
Subklew, *Hauptmann*   112
Swaby, A, Guardsman   134, 218

Tennant, WG, Capt   180
Thorne, AFAN, Major Gen   19, 64
Thorne, G, Capt   152, 154
Turner, GF, Lt   74

Valentine, Capt   21
Vaughn, EBM, 2nd Lt   24
Vernon, MSB, Capt   35
Villiers, WNSLH, 2nd Lt   24

Wade, Corp   119, 120
Wake-Walker, WF, Rear Admiral   164
Warde-Adam, DJ, 2nd Lt   75
Walther, W, *Oberleutnant*   71
Wenzel, H, *Oberfeldwebel*   73
Weygand, General   148
Whitaker, J, Brig   95
Wilkes, Guardsman   176
Windsor, HRH, The Duke of   40, 58
Windsor-Clive, RC, 2nd Lt   75, 134
Winkler, *Leutnant*   129
Woods, R, Lance Corp   188
Worrall, Guardsman   20
Wyatt, FT, Major   75, 132, 176, 177

Ziermann, *Leutnant*   111

APPENDIX ONE

Roll of Honour

When you go home,
tell them of us and say:
For your tomorrow,
we gave our today

Details follow of the known casualties from the 1st Guards Brigade's Battalions (and 2nd Bn North Staffordshire Regiment which fought alongside the 3rd Bn Grenadier Guards on May 21st, 1940) whilst serving with the BEF. Places of burial are indicated where known (details of all casualties are held by the Commonwealth War Graves Commission, so if any reader requires further information the Enquiry Section located at 2 Marlow Road, Maidenhead, Berks, could help). Those who remain officially Missing in Action are indicated by the abbreviation: 'MIA'. Unless otherwise indicated, all of the below listed were killed in action.

3rd Bn Grenadier Guards

Officers: Fatal Casualties

Second Lieutenant P Baring:	May 19th, 1940
Major WRJ Alston-Roberts-West:	May 21st, 1940 (MIA)
Captain RE Abel-Smith:	May 21st, 1940 (Esquelmes BWC)
Lieutenant the 9th Duke of Northumberland:	May 21st, 1940 (Esquelmes BWC)
Lieutenant H Reynell-Pack:	May 21st, 1940 (MIA)
Second Lieutenant AN Boyd:	May 21st, 1940 (Esquelmes BWC)
Lieutenant R Crompton-Roberts:	May 27th, 1940

The following Officers were to die later from wounds received:-

Lieutenant The Hon. GL Hamilton Russell:	June 2nd, 1940
Captain PJC Radford-Norcop:	May 21st, died July 13th, 1940

The following Officers were wounded during this campaign:-

Captain PT Clifton:	May 21st, 1940
Captain C Earle:	May 28th, 1940
Lieutenant The Master of Forbes:	May 21st, 1940
Second Lieutenant JH Lane-Fox:	28th, 1940

Captain RN Brinckman: May 27th, 1940; captured, escaped.
Lieutenant LP Aubrey-Fletcher: May 28th, 1940; captured
Major OWD Smith: May 28th, 1940
Lieutenant PF Thorne: May 28th, 1940

Other Ranks: Fatal Casualties

2616840 Ansett, Guardsman V: May 27th, 1940 (of wounds)
2613216 Atherton, Guardsman J: May 21st, 1940 (Esquelmes BWC)
2613348 Bakehouse, Guardsman J: May 26th, 1940 (of wounds)
2613556 Barton, Guardsman A: May 28th, 1940
2615775 Bennett, Guardsman W: Feb. 26th, 1940 (on active service)
3652644 Bellis, Guardsman H: May 28th, 1940
2615316 Brown, Guardsman G: May 21st, 1940 (MIA)
2614989 Bradbury, Guardsman S: May 21st, 1940 (MIA)
2615314 Bradley, Guardsman W: May 27th, 1940 (of wounds)
2615328 Brimilcombe,Lance Sergeant A: May 19th, 1940
2614989 Bradbury, Guardsman S: May 21st, 1940 (MIA)
2613488 Burnett, Lance Corporal W: May 21st, 1940 (EsquelmesBWC)
2613138 Buckley, Lance Corporal W: May 21st, 1940 (Esquelmes BWC)
6286759 Button, Guardsman G: May 21st, 1940 (MIA)
2613030 Cassford, PSM A: May 29th, 1940 (of wounds)
 823356 Caley, Guardsman G: May 21st, 1940 (Esquelmes BWC)
 873182 Carter, Guardsman J: May 21st, 1940 (Esquelmes BWC)
2613348 Cattermole, Guardsman A: May 21st, 1940 (MIA)
2615800 Chapman, Guardsman W: May 21st, 1940 (Esquelmes BWC)
2615902 Cosser, Guardsman D: May 28th, 1940 (of wounds)
2616260 Cottrell, Guardsman A: May 21st, 1940 (Esquelmes BWC)
2616235 Cook, Guardsman R: May 21st, 1940 (Esquelmes BWC)
2613459 Cracknell, Guardsman S: May 27th, 1940 (of wounds)
2614946 Daniels, Guardsman M: May 21st, 1940 (MIA)
 557505 Dexter, Lance Corporal H: May 21st, 1940 (MIA)
2610908 Ditchett, Guardsman E: May 21st, 1940 (Esquelmes BWC)
2613568 Doyle, Guardsman W: May 21st, 1940 (Esquelmes BWC)
2611284 Dobson, Guardsman J: May 28th, 1940
2615003 Draycott, Guardsman J: May 28th, 1940
2611693 Dryden, Sergeant C: May 19th, 1940
769279 Durdle, Guardsman T: May 28th, 1940
2615556 Dutton, Guardsman W: May 21st, 1940 (Esquelmes BWC)
2616082 Easton, Lance Corporal F: May 28th, 1940
2614925 Ellerington, Lance Corporal W: May 21st, 1940 (Esquelmes BWC)
2613320 Falls, Guardsman J: May 18th, 1940 (1st GB)
1066403 Frewin, PSM W: June 22nd, 1940 (of wounds)
2612111 Gash, Guardsman W: May 21st, 1940 (Esquelmes BWC)
5182911 George, Guardsman R: May 28th, 1940 (of wounds)
2613606 Gibbs, Guardsman F: May 27th, 1940 (of wounds)
2616215 Grandfield, Guardsman L: May 21st, 1940 (MIA)

2615954 Hawkins, Guardsman H:	May 21st, 1940 (MIA)
2612418 Hayes, Guardsman S:	May 21st, 1940 (Esquelmes BWC)
2613354 Hardy, Guardsman W., MM:	May 27th, 1940 (of wounds)
2613779 Harris, Lance Corporal R:	May 28th, 1940 (of wounds)
2615242 Hewitt, Lance Corporal H:	August 19th, 1940 (of wounds, POW)
2612555 Hewitt, Guardsman A:	June 10th, 1940 (of wounds)
2610868 Hicks, PSM R:	May 21st, 1940 (Esquelmes BWC)
2613137 Hope, Guardsman J:	May 27th, 1940 (of wounds)
2615399 Howe, Guardsman W:	May 21st, 1940 (Esquelmes BWC)
2614938 Hull, Guardsman H:	May 30th, 1940
2615506 Hudson, Lance Corporal J:	May 21st, 1940 (Esquelmes BWC)
2615212 Hyde, Guardsman F:	May 30th, 1940
2613579 Jarrold, Guardsman C:	May 22nd, 1940 (died of wounds)
2612556 Jay, Corporal J:	May 21st, 1940 (Esquelmes BWC)
2613361 Jenkinson PSM AS:	May 21st, 1940 (Esquelmes BWC)
2614861 Johns, Sergeant S:	May 21st, 1940 (Esquelmes BWC)
2613339 Johnson, Guardsman A:	May 21st, 1940 (Esquelmes BWC)
820757 Lindsay, Guardsman H:	May 23rd, 1940 (of wounds)
2614860 Little, Guardsman H:	May 21st, 1940 (Bailleul)
2614096 Lines, Guardsman R:	May 19th, 1940 (of wounds, Tournai)
2612213 Lindley, Guardsman T:	May 21st, 1940 (Esquelmes BWC)
2611424 Lyons, Guardsman D:	October 13th, 1940 (of wounds, POW, Edingen)
2615350 Marriott, Guardsman C:	May 29th, 1940 (of wounds)
2615074 Mannion, Guardsman W:	May 27th, 1940 (of wounds)
2613344 Meade, Guardsman W:	May 21st, 1940 (Esquelmes BWC)
2613442 Moring, Lance Sergeant G:	May 28th, 1940
783275 Morris, Guardsman A:	May 28th, 1940
2616211 Neale, Guardsman B:	May 21st, 1940 (Esquelmes BWC)
2613533 Pinkney, Guardsman A:	June 4th, 1940 (of wounds)
2616389 Portsmouth, Guardsman E:	May 28th, 1940 (Esquelmes BWC)
2612419 Porter, Guardsman C:	May 19th, 1940
2614931 Powell, Guardsman C:	May 27th, 1940 (of wounds)
2613997 Reardon, Guardsman G:	May 28th, 1940
2613551 Reynolds, Guardsman E:	May 21st, 1940 (Esquelmes BWC)
2615321 Rimell, Lance Sergeant A:	May 21st, 1940 (Ramignes)
2614724 Riches, Guardsman D:	May 21st, 1940 (MIA)
2616802 Riding, Guardsman K:	May 28th, 1940
2611976 Rowlands, Guardsman W:	May 21st, 1940 (Esquelmes BWC)
2615721 Rosenberg, Guardsman J:	May 28th, 1940
2615653 Roberts, Lance Corporal E:	May 25th, 1940
2614815 Rubie, Guardsman R:	May 31st, 1940
2615207 Ryder, Sergeant J:	July 25th, 1940 (of wounds POW)
2614837 Smith, Guardsman E:	May 20th, 1940
2608592 Smith, Guardsman C:	May 19th, 1940
2612729 Swallow, Lance Corporal W:	May 27th, 1940 (of wounds)
2616697 Thompson, Guardsman E:	May 21st, 1940 (of wounds)
2613248 Titmus, Guardsman J:	May 21st, 1940 (Esquelmes BWC)

2612157 Turner, Guardsman J:	May 21st, 1940 (Esquelmes BWC)
2612591 Vincent, Guardsman F:	May 18th, 1940 (1st GB)
2611402 Walker, Guardsman C:	May 31st, 1940 (of wounds)
2613069 Wentworth, Lance Corporal W:	May 21st, 1940 (Esquelmes BWC)
2616066 Whelpdale, Guardsman L:	May 21st, 1940 (of wounds)
2614494 Wilkes, Guardsman A:	June 10th, 1940 (1st GB)
2615927 Wigglesworth, Guardsman R:	June 1st, 1940 (of wounds)
2614943 Williams, Guardsman J:	May 31st, 1940
5499840 Woodley, Lance Corporal S:	May 30th, 1940

In total, the 3rd Bn Grenadier Guards lost seven Officers and 96 Other Ranks killed during this campaign.

Of the foregoing Officers and men killed in action on May 21st, 1940, two Officers and 10 Other Ranks remain Missing in Action. At Esquelmes British War Cemetery, the 3rd Bn Grenadier Guards and 2nd Bn North Staffordshire Regiment casualties from this battle lie in the same plot. Within there are 10 unidentified soldiers, including one Grenadier Guards Officer and one burial definitely identified as a Grenadier Guardsman. Assuming that all of these particular 'unknowns' are Grenadiers, then two casualties from the River Escaut battle remain unaccounted for. Those BEF servicemen who have no known grave are, in fact, commemorated on the Dunkirk Memorial; sadly this bears the names of 4,516 casualties.

3rd Bn Grenadier Guards: Prisoners of War

After such a battle, a roll call established which men were missing. Some of their number could be confirmed as dead through eye-witness accounts, others would be posted 'Missing in Action'. Some of them would be dead, others captured by the enemy. It took months before a final reckoning was possible, and as evidenced by the foregoing, some casualties would never be accounted for. Unfortunately, the Grenadier Guards Regimental Archive was unable to provide a list of prisoners of war, and the dates each man was taken. From 31 ID records we know that 20 Guardsmen were captured on May 21st, 1940. Of these I can only identify the following:-

2614910 Nicholls, Lance Corporal H VC:	(wounded)	died 1975
2614908 Everett, Lance Corporal B:		died 1988
2611042 Smith, Guardsman HH:	(wounded)	died 1983
Brighton, Guardsman W:	(wounded)	died 1997

Tragically Mr Brighton died just a few months before I learned of his whereabouts. Apparently he was badly wounded on May 21st, 1940, and consequently amongst the first prisoners to be repatriated.

Despite appeals in the *Grenadier Gazette*, any surviving prisoners of war from May 21st,

1940, have defied discovery. It seems that after the war these men in particular wanted to forget the past and did not generally become, it seems, active members of the Grenadier Guards Association. Should any reader be able to offer any help in this respect I would be most grateful, as I still have an interest in establishing the sequence of events during the first few hours of their captivity.

German records concerning the 31st ID, elements of which engaged the 1st Guards Brigade on May 21st, 1940, indicate that the following numbers of prisoners were taken day-by-day throughout the *Blitzkrieg*. It is impossible to say how many Grenadiers were amongst the 50 *Gefangegen* reportedly taken on May 21st.

Date	31 ID: Allied POWs
10.05.40:	750
11.05.40:	6
12.05.40:	166
13.05.40:	Nil
14.05.40:	3
15.05.40:	5
16.05.40:	30
17.05.40:	2
18.05.40:	50
19.05.40:	20
20.05.40:	Nil
21.05.40:	50
22.05.40:	12
23.05.40:	1,000
24.05.40:	Nil
25.05.40:	2,900
26.05.40:	Nil
27.05.40:	Nil
28.05.40:	350
29.05.40:	1,250
Total:	6,594

2nd Bn Coldstream Guards

Officers: Fatal Casualties

Major A McCorquodale:	June 1st, 1940
Major ET Wyatt:	June 2nd, 1940
Captain CN Fane:	May 21st, 1940 (Pecq)
Captain EL Gibbs:	June 1st, 1940

Captain RT Combe:	June 2nd, 1940
Lieutenant The Hon. EFV Boscawen:	May 20th, 1940 (Pecq)
Second Lieutenant CA Blackwell:	June 1st, 1940
Second Lieutenant RDE Speed:	June 1st, 1940

Other Ranks: Fatal Casualties

2653732 Court, PSM F:	May 21st, 1940 (Bailleul)
5098453 Dance, PSM G:	June 1st, 1940
2656884 Burnett CQMS J:	May 21st, 1940 (MIA)
2655394 Fenwick J:	May 14th, 1940
2653922 Beckett, Segeant W:	June 1st, 1940
2655609 Escott, Sergeant B:	May 31st, 1940
2655287 Hardwick, Sergeant E:	June 1st, 1940
821140 Newton, Sergeant S:	May 31st, 1940
2657873 Greig, Lance Sergeant T:	June 1st, 1940
2657989 Hunter, Lance Sergeant R:	May 23rd - 24th, 1940
2657377 Light, Lance Sergeant W:	December 9th, 1939 (on active service)
265463 Warren, Lance Sergeant H:	June 2nd, 1940
2653483 Bowery, Lance Corporal S:	May 29th, 1940
409812 Bowles, Lance Corporal G:	April 20th, 1940 (on active service)
4687721 Dean, Lance Corporal G:	May 21st, 1940 (Pecq)
2656266 Hawthorn, Lance Corporal J:	June 2nd, 1940
2658793 Lawless, Lance Corporal F:	May 21st, 1940 (Pecq)
2658798 Nevett, Lance Corporal H:	January 8th, 1940
2658810 Reay, Lance Corporal R:	June 1st - 30th, 1940
4747404 Allcroft, Guardsman F:	May 30th, 1940
2658864 Bartlett, Guardsman T:	May 21st, 1940 (Pecq)
2655372 Bennett, Guardsman J:	June 1st, 1940
2655701 Bennett, Guardsman T:	May 21st, 1940 (Pecq)
2658448 Brand, Guardsman R:	May 31st, 1940
2654876 Caddy, Guardsman H:	May 31st, 1940
2653937 Carr, Guardsman G:	May 22nd, 1940
2654833 Coope, Guardsman B:	May 21st, 1940 (MIA)
2658601 Dye, Guardsman D:	June 1st, 1940
2655592 Edmonson, Guardsman J:	June 1st, 1940
858644 Edwards, Guardsman N:	June 1st, 1940
2656333 Gooch, Guardsman F:	June 1st, 1940
2658880 Graham, Guardsman J:	May 22nd, 1940 (Esquelmes BWC)
2568087 Harper, Guardsman C:	June 4th, 1940
2655360 Harris, Guardsman R:	June 13th, 1940
2658916 Hasman, Guardsman L:	June 1st, 1940
2658069 Hazell, Guardsman C:	May 31st, 1940
2658549 Hinchcliffe, Guardsman J:	June 6th, 1940
407267 Holdom, Guardsman J:	May 21st, 1940 (Pecq)
2658066 Horton, Guardsman C:	May 23rd-24th, 1940
2658670 Hudson, Guardsman M:	May 24th, 1940

2657158 Hudspith, Guardsman W:	May 21st, 1940 (Pecq)
2658827 Hunt, Guardsman H:	May 20th, 1940 (Pecq)
2654087 Jones, Guardsman R:	May 21st, 1940 (MIA)
2658854 Knowles, Guardsman H:	May 21st, 1940 (Pecq)
2658613 Laignel, Guardsman F:	May 28th-June 1st, 1940
2658811 Lake, Guardsman A:	May 21st, 1940 (Pecq)
2654908 Newton, Guardsman T:	February 18th, 1940 (on active service)
2654826 Nixon, Guardsman E:	May 31st, 1940
2656888 Parsisson, Guardsman F:	June 1st, 1940
4802012 Pay, Guardsman A:	June 1st, 1940
2655233 Purdue, Guardsman K:	June 2nd, 1940
2658853 Quant, Guardsman S:	May 23rd-24th, 1940
2655675 Shufflebottom, Guardsman A:	May 31st, 1940
2654938 Smith, Guardsman A:	May 21st, 1940 (Pecq)
2655756 Smith, Guardsman J:	May 21st, 1940 (Pecq)
2657894 Streeting, Guardsman R:	June 1st, 1940
2658206 Sumner, Guardsman G:	June 1st, 1940
2658568 Ward, Guardsman C:	May 21st, 1940 (Pecq)
2657075 Wriglesworth, Guardsman R:	May 19th, 1940
2656734 Yates, Guardsman J:	June 1st, 1940

In total, the 2nd Bn Coldstream Guards lost eight Officers and 60 Other Ranks during its period of service with the BEF.

The 2nd Coldstream casualties of May 21st, 1940, are largely buried at Pecq Communal Cemetery (the exception being PSM F Court who lies at Bailleul Communal). Of these casualties, two remain Missing in Action: Guardsmen Coope and Jones. At Pecq Communal Cemetery lie two unknown British soldiers: one is specifically identified as a Coldstream Guardsman.

2nd Bn Hampshire Regiment

Officers: Fatal Casualties

Captain DM South:	January 13th, 1940 (on active service, St Aubin BWC)
Second Lieutenant RA Straton:	May 30th, 1940 (Dunkirk Cemetery)

The following officer died later of wounds whilst a POW:-

Captain RFM Humphrey MBE:	July 27th, 1940 (Edingen)

Other Ranks: Fatal Casualties:-

5498256 Adams, Private AHB:	June 2nd, 1940 (MIA)

5494596 Bunker, Private PR:	May 31st, 1940 (MIA)
1442079 Burrows, Private G:	June 10th, 1940 (Dunkirk Cemetery)
5101190 Butlin, Private W:	May 21st, 1940 (Estaimbourg)
2694234 Cobb, Private ARJ:	June 17th, 1940 (MIA)
799154 Davis, Private WA:	May 31st, 1940 (MIA)
5502676 Keeble, Private GG:	May 19th, 1940 (MIA)
5500086 Norris, Private AW:	May 10th/June 16th, 1940 (Malo-Les-Bains Cemetery)
5492437 Stubbs, Private AW:	May 31st, 1940 (Dunkirk Cemetery)
5495058 Tyler, Private TJ:	February 26th, 1940 (on active service, Chambieres French National Cemetery)
5495617 Ward, Private A:	May 31st, 1940 (MIA)
5495617 Williams, Private H:	May 31st, 1940 (MIA)
5499630 Wood, Private AE:	June 1st, 1940 (Dunkirk Cemetery)

2nd Bn North Staffordshire Regiment

The following Officer and soldiers of the 2nd North Staffordshire Regiment perished fighting alongside the 3rd Bn Grenadier Guards at Esquelmes:-

Matthews, Major FG:	May 21st, 1940 (Esquelmes BWC)
5049586 Bolton, Lance Corporal GR:	May 21st, 1940 (Esquelmes BWC)
5047504 Wilcox Private AE:	May 21st, 1940 (Esquelmes BWC)
5043332 Bill, Private AW:	May 21st, 1940 (Ramegnies)
5378427 Cook, Private E:	May 21st, 1940 (Ramignes)
5049166 Snook, Private AJ:	May 21st, 1940 (Ramignes)

They shall not grow old, as we that are left grow old,
Age shall not weary them nor the years condemn,
At the going down of the sun, and in the morning,
We will remember them.

Laurence Binyon

APPENDIX TWO

German Casualties

The surviving records of the 31st *Infanterie-Division* (which engaged the 1st Guards Brigade on May 21st, 1940) indicate that it suffered the following casualties, day-by-day, during the *Blitzkrieg*:-

	Killed	**Wounded**	**Missing**
10.05.40:	8	18	
11.05.40:	2	7	
12.05.40:	9	13	
13.05.40:			
14.05.40:	2	18	
15.05.40:	17	133	6
16.05.40:	38	271	1
17.05.40:	1	14	5
18.05.40:	1	8	
19.05.40:	1		
20.05.40:	1	6	
21.05.40:	56	227	8
22.05.40:	5	33	3
23.05.40:	3	4	
24.05.40:	6	55	
25.05.40:	45	126	6
26.05.40:	26	56	
27.05.40:	60	9	
28.05.40:	19	225	
29.05.40:	84	150	28
Total:	383	1,374	33

The foregoing figures can only be considered approximate, however. For example, records provided by the *Volksbund Deutsche Kriegsgraberfursorge* (German War Graves Commission) indicate that on May 21st, 1940, II/IR 12 suffered at least 59 fatal casualties, this number having been buried by *Oberleutnant* Michael's party at Esquelmes. Unfortunately such records relating to IR 82, which fought the 2nd Bn Coldstream Guards at Pecq, have not survived. On that basis, however, on May 21st, the 31st ID definitely suffered more than the 56 fatalities indicated by the table above. After the Second World War, the majority of Germany's casualties from this area were exhumed and re-buried at the huge *Deutscher Soldatenfriedhof* at Lommel, Belgium, which contains the graves of 38, 549 German soldiers.

II/IR 12 soldiers killed on May 21st, 1940:-

Werhstadt, Karl	Obschtz	6/IR 12
Schwartz, Franz	Gefr	6/IR 12
Bies, Walter	Gefr	6/IR 12
Ludwig, Leoplold	Schtz	6/IR 12
Stieber, Otto	Uffz	5/IR 12
Engel, Hans	Leutnt	II/IR 12
Gerotski, Albert	Obschtz	5/IR 12
Schiweck, Lother	Schtz	8/IR 12
Tockern, Kurt	Obschtz	II/IR 12
Hieke, Emil	Schtz	4 Bau. Btl. 252-72
Sanftleben, Wilhelm	Schtz	6/IR 12
Schindler, Willi	Schtz	6/IR 12
Becker, Kurt	Schtz	5/IR 12
Tehn, Erich	Gefr	5/IR 12
Lichtenberg, Emil	Schtz	6/IR 12
Schober, Johann	Gefr	5/IR 12
Muschiol, Ernst	Schtz	8/IR 12
Wagner, Heinrich	Schtz	6/NR 12
Schmidt, Karl	Gefr	8/IR 12
Fricke, Ernst	Schtz	8/IR 12
Kutzner, Erich	Schtz	5/IR 12
Eggers, Karl	Schtz	5/IR 12
Horns, Friedrich	Schtz	5/IR 12
Wiele, Walter	Schtz	5/IR 12
Konnecke, Walter	Schtz	IR 12
Johannsmeier, Heinrich	Gefr	IR 12
Quaas, Friedrich	Schtz	8/IR 12
Scholze, Herbert	Gefr	4/IR 12
Schoppe, Gustav	Schtz	7/IR 12
Jorst, Wolfgang	Schtz	7/IR 12
Gehrt, Otto	Schtz	7/IR 12
Giere, Hans	Gefr	6/IR 12
Spucher, Nikolaus		IR 12
Gobst, Frtiz	Gefr	8/IR 12
Roter, Gunther	Schtz	IR 12
Timme, Frederich	Schtz	5/IR 12
Harre, Heinrich	Schtz	6/IR 12
Colle, Ernst	Obschtz	6/IR 12
Klockau, Lorenz	Schtz	5/IR 12
Sawerborn	Schtz	5/IR 12
Pitcher, Walter	Schtz	5/IR 12
Hespe, Hans	Schtz	5/IR 12
Nengeboren, Erich	Gefr	5/IR 12
Miair, Emil	Schtz	5/IR 12
Neber, Alfred	Schtz	5/IR 12
Schade, Helmut	Gefr	5/IR 12

Heldendorfer, Rudolf	Schtz	5/IR 12
Meyer, Rudolf	Gefr	5/IR 12
Stuck, Gerhard	Gefr	5/IR 12
Heller, Wilhelm	Gefr	5/IR 12
Reuffert, Wilhelm	Schtz	6/IR 12
Saage, Hermann	Uffz	6/IR 12
Sellwind, Walter	Schtz	6/IR 12
Kinder, Hans	Schtz	8/IR 12
Hoffmann, Herbert	Schtz	8/IR 12
Alfenbrulef, Hans	Schtz	6/IR 12
Klododzig, Alois	Schtz	5/IR 12
Mayer, Kurt	Obschtz	4/IR 12
Vrobel, Paul	Schtz	8/IR 12

Comparison of ranks used above (also see Appendix Three):-

German Army

British Army

Schutz:	Private, infantry
Oberschutz:	Translates to 'Senior Private': no equivalent rank
Gefrieter:	Lance Corporal
Unteroffizier:	Lance Sergeant or Sergeant
Leutnant:	Second Lieutenant

Composition of the German 31 *Infanterie-Division*, Infantry Weapons & Equipment, 1940

R eaders may find certain selected data regarding the 31 ID, elements of which fought the 1st Guards Brigade on May 21st, 1940, interesting. This information has been researched from contemporary documents held at the *Bundesarchiv* in Germany, and the histories of the Regiments concerned; unfortunately most of these have so far been published exclusively in German and are therefore not widely available in the UK. I am most grateful, therefore, to my Belgian friend Peter Taghon for providing much of this material.

In my experience, former Allied Servicemen know little about the *Wehrmacht* on a personal basis; our previous publishing projects, however, have been well received due to their balanced nature and German detail. For those reasons I hope that the following information will be of special interest to Dunkirk Veterans. Basic comparative data regarding the BEF exists in Chapter One, although certain books listed in the Bibliography deal with this subject in depth.

31st *Infanterie-Division*, 1940.

This was a Division of the regular German Army which recruited in the Braunchsweig area. Only certain elements of the Division were engaged during the Polish campaign, but the 31 ID saw extensive service in both Belgium and France.

An Order of Battle, marked *Geheim!* (Secret) dated May 1st, 1940, indicates that the *Kommodore* of 31 ID was *Generalleutnant* Kaempfe, his deputy being Major Ulrich. Essentially each ID comprised three *infanterie* regiments, each of three battalions sub-divided into three rifle companies and a heavy weapons company.

In the case of 31 ID, the IRs concerned were 82 (*Oberst* Hossbach), 17 (*Oberst* Berthold) and 12 (*Oberst* Ribstern). The first battalion's (I/IR 12) *Kommandeur* was *Oberleutnant* Hassenstein, II/IR 12's *Hauptmann* Ambrosius; the name of III/IR 12's *Kommandeur* is unfortunately illegible. The strength of each regiment was 95 officers and 2,989 men.

Each IR had its own *Nachrichten Staffel* (Signals Squadron), fire support company (two horse drawn 150 mm guns and six 75 mm guns), and *Panzerjaegerkompanie*: four platoons totalling 12 37 mm anti-tank guns.

The battalions were divided into three *Schutzen Kompanie* (Rifle Companies) of four officers and 183 men). Each SK comprised two rifle platoons, each of four rifle sections and a *Leichter Granatwerfer Trupp* (Light Mortar Section) armed with one 50 mm mortar. In each *Kompanie* was also a *Panzer Buchsen Trupp* (Anti-Tank Rifle Section) of three AT rifles.

Each battalion also had a *Maschinen Gewehr Kompanie* (Machine-Gun Company) - to prove so important at Poplar Ridge on May 21st, 1940 - which consisted of five officers and 183 men. This was sub-divided into three platoons, each with two sections of two heavy machine-guns (MG 34). Also attached to the MGK was the *Schwere Granatwerfer Zug* - Heavy Mortar Platoon: three sections each with two 81 mm mortars.

At Divisional level, answering to the *Stab* HQ (Divisional Staff HQ), in the main were an *Aufklarungs Abteilung* (Reconnaissance Battalion, Major Oertzen) and *Panzerjaeger Abteilung* (Anti-Tank Battalion, Major Ulrich), consisting of three *Kompanies*, each armed with 12 3.7 cm anti-tank guns. Also attached to this *Abteilung* was the Anti-Aircraft *Kompanie* armed with 12 2 cm anti-aircraft guns.

In addition to Hauptmann Friesel's *Nachrichtruppe*, the 31 ID *Stab* controlled a complete *Artillerie Regiment* (artillery Regiment, AR), No 67, commanded by *Oberst* Muller, the Divisional *Artilleriefuhrer*. The AR consisted of three battalions, each of three *Batteries* of four 15 cm guns each. The AR also enjoyed the benefits of an Observation Battalion three *Kompanies* strong (which often used balloons as sighted by 1st Guards Brigade on several occasions).

Also at Divisional level was a Reserve Battalion, *Pioniere Abteilung* (Combat Engineer Battalion, to prove essential during the campaign in the West) commanded by *Oberstleutnant* Bingmann, and *Versongungstruppen* (Supply Troops). There were, in addition, the usual administrative, repair, transport and medical units.

Such a 'First Wave' infantry division possessed approximately 378 light machine-guns, 138 heavy machine-guns, 93 light mortars, 54 medium mortars, 20 light infantry guns, six heavy infantry guns, 76 anti-tank guns, 36 light field howitzers, 12 heavy field howitzers and 12 light AA guns. The total strength was around 17,700 men of all ranks.

German Infantry Weapons & Equipment.

The German infantryman went to war in Belgium and France using basically the same equipment he had used in Poland in 1939. Uniforms and equipment were essentially of a field-grey colour. The M35 *Stahlhelm* (steel helmet) remains a classic symbol of Nazi oppression. On the right-hand side it bore the national tricolour shield, and on the left the German eagle clutching a Nazi swastika (although the tricolour was actually discontinued during 1940). The German soldier was equipped with a leather fighting belt and 'Y' straps which carried the following equipment: M31 breadbag, field flask with cup, messtins, bayonet and ammunition pouches. Each man was also issued with an M34 or M39 knapsack pack, blanket, greatcoat and camouflage *Zeltbahn* 31 shelter section or waterproof. A cylindrical metal canister was also issued which contained a gas mask, although this was often used to store extra ammunition and personal medical supplies. It would be remiss not to mention the German Army 'Jackboot', or marching boot (known as 'Dicebeakers'), which, like the distinctive steel helmet, became a symbol of Nazi tyranny.

The enemy's weapons are of great interest. First of all the German rifleman carried the classic Mauser *Karbine* 98 (K98), which was very similar to the British .303 SMLE. Their infantry officers, and some NCOs, were often armed not only with a Luger pistol, or similar, for personal protection, but also the superb *Maschinenpistole* 38/40 - known to the Allies as the *Schmeisser*. This was a major advantage over the British infantry. A light sub-machine-gun (SMG), this had been developed with the new doctrine of 'Lightning War' very much in mind: high mobility and maximum local superiority. When this weapon was introduced in 1938, it was revolutionary. At that time SMGs were generally in short supply, due to being unnecessarily heavy and expensive, being machined from solid steel billets and fitted with hardwood stocks. The MP 38, however, produced by *Erfurter-Maschinenfabrik* (Erma) was completely the opposite: lightweight, fitted with a folding skeleton stock and plastic handle. The specification lent itself to mass production and proved very effective in close combat. The design was to serve the Germans well throughout the Second World War, 1,047,000 of these weapons being produced. In 1940, these weapons definitely gave German infantry a distinct firepower advantage at close range as there were few SMGs available to the BEF.

The German infantryman also carried the M24 *Stahlgranate* - known to the Allies as the 'Stick Grenade' for obvious reasons. These could easily be shoved inside a belt or even down a boot for ease of access. Referring back to the action fought on Poplar Ridge on May 21st, 1940, so close did Lieutenant Reynell-Pack's Carriers get to the enemy that stick grenades were tossed inside his vehicle - destroying it and killing all three crew members.

Specification: MP40	
Calibre:	9mm by 19mm *Pistole Patrone* '08 (9mm Parabellum).
Ammunition:	Ball; blank.
Weight:	Unloaded 8.87 lbs. Loaded: 10.37 lbs.
Rate of fire:	Approx. 450-550 rounds per minute.
Muzzle velocity:	365mps.
Max. Effective range:	Approx. 200 metres (most effective at close range: 50-150 metres).

On Poplar Ridge, the 3rd Bn Grenadier Guards faced three *Maschinengewehr* 34. The MG34 represented the world's first machine-gun that was fully capable of providing a very high rate of fire (up to 1000 rpm) and could be carried by one man (although generally operated by two or three man teams), thus affording sections tactical flexibility. This excellent weapon was, in fact, the forerunner of the 'weapons system' approach: a basic tool to which could be added various accessories thus fulfilling a variety of tactical roles.

The MG34 was relatively lightweight at 26.7 lbs (but three pounds heavier than the Bren). It featured an attached bipod (similar to the Bren), air-cooling with rapid barrel change, recoil operated selective fire action, fast and simple field stripping without the requirement for special tools, and a high cyclic rate of fire. There was a choice of ammunition delivery: a drum-shaped 50 round belt carrier, a 75 round saddle drum magazine, or from field ammunition boxes containing 50 round metallic continuous link belts. The latter were often joined into longer belts. In effect, the MG34 satisfied the requirement for the 'universal machine-gun'.

Used with the bipod, the MG34 was a light section machine-gun (and was probably so used on Poplar Ridge). When fitted with the *Lafette* 34 tripod it became a heavy machine-gun in a sustained fire role. On the *Dreibein* 34 tripod it was an anti-aircraft gun. The MG34 was used on just about every German military vehicle from motor-cycle and sidecar combinations to the huge King Tiger tank. Developed at *Rheinmetall* and tested extensively during the Spanish Civil War during the late-1930s, by 1939, the MG34 was a standard German infantry weapon. The only drawback was that the MG34's production process required detailed machine work and precise fitting. As the war progressed this was disadvantageous and led to development of the MG42. This was easier to produce (due to extensive use of sheet metal stampings, rivets and spot welds), was mechanically superior and more reliable under harsh battle conditions. Nevertheless the MG34 remained in production throughout the Second World War.

It is worth adding that the British considered their Bren Gun to be more accurate (450 rpm from a 30 round magazine) than the MG34 which, with its high rate of fire (a maximum of 1000 rpm), was wasteful in ammunition. Although the MG34 was less accurate it could produce a high volume of suppressive fire. Subsequently, however, the British Army introduced the belt-fed 7.62mm FN General Purpose Machine Gun (GPMG), a development of the MG42, alongside the re-bored 7.62mm Bren LMG. Nevertheless the *Bundeswehr* (present day German Army) continues to use the MG42 to this day.

Specification: MG34	
Calibre:	7.92mm by 57mm *Gewehr Patrone* 98 (8mm Mauser).
Ammunition:	Ball; tracer; armour piercing; incendiary, blank.
Weight:	26.7 lbs.
Rate of fire:	Approx. 800-900 rounds per minute (optimum).
Muzzle velocity:	760mps.
Max. effective range:	(With bipod) approx. 800 metres.
	(With tripod & telescopic sight) approx. 3,000 metres.

Equivalent Ranks

Finally, it is worth providing a comprehensive comparison of the German and British commissioned ranks used in *this* book:-

German Army	British Army
Leutnant:	Second Lieutenant
Oberleutnant:	Lieutenant
Hauptmann:	Captain
Major:	Major
Oberstleutnant:	Lieutenant Colonel
Oberst:	Colonel
Generalleutnant:	Lieutenant General
Feldmarschall:	Field Marshal

ACKNOWLEDGEMENTS

My project has been provided invaluable assistance by many people and organisations. Firstly, however, I must thank my Mother, Janet Sarkar, for suggesting that I should write this book, and my wife, Anita, for all her support and help with administration, publishing and promoting my work. Our children, James and Hannah, have also had to endure the domestic disruption required to produce yet another book!

Although unwitting catalysts, I must also thank my Grandfather, former 2611042 Guardsman HH 'Bert' Smith and his second wife, Mary, for giving me various wartime souvenirs; likewise my Grandmother, Dorothy Smith. Sadly all three are now deceased; I suspect that 'Granddad' in particular would be astonished by my project.

I owe a particular debt to both Lieutenant Colonels David Hutchison, Commanding Officer 1st Bn Grenadier Guards, for his much appreciated Foreword, and Hugh Boscawen, Coldstream Guards, for reading the first draft of *Guards VC* and making *numerous* constructive suggestions. It was Hugh, in fact, who urged me to undertake more work on the manuscript at a point in time when I was exhausted, and was of great help in producing, to use his words, a 'framework of history' to set these dramatic events in context.

The Veterans:-

We all owe an immeasurable debt to the following BEF Dunkirk veterans, myself especially for their inspiration and kind assistance:-

Headquarters 1st Guards Brigade:-

Captain (Retd) LHT Court (Coldstream Guards), Mr DR Ellingworth (1st Division Signals).

3rd Bn Grenadier Guards:-

The Lord Forbes KBE, Sir Edward Ford GCVO KCB ERD, Mr Arthur Rice MBE, Mr Les Drinkwater, the late Mr Percy Nash, Mr Charles Constantine, Mr W Lewcock, Mr Gil Follett, Mr Bert Middleton & Mr Eric Pounder.

2nd Bn Coldstream Guards:-

Brigadier (Retd) RC Windsor-Clive, Mr Joe Nixon, Mr R Christie & Mr TW Abbott.

Royal Warwickshire Regiment:-

Major (Retd) Denis Dodds & Mr Ken Hawkins.

2nd Bn Royal Norfolk Regiment:-

Mr Ernie Leggett.

1/6th Bn East Surrey Regiment:-

Mr Mike Coyle.

2nd Bn Hampshire Regiment:-

Lieutenant Colonel (Retd) Peter Halliday.

I am also grateful to certain former German soldiers, in particular:-

II/IR 12:-

Dr Albert Bollmann, 1940 veteran and President of the IR 12 *Kameradschaft* (Old Comrades Association).

The Relatives & Friends of Casualties & Deceased Guardsmen:-

Grenadier Guards:-

First of all I must make special mention of Mrs Irene Hazeldine, sister of Lance Corporal Harry Nicholls VC whose kindness, interest and enthusiasm is much appreciated.

His Grace The Duke of Northumberland, & Northumberland Estates (Lieutenant The 9th Duke of Northumberland), Mrs B Clark, Mr David Clark & Mr FV Hayes (Guardsman SJ Hayes), Lieutenant Colonel (Retd) GA Alston-Roberts-West CVO (son of Major WRJ Alston-Roberts-West), Mr Charles Rimell, Mr Dennis Rimell and Mr Ken Ball (Lance Sergeant A Rimell), Mrs Ruth Grocott (Lance Corporal JH Hudson), Mrs IE Bullock (Sergeant N Bullock DCM), Mrs EJ Hancock & Mrs Anne Wall (Lance Corporal B Everitt), Mrs Seager & Mr George Lewis (Guardsman RJ Cook), Christopher A Collins (Military & Heraldic Artist, son of Lance Corporal A Collins).

Coldstream Guards:-

Lieutenant Colonel HGR Boscawen (nephew of Lieutenant The Hon. EFV Boscawen) & Captain (Retd) LHT Court (brother of PSM F Court).

The following Regimental Archivists, former and serving members of the Regiments concerned were of great help; I also wish to acknowledge especially the enthusiasm and assistance given by those Grenadiers of the present day:-

Grenadier Guards:-

The late Major (Retd) EC Weaver MBE, the late Major (Retd) PA Lewis MBE, Lieutenant Colonel (Retd) CJE Seymour (Regimental Adjutant), Lieutenant Colonel (Retd) Sir John Smiley Bt, Mr Alan Kear, Lieutenant Colonel (Retd) GA Alston-Roberts-West CVO, Lieutenant Colonel (Retd) HS Hanning, Lieutenant Colonel AD Hutchison (Commanding Officer 1st Bn Grenadier Guards who kindly wrote the Foreword), Captain SD Marcham, Colour Sergeant Andrew Butcher (who appears on our front cover) and his wife Wendy, Ted 'Boxer' Brown & Bruce Bayliss.

I also owe special thanks to Mr Ray Seale, Honorary Secretary of the Worcester & Hereford Branch of the Grenadier Guards Association, for both recording brief notes concerning my late Grandfather and supporting my project throughout.

Coldstream Guards:-

Lieutenant Colonel HGR Boscawen, Major (Retd) EM Crofton (Regimental Adjutant), & Major (Retd) CJ Louch.

Royal Hampshire Regiment:-

Lieutenant Colonel (Retd) CD 'John' Darroch DL

Organisations:-

The Victoria Cross & George Cross Association, The Dunkirk Veterans' Association, The Grenadier Guards Association, The Coldstream Guards Association, Regimental HQ The Staffordshire Regiment, The Keeper & Staff of the Public Record Office, Imperial War Museum, The Air Photo Library Keele University, The Tank Museum, Commonwealth War Graves Commission, Red Cross Archive & Museum, *Volksbund Deutsche Kriegsgraberfursorge* (German War Graves Commission), *Bundesarchiv* (Military Archive, Freiburg), Malvern Gazette & Ledbury Reporter, Worcester Evening News, The Fleet News, BBC Radio Hereford & Worcester, Nottingham Evening Post, Worcester City Council & the West Mercia Constabulary.

The book's launch at The Guildhall, Worcester, on May 22nd, 1999, was greatly assisted and supported by the Grenadier Guards, Grenadier Guards Association, Worcester City Council (The Right Worshipful Mayor of Worcester, Councillor Joan Hodges JP, Mrs Ursula Jones and Mrs Jacki Potts) and the West Mercia Constabulary (Chief Inspector David Price, Sergeants Chris Allen, Graham Cooke and Richard Robson).

As ever, a number of enthusiasts and like-minded friends rallied to the cause, namely Frank Kamp (a former WWII German combat engineer who kindly undertook all translation work), Ray Loveslife-Brown, Ernie Hardy (commissioned to undertake much PRO work), Winston Ramsey of *After the Battle* magazine, Larry McHale, Jim Langford, journalists David Edwards, Steve Snelling & Andy Smart; Carol & Alan Hill, Francis Huibrechts, Mrs Pat Jordan (daughter of Major FG Matthews), Neil Sarkar (my brother), Christopher Gale (my cousin) and Margaret Woodward (my Mother's cousin). My Mother and Father also provide an essential support service for which I am most grateful!

This is the sixth book which Ramrod Publications has produced in conjunction with Aspect Print & Design of Malvern, so, once more, many thanks to Allan, Sue, Simon & Paul.

Finally, a special debt is owed my fellow 'War Pilgrims', whose knowledge, enthusiasm and energy both encouraged and sustained me throughout this project:-

Andrew Long (who kindly undertook all photographic copying), Allan White (only ever a phone call away to offer sound advice and encouragement), Peter Taghon (who supplied otherwise unobtainable German records and photographs), Dr Bernard-Marie Dupont (my French 'brother') and Antony Whitehead (who, as ever, bought the beer!).

BIBLIOGRAPHY

During the course of my research, I consulted the following documents at the Public Record Office; such records can be inspected by anyone holding a valid reading ticket:-

War Diaries:-

1st Guards Brigade:	WO 167/346
3rd Bn Grenadier Guards:	WO 167/702
2nd Bn Coldstream Guards:	WO 167/699
8th Bn Royal Warwickshire Regiment:	WO 167/841
2nd Bn Royal Norfolk Regiment:	WO 167/794
1st Bn Suffolk Regiment:	WO 167/832
2nd Bn East Yorkshire Regiment:	WO 167/850
2nd Bn Hampshire Regiment:	WO 167/42801
1st Bn Loyal Regiment:	WO 167/773
2nd Bn North Staffordshire Regiment:	WO 167/830
6th Bn Gordon Highlanders:	WO 167/747

Other Documents:-

Ill-Treatment of British POWs, Stalag XXB:	WO 309/34

Previously unpublished sources:-

Memoirs of The Lord Forbes, 3rd Bn Grenadier Guards.
Memoirs of Lance Sergeant Charles Constantine, 3rd Bn Grenadier Guards.
Memoirs of Lieutenant Colonel Peter Halliday, 2nd Bn Hampshire Regiment.
Memoirs of Corporal Ken Hawkins, 1/7th Bn Royal Warwickshire Regiment.
Casualty list II/IR 12, May 21st, 1940.

I have also quoted extensively from my personal correspondence and taped interviews with veterans, and the relatives and friends of various casualties. The personal service records of certain Grenadiers, provided by the Regimental Archive, were invaluable, as were the German records found by Peter Taghon; these included:-

IV *Armeekorps* War Diary
18 ID War Diary
31 ID War Diary
IR 12 War Diary
IR 82 War Diary
IR 54 War Diary
Various Daily Intelligence Summaries

Published sources:-

In addition to various issues of the *Grenadier Gazette*, Dunkirk Veterans' Association *Journal*, and Newsletter No 6 of the Worcester & Hereford Branch of the Grenadier Guards Association, the following works proved most helpful:-

The War in France & Flanders, Major LF Ellis, London 1953.
The Bartholomew Report, a report by the War Office into the campaign, 1940.
War Dead of the British Commonwealth 1939-45, Register Belgium 119-161, CWGC, 1982.
First & Second Despatch by General the Viscount Gort covering the period September 3rd, 1939 - May 31st, 1940, published in the *London Gazette*, March 1941.
A Guards General: The Memoirs of Major General Sir Allan Adair, Edited by Oliver Lindsay, Hamish Hamilton Ltd., 1986.
The Grenadier Guards In The War Of 1939-45, Volumes One & Two, Patrick Forbes & Nigel Nicholson, Gale & Polden Ltd., 1949.
No Dishonourable Name, compiled & edited by DC Quilter, SR Publishing Ltd., 1972.
Nulli Secundus: The Record of the Coldstream Guards 1650-1950 & 1951-1974, Published by the Regiment 1950, with additions in 1975.
History of the Coldstream Guards 1920-46, Michael Howard & John Sparrow, Oxford, 1951.
British VCs of World War 2: A Study in Heroism, John Laffin, Sutton Publishing 1997.
The Bronze Cross, F Gordon Roe, PR Gawthorn Ltd., 1945
Blitzkrieg in the West Then & Now, Jean Paul Pallud, After the Battle, 1991.
Blitzed: The Battle of France May-June 1940, Vic Bingham, Air Research publications, 1990.
The Fall of France: Disaster in the West 1939-40, George Forty & John Duncan, Nutshell Publishing, 1990.
Mai 1940: La Campagne Des Dix-Huit Jours, Peter Taghon, Belgique Loisirs, 1989.
60 Days That Shook the West, J Benoist-Mechin, Jonathan Cape Ltd.,1963.
Blitzkrieg: From the Rise of Hitler to the Fall of Dunkirk, Len Deighton, Joanathan Cape Ltd., 1979.
Destination Dunkirk: The Story of Gort's Army, Gregory Blaxland, William Kimber & Co. Ltd., 1973.
The Miracle of Dunkirk, Walter Lord, Allen Lane 1983.
Dunkirk: Pillar of Fire, Ronald Atkin, Sidgwick & Jackson Ltd., 1990.
Dunkirk: Anatomy of Disaster, Patrick Turnbull, BT Batsford, 1978.
The Second World War, Volume II: Their Finest Hour, Winston S Churchill, Cassell & Co. Ltd., 1949.
German Army Uniforms & Insignia 1933-45, Brian L Davis, Arms & Armour Press Ltd., 1971.
German Army Handbook 1939-45, James Lucas, Sutton Publishing Ltd., 1998.
A Collector's Guide to Third Reich Militaria, Robin Lumsden, Ian Allen Ltd., 1987.
Life of a British POW in Poland, May 31st 1940 - April 30th 1945, J Stedman, Merlin Books 1992.
The British Army Handbook 1939-45, George Forty, Sutton Publishing 1998.
The Battle of the Ypres-Comines Canal 1940, M. Henri Bourgeois, Royal Warwickshire Regiment Association, 1994.